REASSESSING ANGLO–SAXON ENGLAND

'It is an extraordinary, and in important ways, an extraordinarily interesting book. It is not a survey of all aspects of Anglo-Saxon England and nor does it claim to be such. Rather it is a commentary on Anglo-Saxon history, paying special attention to areas and aspects which have engaged Mr John's attention over his long and distinguished scholarly career; ... the cult of Woden, bookland, the nature of the 'tenth-century Reformation', the thought world of Ælfric and other themes dear to Mr John.'

James Campbell, Worcester College, Oxford

Eric John is one of the most distinguished and provocative of Anglo-Saxonists. This new and original analysis is the fruit of thirty years of scholarship and therefore has something of the nature of a testament. Mr John seeks to make use of social anthropological insight to understand the type of primitive people the Anglo-Saxons were and sets them (unusually) in their European context. He starts at the beginnings of English society, looks then at Anglo-Saxon pagans, Mercian hegemony, English politics in the ninth century, the West Saxon conquest of England, holiness and *hubris*, the restoration of learning, the ruin of the house of Cerdic, the northern empire and the avoidance of chaos.

Brilliantly and entertainingly written, this is an interesting and remarkable book.

ERIC JOHN

Reassessing
Anglo-Saxon England

MANCHESTER
UNIVERSITY PRESS
MANCHESTER AND NEW YORK

distributed exclusively in the USA
by St. Martin's Press

Copyright © Eric John 1996

Published by Manchester University Press
Oxford Road, Manchester M13 9NR, UK
and Room 400, 175 Fifth Avenue, New York, NY 10010, USA

Distributed exclusively in the USA
by St. Martin's Press, Inc.,
175 Fifth Avenue, New York, NY 10010, USA

British Library Cataloguing-in-Publication Data
A catalogue record is available from the British Library

Library of Congress Cataloging-in-Publication Data
John, Eric.
  Reassessing Anglo-Saxon England / Eric John.
    p.   cm.
  ISBN 0–7190–4867–2.—ISBN 0–7190–5053–7 (paper)
    1. Great Britain—History—Anglo-Saxon period, 449–1066.
  2. England—Civilization—To 1066.   3. Civilization, Anglo-Saxon.
  4. Anglo-Saxons.   I. Title.
DA152.J65   1996
941.01—dc20   96-2687

ISBN 0 7190 4867 2 *hardback*
ISBN 0 7190 5053 7 *paperback*

First published 1996

00 99 98 97 96   10 9 8 7 6 5 4 3 2 1

Typeset in Bembo
by Northern Phototypesetting Co Ltd, Bolton
and printed in Great Britain
by Biddles Ltd, Guildford and King's Lynn

CONTENTS

PREFACE   vii

INTRODUCTION   I

1   The beginnings of English society   4

2   Anglo-Saxon pagans, saints and sinners   22

3   Thought and action under the Mercian hegemony   50

4   English politics in the ninth century:
     problems, solutions and more problems   66

5   The West Saxon conquest of England   83

6   Holiness and *hubris*   99

7   The restoration of learning   124

8   The ruin of the house of Cerdic   139

9   The northern empire   151

10   The avoidance of chaos   161

11   *Götterdämmerung*   171

INDEX   197

IN MEMORY OF NUMA DENIS FUSTEL DE COULANGES

Ask him courteously and he will speak history and tell you no lies
Homer, Odyssey

PREFACE

REASSESSING ANGLO-SAXON ENGLAND was not my original title but it does seem to express what the book is about. It is a resonance of the title of Sir Frank Stenton's famous book *Anglo-Saxon England*. In the preface to my first book, *Land Tenure in Early England*, I noted the many points of disagreement with Sir Frank. This was because the subject of feudalism was a central part of the discussion and Stenton was not at his best on the topic. It might be asked, 'Who is?' I was aware, like anyone else, how much I owed to *Anglo-Saxon England* but not until I wrote this book of the extent and depth of that indebtedness. It was pointed out to me that the *apparatus* of every chapter begins with a quotation from Stenton and there are innumerable other citations in the course of the argument. Since its publication half a century ago is a fairly recent event, it seemed suitable to attempt a reassessment of the book as well as to try to describe the relationship of my book to Stenton's.

It is important to note that there is nothing like it in either French or German historiography. The nearest I can recall is Robert Holzmann's *Das Sächsische Kaisertum*. This is a work on a similarly large scale but of much smaller scope. It is a work of great value to historians but a comparison shows its inferiority to Stenton's book. Holzmann's subject is the *Reich*: we get a lot of *Adel* alongside the kings and a lot of other not very clearly socially delineated people in the background. His subject is the *Reich* and there is little differentiation between provinces and their inhabitants. Stenton was acutely aware of social and regional differentiation, and that is one of his strengths.

Many of us have thought a weakness of *Anglo-Saxon England* was the allegiance it acknowledged to the old tenets of Germanist historiography. But a closer look shows how chary Stenton was of committing himself too far to an early England that was an egalitarian community of free peasants. The fundamentals of the old historiography are pushed deep into the past. The egalitarian – for want of a better word – structure of early English society only appears on p. 304, where Sir Frank wrote:

> In general it would seem that the circumstances of the migration to Britain had disintegrated whatever forms of primitive aristocracy had existed amongst the continental English, leaving few representatives of a genuine aristocracy of birth, apart from the king and his kinsmen.

But Hengest was an exception. 'The historic Hengest is best regarded as a chief of very noble descent who brings his own retinue from overseas to Britain' (p. 17). There are plenty of aristocratic Anglo-Saxons in the first three hundred pages of *Anglo-Saxon England* but if we take Stenton literally they must have been members of royal kindred groups. (This is perfectly plausible. The Saudi Arabian aristocracy is, or, perhaps better, was, composed of more or less minor royals.)

But the nitty-gritty of discussion of class distinctions in early English society comes when we tackle the problem of land tenure. In *Anglo-Saxon England* land tenure is considered under two forms, bookland and folkland. Bookland was introduced for the convenience of the Church and created perpetual tenure. Folkland was the primitive form of land tenure. It meant land of the people in some way, and for several generations was misinterpreted as a sort of primitive communism. (Possibly the rise of Marxism rendered this interpretation less attractive.) In fact, whatever else folkland was, it was not a form of primitive communism, and Stenton made sense of folkland in very ingenious ways. It has been supposed that the discussion in *Anglo-Saxon England* exhausted his views on the subject. It did not. In 1955, twelve years after the publication of *Anglo-Saxon England*, Stenton took up the subject again in his *Latin Charters of the Anglo-Saxon Period* (Oxford, 1955). His views, as expressed there, have been ignored. We are no longer dealing with a primitive commonwealth:

> This society was familiar with great landowners; the king above all, and men representing different branches of the royal family. It may have included men not of royal descent, whose families were regarded as inherently noble … It was certainly familiar with men who served the king in his *comitatus* and at an appropriate time had been provided with land on which they could marry and live in accordance with their rank. But the stages by which these rewards to faithful companions passed into hereditary properties are unrecorded. For many generations it is probable that a young man of this class who wished to inherit his father's land knew that in due course he must earn a new grant of it from his father's lord or his successor. In Bede's Northumbria, at least, the grants of land which kings were making to their followers seem to have been limited to the recipients' lifetime. It may have been long under such conditions before the need was felt in lay society for the solemn charter with its insistence on perpetuity and hereditary right. [pp. 60–1]

The contrast here is not between folkland – that is, land tenure traditional and primitive or at least unsophisticated – but between bookland and lænland. I do not think he had arrived at this view when he wrote

Anglo-Saxon England. But his mind was open on the question of hierarchy which he had come to see was something developing in Anglo-Saxon society, though not primitive. In his last paper on the ceorl, 'The thriving of the Anglo-Saxon Ceorl', in *Preparatory to Anglo-Saxon England* (ed. D. M. Stenton, Oxford, 1970) the movement of his thought is clear enough. The ceorl is a slaveholding landowner, more prosperous and a member of a more socially variegated social class than he is presented as being in *Anglo-Saxon England.* This revision of opinion has obviously very drastic implications, and Stenton at that time could not be expected to follow them through. But there were plenty of people around who could and would have, and they might have expected, if not encouragement, at least sympathy with the enterprise. If they did they did not get it.

I think Stenton saw that although from Bede's Northumbria at least Anglo-Saxon England was becoming more and more hierarchical (this is what makes *Anglo-Saxon England* capable of giving convincing interpretations of the reigns of Cnut and Edward the Confessor) deep in the historical past it had not been like that. He thought that the lost generations were important but remote and largely unknowable. My own book really gets going precisely with the appearance of written sources but there is no doubt that the the first, illiterate, generations had a history. I was inclined to think it was irrecoverable but some of James Campbell's essays give one pause.

Putting all this together also throws light on the problem of the nature of the English invasions. What is clear is that the upper classes of English society were purely Germanic. There is no evidence whatever of any significant Celtic element in the English aristocracy. At the level of slaves or thralls there must have been a considerable Celtic element and there is no compelling evidence of thralls of Germanic descent. The ceorl seems to have been purely Germanic but in Stenton's later thought he had moved up-market.

I have mentioned already that in contrast to Holzmann Stenton is very sensitive to differences of place and the importance of local geography. I cannot believe that any reader of *Anglo-Saxon England,* however inattentive, can have failed to notice that.[1] But there is one very remarkable passage that deserves at least passing attention.

> The Northumbrian revolutions of the eighth century would have been impossible if any single branch of the royal house had been regarded as indefeasibly entitled to the kingship. But in every English kingdom the mere fact of royal descent gave a title to rule, and in Northumbria the configuration of the country made rebellion easy. Deira, or at least the original Deira of

the eastern Wolds and central plain is in structure a detached fragment of southern England. But the great mass of the Pennines and the central hills of southern Scotland which are its continuation gave a distinctive character to the life of western Deira and of all Bernicia. Even in the habitable country between the eastern and the western sea, the poverty of the soil under ancient methods of cultivation meant that a vast estate was necessary for the support of a nobleman's rank. It was therefore possible for a few disaffected lords to withdraw a wide region from the king's obedience, and the difficulties of Northumbrian travel were so great that a royal army could not easily be concentrated for their suppression. Between the east and west of the kingdom the Pennines formed a barrier, passable at many points, but everywhere hindering the movements of large masses of men. For forty years after the destruction of the Northumbrian kingdom by the Danes, an English aristocracy was able to maintain itself in independence beyond the mountains. There was no part of England where the physical obstacles to government were so formidable as in Northumbria, and nowhere else was it so difficult for a king to be forewarned against the movements of his enemies. [p. 91]

The implications of all this for the Easter controversy and the synod of Whitby in 664 are obvious.

There is only a handful of ordinary historical facts here, including the small amount of archaeological evidence that Deira was settled much earlier than Bernicia. But these facts are made into a firm historical structure by being set in an inescapable context determined by the facts of geography.

Perhaps most striking when one notices it is the way Sir Frank moves from treating Anglo-Saxon England as a whole, a unity, to stressing the detail, the particular. A good example is his treatment of the overlordship. This makes one want to say, 'You could go a little further here. This overlordship is a factor making for unity you are underestimating.' Just as with his claim that, in the tenth-century mess that was the politics of the kingdom of York, the descendants of the Vikings behaved like Englishmen, one would want to say, 'This is a little premature.' The point being that he makes you think in a long perspective or in a restricted one as seems appropriate. What matters is that he imparts a sense of the importance of choosing the right perspective in his readers. In reading Stenton one is not just informed, one is educated.

One cannot overlook his mastery of the telling detail. There is the footnote on p. 390 recounting the early eleventh-century feud in Northumbria that is not only important in itself but reminds one – as I think it was meant to – that feuds were still a fact of life for all walks of life, including the aristocracy. One cannot make sense of the relations between Earl Godwin and Edward the Confessor – though plenty have tried – without taking the feud seriously.

Again, almost at random (almost, but never quite with Stenton):

> One of the most instructive documents of the reign is a grant of land by Oslac, *dux* of the South Saxons, to which Offa at Irthlingborough, on the Nene, added a confirmatory endorsement. The contrast between the crude provincial script of the text and the practised, almost official, hand of the endorsement represents a real distinction between the primitive government of the local kingdoms and the beginnings of administrative routine in a court which had become the political centre of England south of the Humber. [p. 211]

A mere difference in handwriting but also a stage in the making of England.

In the volume of essays published by the University of Reading to commemorate the fiftieth anniversary of the appearance of *Anglo-Saxon England*[2] James Campbell remarked, 'Stenton, like other great men, may not have been best served by the loyalty of his disciples.' Loyal and devoted they were, but there is precious little evidence that they read him much, still less understood him.

Michael Wallace-Hadrill once spoke of the early medieval period as a time when the historian hardly knew what was happening but could find out what was going on. No mean practitioner at this himself, he was, like the rest of us, surpassed by Stenton. It will at any rate be obvious how deep is my debt to Stenton, which I gladly acknowledge here.

I should like to acknowledge other debts too. To Dr C. R. Hart, who let me read much of his work, to my and the book's profit, though the main fruits of that will not be apparent until my article on the *Annals of St Neots* and the defeat of the Vikings, a spin-off from the book, appears. I have to thank Herbert McCabe, OP, who read a draft of the book from the point of view of the interested layman and saved me from obscurity at several points. I owe a general debt to James Campbell for the many occasions I have enjoyed his hospitality at Worcester and the enormously valuable discussions that ensued. I owe him a more particular debt. He gave up much of his long vacation to a minute scrutiny of the book, saved me from errors and gave me much improving advice.

E. J.

NOTES

1   It is fair to point out that since Holzmann wrote a number of local and regional stud-
     ies of medieval Germany has been published.
2   Donald Matthew (ed.), *Stenton's* Anglo-Saxon England *fifty years on*, Reading Histor-
     ical Studies 1, University of Reading, 1994.

INTRODUCTION

IT IS COMMONLY SAID nowadays that historians are abandoning history for a kind of bastard sociology. Teachers of history at every level have a suspicion and ignorance of sociology: this is especially true of students of early English history.[1] They constantly commit the classic fallacy of social anthropology: 'if I were a horse'. This derived from the supposed American whose horse broke out in the night and bolted. Next day he was seen on all fours eating grass. Asked what he was doing, he said, 'Finding out, if I were a horse, where I would have gone.' If a historian does not understand the bounds of the social space within which the events he is studying occurred, all he is doing is to paint a picture of his own society in fancy dress. In his very fine biography of Alexander the Great Robin Lane Fox says: 'I am bored by institutions and I do not believe in structures.' It is ironic that what makes his book so remarkable is his elucidation of the structures of the Persian empire and the institutions by which it was governed, which in turn makes it possible to understand why Alexander did what he did and achieved what he achieved. Inconsistency is a virtue here. Let me take what at first sight appears a humbler example. Many primitive peoples – including the Anglo-Saxons and their Irish contemporaries – leave the protection of the individual to the kindred group to which he or she belongs, backed by the blood feud or the threat of it. Unless we grasp this we cannot understand what the early Christian missionaries from those parts were doing. By going on a *peregrinatio* or pilgrimage they were putting themselves outside the normal forms of protection. They were casting themselves utterly on the mercy of God and facing probable martyrdom. Some, the successful ones who got their names into the history books, found powerful protectors to stand in place of their kindred and so make it possible for them to work in peace. Even then, so famous and successful a missionary as St Boniface, who secured the favour and protection of the most powerful family in Europe, still died a martyr.

Dr Richard Wenskus, in a book on the origins of the Germanic states[2] denies the relevance of social anthropology to his studies.[3] He says that what went on in a Kaffir kraal throws no light on his subject. Aside from the disgusting use of the word 'kaffir' – of the significance of which he may be ignorant – he has simply looked in the wrong place. In the end he decides that the ultimate factor in the making of his Germanic states is something he calls *Zusammengehörigkeitgefühl* which I keep in the original because it is less risible than its English equivalent, 'feeling of togetherness'. Had Dr Wenskus read Evans-Pritchard's classic studies of the Nuer and the Azande,[4] he could have got further than that. Evans-Pritchard pointed to the fundamental importance of the feud in tribal structure. (The late Michael Wallace-Hadrill, in the kind of apparently innocent throwaway remark he was rather good at, once wondered if the origins of the various Germanic tribes that took over the Roman empire did not lie in some long-forgotten feud.[5]) The degrees of kinship liable to share a feud determine the boundaries of the tribe. If a man's degree of kinship was too remote to draw him into any feud or its composition he was to all intents and purposes outside the network of kinship and consequently of the tribe itself. It was kinship and the workings of the feud that comprised *Zusammengehörigkeitgefühl*. It is worth pointing out that feuds do not arise from bloodlust or a taste for fighting. Each individual depended for life and limb on the sanction of the feud. Consequently public opinion – public opinion here meaning tribal opinion – provided powerful pressure to enforce these duties. I do not apologise therefore that the first chapter of this book is devoted to structures, and I have not avoided discussion of structural issues *passim*. I have also attempted to add another, not usual, dimension to the book. In his foreword to the collection of essays entitled *Ideal and Reality*[6] the editor, Dr C. P. Wormald, says one of the themes 'is the parallel development of Frankish and Anglo-Saxon history'. Literally parallel, they only occasionally meet in his book. I have tried in mine to place the entire Anglo-Saxon experience in its European setting, the sub-Roman world and its successor states, of which Francia and Anglo-Saxon England were two of the most important. This is not an easy task and I do not claim to have more than tried. It will be done again and done better but at least this is a beginning.

NOTES

1   There are honourable exceptions, of course. The late K. J. Leyser, notably in his *Rule and Conflict in an Early Medieval Society*, Oxford, 1979 and especially Dr J. L. Nelson, whose essays on *Politics and Ritual in Early Medieval Europe*, London, 1986 are always sensitive to social anthropological insights.
2   Richard Wenskus, *Stammesbildung und Verfassung. Das Werden der frühmittelälterlichens Gentes*. Cologne, 1961.
3   *Ibid*.
4   E. E. Evans–Pritchard, *Witchcraft, Oracles and Magic among the Azande*, Oxford, 1937.

5 In a review of Wenskus, *Stammesbildung*, in the *English Historical Review*, lxxix, 1964, pp. 137–9.
6 C. P. Wormald (ed.), *Ideal and Reality in Frankish and Anglo-Saxon Society*, Oxford, 1983.

CHAPTER I

The beginnings of English society

IN A CLASSIC VOLUME, *The Grandeur that was Rome*,[1] J. C. Stobart wrote, 'The destiny or function of Rome in world-history was nothing more or less than the making of Europe.' The achievement of the Anglo-Saxons was the making of England: not, that is, the making of the United Kingdom or of Great Britain but more or less what we mean by England now. The making of Great Britain was left to later generations, who did not make it half so well. Like the origins of Rome, the origins of Anglo-Saxon England are wrapped in myth and legend. Shorn of Venus and Juno, who somehow do not seem at home in the Anglo-Saxon world, the myths have a certain family resemblance. The Anglo-Saxons had a remarkable historian, the Venerable Bede, as he is called by custom, but rightly St Bede, to record their origins. His story is vivid and picturesque. A British king called Vortigern – it is possible Vortigern was not a personal name but the Celtic term for a high king – was troubled by a mysterious group of people from North Britain called Picts. He hired mercenaries from three peoples called the Angles, Saxons and Jutes, led by two brothers called Hengest and Horsa. They arrived in three boats and, seeing the pickings were rich, sent home for 'more'. No indication of large armies is given, and certainly nothing in the nature of a *Völkerwanderung*, an immigration of whole tribes.[2] Although English historians for the last hundred and fifty years have supposed that what Bede meant was a *Völkerwanderung*, it is a very forced interpretation that so describes 'three boatloads' and 'more': but it is an interpretation to which constant repetition has given canonical authority. The reinforced mercenaries were not satisfied to remain employees but set up for themselves and began the take-over of Roman Britain.

Hundreds of books have told the story in these terms but the passage from Bede on which the story depends is not by him. It seems to have come from a Kentish source contemporary with Bede – that is, nearly three hundred years after the events it purports to describe. The passage – that which concerns the Angles, Saxons and Jutes – has been cobbled clumsily into Bede's text. I do not know whether Bede was aware of the interpolation into his text but it is done so clumsily that I cannot believe he did it himself.[3] Later in his *Ecclesiastical History*,[4] Bede gives what is indubitably his own view of English origins in a passage hardly ever cited. He lists what seem to be the names of all the tribes he had ever heard of – the list includes the Huns – who lived in what we should call southern and central Germany. I think he means to tell us that he only knew that the ancestors of the English came from those parts. What then of Hengest and Horsa?

The names mean literally 'horse' and 'mare'. This does not immediately inspire confidence, though the Anglo-Saxons did use animal names for persons. There is the obvious case of the sermon preached by Archbishop Wulfstan of York, the *Sermo Lupi*, the sermon of the Wolf to the English. If a wolf could preach a sermon to the English, a horse could lead them into battle. In his classic book *The Origins of the English Nation*[5] the late H. M. Chadwick made a case for supposing that a late Roman source knew of a man, probably called Hengest, who was the leader of the invaders of Roman Britain. In the event we have only two sources, both written generations later than the events they describe, both coming from very recently literate societies. The Bede interpolator is suspiciously precise about personal and geographical names; Bede himself has the imprecision of honest ignorance. There can be no doubt that a people called the Jutes played some part in early English history and they probably came from Denmark. But it seems improbable they would form an alliance with two other peoples and that the ensemble would fit in three boats. A tribe per boat? The three boats seem about as historical as the Three Bears, and they – the boats, not the bears – occur in other contexts, notably the arrival of Ælle and the South Saxons. Cerdic and his West Saxons arrived in five boats to conquer the middle portion of southern England.

A notable feature of the early sources before and after Bede is that they treat *Angli* and *Saxones* as the same people.[6] Some more light is thrown by the Continental traditions of the origins of the Saxons.[7] These suggest that the Saxons were a segment of a larger group called the Angles. If all this seems hideously complicated, it is none the less certain that it is a gross oversimplification. We have only a handful of facts, and we must do what we can with them.

It seems certain that the Germanic tribes of the sub-Roman world were not discrete entities held together by *Zusammengehörigkeitgefühl* but racially, or at least tribally, diverse in origin. Those origins are now beyond hope of unravelling. What held them together was probably the search for loot;

what kept them together was the transformation of loot into land and the necessity of defending that land.

At the same time a man called Cerdic was invading Hampshire and founding the kingdom of Wessex.[8] We depend for our information on the early portion of the *Anglo-Saxon Chronicle*, which I shall discuss more fully when it becomes a serious historical source. At the time of Cerdic the West Saxons were pagan and illiterate and could not have produced any written source, let alone one that uses the year of grace, as the Chronicle does. Social anthropologists have shown how prodigious the memories of illiterate peoples can be. Now Cerdic is a Celtic name: the West Saxons had two more kings with Celtic names during the next century. They could not have been invented. West Saxon kings with names beginning with C are the rule until the late seventh century. They cease with the accession of Ini, whose own father, a probable king of the West Saxons, had a C name. (Is this a form of ethnic cleansing? Had the C rule continued, the Celtic names must have recurred.) At about the same time the West Saxons began the conquest of south-west England. The most prestigious memorial of this is the abbey of Glastonbury, all of whose abbots henceforth had English names.

The centre of the English invasions, the area of their greatest intensity, was southern England, at first south-eastern England. In western and northern England the people were still Romano-British by culture and Christian by religion. It now seems certain that Christianity was more tenacious and deeply rooted than used to be thought.[9] In the fifth century the northern parts were capable of producing a missionary, St Patrick, who started the conversion of northern Ireland. He was the premier missionary but he did not work alone. There was an important Continental and Roman side to the whole enterprise.[10]

The late Romano-Britons had their own historian, called Gildas,[11] who is generally thought to have written about 550. He never gives dates, but in an important passage he seems to mean there was a battle soon after 500 between the descendants of the Romano-Britons and the English newcomers at a place called Mons Badonicus (Mount Badon) that the British won. Somewhere in this British revival came King Arthur. Only a romantic novelist would seek to find the real Arthur. But traditions of some antiquity say he was a real person and in sufficient number to make it difficult to explain them away. They never call him king but present him as a successful general. They say he won battles in places they name and there is general agreement where those places were. None of this sounds like myth.[12] The place above all associated with Arthur is Camelot, and here there is much disagreement. Popular opinion identifies Camelot with Cadbury Rings in the west of England. It seems likely to have been much farther north, near Hadrian's Wall.

The Englishing of the north of England proceeded very differently from that of the south. The first northern English kingdoms were Deira (whose early centre we cannot identify, although its ecclesiastical centre was Whitby and its political centre York) and Bernicia (whose centre was Bamburgh). At some point – when or how we do not know – the two joined to form a single kingdom of Northumbria. It is unlikely that one conquered the other, since members of both the Deiran and the Bernician royal families ruled Northumbria from time to time, though there was always friction between the northern and southern parts of the kingdom. King Æthelfrith of the Bernician dynasty (592–616) put Northumbria on the map. He subdued northern England to Northumbrian rule so quickly as to make any suggestion of a folk migration totally implausible. It is obvious – as archaeology confirms – that the bulk of the inhabitants of Northumbria at its widest extent must have been of Celtic origin, although its ruling class was entirely Northumbrian, and it seems that Christianity survived on a larger scale than used to be thought. There is, then, a marked difference between English origins in the north and the south of the country especially where ecclesiastical matters were concerned. The river Humber became a political barrier and sometimes a political frontier. This remained the case throughout the Anglo-Saxon period.

We must now switch to the numbers game and consider the scale of the invasions. In the nineteenth century most – though not the best – historians supposed that what took place was a folk migration. It is no accident that the technical term, *Völkerwanderung*, is a German word, because the dominant school both on the Continent and in Britain, was that known as the Germanist school. Although a lot of what the members of this school taught is quite dead, it has for many historians a residual fascination that seems to me entirely deplorable. The Germanist school placed great emphasis on racial factors as formative of primitive institutions which they believed were favourable to freedom. The more extreme believers extended this view to seeing race – Germanic race in particular – as determining all that was good in European history. (Even French historians subscribed to this guff.) In later centuries Luther, who was German from the soles of his feet to the crown of his head, nearly destroyed the effete remains of Roman Christianity by effecting a reformation of the Church: anyway liberty broke out, though contemporary German peasants may have begged to differ. The last protagonists of this paean to race and liberty made it the bedrock of Nazi ideology, which shows how hollow and deceitful it all was. In looking at early European society the protagonists of this ideology always sought to maximise the scale of the invasions and emphasise their Germanic character. It is with this in mind that we must consider the way in which three boatloads of Germanic booty hunters, augmented by 'more' – if there is any reality behind the story of the Bede interpolater – were made into nations and, willy nilly, the ancestors of the English.

The only hard evidence for the folk migration theory comes from place names. English elements in place names seem predominant in the east of the country and become progressively less so as we move westwards. We need caution here. All place name experts know Old English, almost none know Old Celtic. Some of the English place names could be Celtic (just as what appear to be typical Welsh names, like Rhyl and Prestatyn, are in fact English in origin). Some names, like Dover, are simply translations of the original Celtic name. English place names are as common in the north as they are in the south-east, but we know there was no folk migration there. The late Provost of Kings, in a masterly study of the hill tribes of Burma, showed that language is a status symbol, not evidence of race.[13] It is possible to argue by analogy that the larger proportion of Celtic place-name elements that survives in the West of England proves the survival of a Celtic-speaking upper class. I do not think we can make meaningful guesses at the number of Germanic invaders, although it is obvious that they were fewer than used to be thought. It helps, however, to go round the problem by looking at early English social structure.

Scholars used to suppose that Germanic society in general and English society in particular were classless – hence the notion of Germany as the source and fount of freedom. In the Anglo-Saxon volume in the *Oxford History of England* Stenton claimed that if the Anglo-Saxons ever had an aristocracy they lost it *en route* from the Continent. In other words the Anglo-Saxons were the only invading army in history that lost its entire officer class and won.[15] There can be no doubt, however, that the Anglo-Saxons did have a class structure, and a hereditary one at that. The most important evidence is the wergeld, or man price. We are back to the feud. As has already been pointed out, the individual depended on his kindred for protection. It was their duty to wage a feud for one of their number if he were killed, unless the killer's kindred paid the man price. It would always be beyond the means of the killer alone and would in effect have to be paid by the man's kindred. The extent of the degrees of kinship liable for the feud is unknown for English society but, as has already been said, if men were too remotely related to be involved in the feud, except in the biological sense, they were not kindred at all.

The natural assumption of a modern student would be that the feud was a force making for social anarchy, but it was not necessarily so. In the 1920s and '30s the feud still obtained among the Nilotic peoples of the southern Sudan, now threatened with extermination by the Sudanese government. The social anthropologists who studied them (notably E. E. Evans-Pritchard) found that they enjoyed neither feuding nor finding large sums to avoid it. One joined a feud not from love of a first cousin once removed but because the feud was the only institution society had to protect the individual. Equally, it was all the protection the individual could look for from society. The family were likely to know which of its members were most likely to provoke a feud – those violent in drink for instance – and to take measures to control them. The feud is not necessarily an invitation to a permanent brawl but a way of containing violence.[16]

For this to be so, however, the feud must be confined to the paternal kindred group. Where maternal kindred were involved scatter feuds could result which could tear a society to pieces.[17] In England the feud was traditionally confined to the paternal kin group until the exigencies of the Viking wars forced King Ælfred to extend it to the maternal kindred as well. Even so the evil consequences of the scatter feud were held off or controlled in England for reasons that will presently appear.

When the English became Christian they became subject to the rules of the prohibited degrees within which a man or woman might not marry. The rules meant that two people who had a common great-grandparent might not lawfully marry. As a result, England, like the rest of Christendom, was an extreme example of what the social anthropologists call an exogamous society.[18] A wide degree of exogamy also limited the feud. If, by reason of the marriage taboos, a man was compelled to marry outside his native village he might easily be involved in a feud with his in-laws, which would hardly make for domestic bliss.

Such taboos are not necessarily a way of life. In any society there is a difference between what is the law and what are the rules public opinion compels people to obey. In the case of marriage within the prohibited degrees, in the absence of strong moral prejudices against many of the prohibitions there was nothing much the Church could do whilst the parties were living. Any study of the matrimonial attitudes of the later Carolingian aristocracy,[19] including the higher clergy, will show what a cavalier attitude was taken to what the stricter churchmen would have called lawful matrimony. But when a wealthy aristocrat died the Church had important powers of retaliation. It could pronounce the offspring of any such incestuous union illegitimate and give a remoter relative title to the dead man's property.

The wergelds by which feuds were avoided are the principal evidence of the class structure of Anglo-Saxon society. The king had the highest wergeld but we do not know what it was. His closest associates were the ealdormen and kings' thegns, who formed a power elite and had a higher than usual wergeld. For the rest the law recognised two main classes among men legally free, one with a wergeld of twelve hundred shillings the other with a wergeld of two hundred shillings. Throughout most of the period the first category were known as *twelfhyndemen* and the second as *twyhyndemen*. In the earlier sources the *twelfhyndemen* were also known as gesiths – that is, companions, presumably of the king. The *twyhyndemen* were also known as ceorls throughout the period. In the laws of Edgar in the second half of the tenth century the term 'twelfhyndeman' was replaced by the word 'thegn', which had hitherto been reserved for the highest class of magnate. The word seems to have had a connotation of service, but distinguished and honourable service. The higher class was distinguished as kings' thegns still. It is likely this was deliberate and part of Edgar's not very successful efforts to tighten the bonds of society.

The ceorl was the Germanists' favourite creature, the carrier of the new freedom the Anglo-Saxons were supposed to have injected into the body politic. In fact we know very little about the ceorl's status. 'Ceorl' is a word for a husband of any social class. In the early tenth century the laws of Æthelstan reveal that ceorls could become so powerful it took ealdormen and bishops together with their posses to put them in their place. Socially the ceorls were, or could be, upwardly mobile. They could, though we do not know when, achieve the status and wergeld of a thegn if they performed the services – principally military – due from an estate of five hides of land. That is, they had to have a landed estate the extent of which might vary but which was rated at five hides for the purposes of its obligations. If they maintained this enhanced status over three generations it became hereditary. The only ceorl whose status is defined in a literary source is one Dunnere,[20] a ceorl who fought at the battle of Maldon in 991. He is plainly the man of Ealdorman Byrhtnoth and part of his retinue. The only ceorl to be individuated in history turns out to be one of the upwardly mobile ones. On reflection this is not really surprising. The laws also reveal that ceorls were commonly slave-owners. The slaves were called thralls. We have no statistics but, on the rule of thumb that the lowest class in a hierarchical society is likely to have been the most numerous, there must have been more of them than ceorls. In spite of which the thralls rate only a single mention in *Anglo-Saxon England*.[21] It is obvious that in no sense was Anglo-Saxon England a free society and only wishful thinking ever made it seem so.

The power elite was composed of the king, the ealdormen and the kings' thegns. If we ask, 'From when?' the question admits no easy answer. When charters become plentiful the composition of the 'establishment' becomes obvious but many generations of society preceded the plenitude of charters. There must, I think, have been continuity in the early establishment but we must wait for James Campbell's new book to explore this further. From a study of the witness lists of the charters it is clear the ealdormen were recruited from the kings' thegns. The ealdormen were close to the kings, who normally married their daughters. The ealdorman governed a *scir*, the ancestor of the modern shire. The term comes from the Anglo-Saxon word 'to cut'. The idea behind it was that the kingdoms were cut up into areas of jurisdiction, each headed by an ealdorman. In many cases, especially in the south of England, the modern shires, or at least the pre-1974 variety, can be identified more or less with the ancient scirs. In the tenth century the expansion and consolidation of the kingdom under the house of Cerdic made the ealdormen very great magnates indeed. They now frequently ruled several shires. Some of them left wills that showed they had amassed, or perhaps inherited and maintained, enormous fortunes. Some of them left great estates to the Church – that is why their wills were preserved – and a very great deal to their families. East Anglia was ruled by a single family through nearly all the tenth century. It is hard to escape the conclusion that the power elite were what is usually called a hereditary aristocracy. Whether we look to the top or to the bottom of Anglo-Saxon society, it is apparent that the notion of a free Anglo-Saxon commonwealth waiting for William the Conqueror to clamp the Norman yoke on it belongs in the dustbin of discarded historical myths.

Fairly recently the means the Anglo-Saxons used to exploit the wealth of the land they had taken over have become a good deal more intelligible than they once were. For the best part of a century historians have debated the problem of the origins of the manor. The manor was a – if not the – basic unit by which the upper classes exploited the lower. The majority of historians have supposed that the manor was invented in the late Anglo-Saxon period. (Some have even supposed it was introduced by the Normans.) There has always been a minority opinion, expressed most notably by H. M. Robertson, that the manor was inherited by the Anglo-Saxons from the Romans. The scholars who held this view argued for a basic continuity between Roman Britain and Anglo-Saxon England. The other party rejoined that if, as they thought, the manor was introduced in the late Anglo-Saxon period, there was no evidence to indicate any such continuity. There is no doubt that the manor was an institution in the course of development, some of which is late Anglo-Saxon. But what is important is the means by which a minority Germanic elite organised and ruled an alien population, means which may be very old indeed. It now seems that both parties were debating the wrong question. The manor was indeed ancient but it was neither Roman nor Anglo-Saxon, nor can it be discussed as though it were a discrete social entity: the manor had a context. Recently the existence of what are now called multiple estates (or federal manors) has been recognised.[22] These were noticed by scholars looking not for traces of the origins of the manor but for evidence of the early economies of Celtic Britain, notably North Wales and Scotland.

They discovered a striking family resemblance between these Celtic economic arrangements and those of the early English. The first to be identified was the multiple estate of Aberffraw in south-west Anglesey. Several more have been identified in other parts of Britain, notably one near Leeds in what was once the kingdom of Elmet, a Romano-British succession state that retained its independence until a generation before the coming of Christianity to the Anglo-Saxons. In England the multiple estates were called shires, though they had no direct connexion with the later counties. One of the earliest we have evidence of is the great estate near Sheffield called Hallamshire. Another was Islandshire in Northumberland (the island was Lindisfarne), near Bamburgh. An important example lay in what used to be called Lancashire, the area between the Ribble and the Mersey.[23] Since there are Welsh and Scottish parallels that direct influence or institutional diffusion cannot explain, it would seem that the multiple estate was a Celtic institution and a very ancient one.

It has also been noticed that these estates could explain an anomaly that has puzzled students of place names for a long time. This is the significance of the common place name Walton. The two elements that compose it are certainly Old English and mean the *tun*, village of the foreigners. The Anglo-Saxon word for foreigner was *weahlish*. The foreigners the Anglo-Saxons most frequently encountered were Romano-Britons and the word moved from meaning foreigners in general to one particular kind of foreigner, hence our modern word 'Welsh'. Walton was the village of the Welsh. Waltons are commoner in the east of England than they are in the west. The explanation seems to be that it was the part of the estate the Welsh were kept in. It is becoming apparent from several directions that the 'English' are much more racially mixed than nineteenth-century historians liked to believe. Again one must stress one is not talking about a homogeneous population but a socially and racially divided one.

They could fragment into what historians called the classical manor[24] or the multiple estate could grow, sometimes very rapidly, into much bigger units. Aberffraw was the kernel of the later principality of Gwynedd. Islandshire grew into Bernicia, then into Northumbria. Another disputed question concerns the way the warrior class held its land. We are fortunate in having a letter written by the Northumbrian monk Bede, the greatest intellectual of his day.[25] He wrote it towards the end of his life to his bishop, Ecgberht of York. The point of the letter was to tell the bishop what Bede thought of the state of the Northumbrian Church. His comments are critical and sometimes scathing but when he comes to speak of Northumbrian monasticism he is most revealing about the prevailing forms of land tenure. Bede is speaking only of the Northumbrian situation but it seems certain that what he has to say would be true of some parts of southern and western England but certainly not of the Midlands. Bede says that warriors earned land in a way that leaves no room for us to suppose that they inherited any.[26] Monasteries cannot survive on purely precarious tenure any more than universities can in the twentieth century. They needed continuity of land-holding to maintain their schools, feed their members, house their libraries and maintain the constant round of prayer that was their *raison d'être*. Before Bede wrote his letter a way had been found of meeting these needs by the introduction of a new system of land tenure called bookland. Land was held by book, that is by a written charter. No Northumbrian landbooks have survived, not even plausible fakes. But it is unlikely that they differed much from their southern counterparts that have. The charters of two of the main centres that early produced charters, Canterbury and Worcester, differ in some ways but have a striking family resemblance.

The formulas of the landbooks confer perpetual possession of the land named, always at first on a church, sometimes personified by its patron saint. Bede explains that noblemen are turning their families into pseudo-monasteries to enjoy the privileges of *ius perpetuum*, perpetual possession, for themselves and their descendants. As a result there is no land to endow warriors *emeriti*, that is, young warriors who have proved their military capacity in the king's service and now expect an estate called a *læn* or loan on which they can marry and bring up a family. The disappointed men are going elsewhere for employment and Northumbria is being denuded of its gesiths as a result.

It would seem that a society under constant military pressure could scarcely afford the luxury of hereditary tenure. It needed evidence that a new landholder was a competent fighter. In Bede's day the hegemony of England was passing from Northumbria to Mercia, the Midland kingdom. Bookland may well have had something to do with this. In the kingdom of the Hwicce – roughly Worcestershire, Warwickshire and Gloucestershire as they were before 1974 – land was booked to churches, real or imaginary, on some scale. The Hwicce then fell under Mercian domination. The Mercian kings did not attempt to abolish the bookland the rulers of the Hwicce had created but they supervised it closely. In Mercia proper, land was not booked until ways had been found of imposing various forms of military service on bookland, whether held by churches or laymen. (Charters booked to laymen with no pretence about them are found from the late eighth century, when the structure of military service on bookland was in place.) It could be argued that the monasteries of the Mercian heartland had all their muniments destroyed by the Vikings. What seems to me against this is the fact that it took all the learning of a Stubbs to show that the early Evesham charters were forgeries. The forged charters from Crowland could not deceive a schoolboy. The Evesham forger knew what Anglo-Saxon charters looked like; the Crowland forger did not. Thus bookland seems to have played some part in the rise of Mercia and the fall of Northumbria and the kingdom of the Hwicce.

We know from experience how expensive the maintenance of institutions of learning and culture is. The early Church is unlikely to have come for nothing. We have no evidence of the incomes of particular churches but there are the physical remains of buildings, books, precious objects for liturgical use, which show that some churches must have commanded enormous incomes. The most famous single surviving book is the Lindisfarne Gospels. It has been calculated that hundreds of calves must have been slaughtered to provide the parchment. In addition some sixteen hundred calves would have been needed to make the *Codex Amiatinus* and its siblings. Near Northampton is the finest of the surviving pre-Viking churches, Brixworth. It may have been built in a single operation in the late eighth century; at any rate, it was completed then (although there are those who would date it in the ninth century). It is a very creditable version of a Roman basilica. We do not know who built it but it was not connected with any centre of wealth or power.

The scholarly achievements of Bede are rightly celebrated but they would not have been possible unless he had had access to a great library. The books he quotes show him to have been very widely read and he must have read many books he does not quote. The books were made from expensive materials and, of course, by hand. Many objects, often obviously of secular provenance, made from precious metals survive from all over England. There were lean times. After the rise of Mercia very little original comes from Northumbria. Bede himself wrote his history after Æthelbald had become the dominant ruler south of the Humber. But the impression is strong that the Northumbrian Church was living on its capital (not only its intellectual capital). The two most famous Northumbrian churchmen of the generation after Bede, Willibrord and Alcuin, both found their careers on the Continent. But there was always money somewhere in England and it was spent on sumptuous things.

We know a little about how the money was raised and where it came from. We have an eighth-century document called the Tribal Hidage. It is a Mercian financial record. It lists what is probably a complete tally of Anglo-Saxon tribes south of the Humber and assigns each a round number of hides – which I have already pointed out are units of service, not area. Perhaps the most striking proof is the hundred hides of Chilcomb. This was a well defined area of several square miles surrounding Winchester. The hundred was held by the monks of Old Minster, who got one hundred hides of food rents and labour services from their peasantry. They in turn rendered only one hide's worth of services to the king. Thus a great estate had two different hidations, one looking down and one looking up. The Tribal Hidage not only rated the tribes in hides but where possible in hundreds.

The hundred was one of the most ancient units of Anglo-Saxon local government, although it finds its way into the sources only in the tenth century. It is clear that by then it had a long history behind it. It was not invented in England but is found in Francia, where it has the Latin name *centena*. From the first life of Wilfrid, written about 700, it seems that the Northumbrians and the Mercians fought a war over who should pay the other tribute. On that occasion the Northumbrians won, though their victory did not endure for long. It was the liability for this tribute that the Tribal Hidage was meant to record. No Northumbrian version of the Tribal Hidage survives but it obvious from Bede that there was one among his sources. The tribute must have paid for a lot of the treasure.

Hundreds did other things than raise taxes. The counties were subdivided into hundreds, each of which lay in one county only. Whether this was because counties were divided into hundreds or whether counties were originally combinations of hundreds we do not know. The hundred had a court that met once a month and settled lawsuits. We have seen that the lord of the shire was the ealdorman. He had minions called hundred exactors: the name speaks for itself. Not the least important function of the hundred was military. In the tenth century the royal ealdorman and author Æthelweard[27] calls the local army the hundreds. In an important sense English government and English cultural achievements rested on hides, hundreds and shires. After the creation of the Danelaw the hundred was replaced by the wapentake in that part of England. While in some ways the wapentakes were very similar to the hundreds it is not likely, given the different cultural backgrounds of the Vikings and the Anglo-Saxons, that they were identical. I repeat, we know more about what hundreds did in the tenth century than in the earlier period but I am convinced that in the tenth century it was the records that were new, not the functions.

Having said something about English social groupings and the sources of English wealth, it is time to turn to the top of society and find out how English government worked. Traditionally England was a heptarchy of seven kingdoms. There were in fact more than seven at first, though some of the smaller ones were really dependencies of the larger. The greatest kingdoms numbered far fewer than seven. The Anglo-Saxons could not imagine any form of government other than monarchical. Their kings were above all generals. A rare defeated king who survived the battle he lost was usually deposed. The king was advised by his *witan*. For a long time this was, and sometimes still is, seen as the king's council. *Witan* is a plural but not a collective noun. It means literally 'wise men': in the Middle Ages the men who mattered were automatically deemed wiser and better than their inferiors. They were *maior et sanior pars* – the great and the good, we should say. In most periods such men are wealthy: in the Anglo-Saxon period they certainly were. The *witan* consisted of ealdormen, king's thegns and bishops, and a correct translation of the word would be 'magnates'. Very occasionally the sources use a collective noun, *witenagemot*. This term was horribly misused by Victorian scholars to give Anglo-Saxon politics a democratic flavour they did not possess. The Regius Professor of Modern History in the university of Oxford, Edward Augustus Freeman, could speak of the *witan* as voting and describes courses of action as implementing majority decisions. None of this was based on evidence: it rested purely on assumptions of a Germanist character.

There were no constitutional guidelines. Kings took decisions because they were expected to. How far they sought advice, how much they heeded it, how far their advisers felt free to speak their mind, is usually unclear and was probably largely undefined. In the few cases when it is clear there is little comfort for those looking for Anglo-Saxon democracy. In the interesting eleventh-century work the *Encomium Emmae Reginae*, Encomium of Queen Emma, Emma's husband, the future King Cnut, is consulted, along with other counsellors, by his father, King Sweyn of Denmark, as to whether he should invade England. It is obvious that Sweyn had already made up his mind, that the counsellors, including Cnut, knew it and that they hastened to say what Sweyn wanted to hear. In the earlier period Bede makes it plain that it was Æthelberht who decided that Kent should accept Christianity and many of his people followed him only out of fear. In both these cases the decision was about very grave matters but there seems no doubt that the king alone took it. When there appears to be evidence of genuine debate it is unwise to make too much of it. In the next chapter we shall encounter a Northumbrian king faced with a very serious ecclesiastical decision which, if we accept Bede at face value, he took after a free and independent debate. But the best source makes it clear that the king had made his mind up already. The debate was a farce.[28]

This brings us to another element in Anglo-Saxon kingship that seems at first sight very strange, although it is not unique to England and is explicable, given the strongly authoritarian version of kingship that obtained in the early Middle Ages. This is the importance of the length of a king's lifetime. When the king died or was killed political order began to disintegrate. The new king had to restore order before normal political life could be resumed. His success in doing so, the speed with which he did it, and the concessions he had to make in the process, determined how normal that political life would be. Nothing prevented the East Frankish kingdom turning from into a strong nation state, a real Germany, as the West Frankish kingdom turned into a strong nation state, a real France, more than the series of short reigns, with a change of dynasty, that followed the death of Otto the Great. In France, a little later, three men of exceptional ability ruled for the best part of a century. In the eighth century the Mercian hegemony transformed England, largely because it was exercised for almost the whole century by two very strong men.

Not all Anglo-Saxon kings were equal. From early in their history one king seems to have exerted hegemony over the others. Bede lists seven kings who held this position. The position was not hereditary until it settled in the hands of the Northumbrian and Mercian royal families in the seventh and eighth centuries, and even then it is better described as heritable. In the vernacular such a ruler was called *brytenwealda*, which means literally 'broad ruler' and seems to have been a very ancient Germanic way of describing the Roman *imperator*, emperor.[29] Sometimes, in English charters, the title is glossed in Latin, and by the eighth century it means not broad ruler but ruler of Britain. The correct word for this title would be *bretwalda*, and most scholars prefer the term. *Bretwalda* occurs only once, whilst *brytenwealda* occurs on a number of occasions, and must surely be the original Anglo-Saxon term. The similarity between *bryten* and *Britannia* made the meaning shift, and a single pedantic author made word and meaning coincide whilst everyone else went on using the traditional term, though with a different meaning. It is difficult to say what exactly the office entailed but it must have involved the taking of tribute. The *brytenwealda* was the man who used the Tribal Hidage.

The Church certainly took the hegemony seriously. When Gregory the Great despatched his mission to convert the English, he sent the leader of the mission, Augustine, to the then *brytenwealda*, Æthelberht of Kent. It is true that Æthelberht was married to a Christian, Merovingian, princess who brought her own bishop with her. Nothing suggests that Æthelberht was influenced either by her or by him. Gregory had a considerable patrimony in Gaul and he was in a good position to obtain intelligence about the state of England. He addressed Æthelberht as *rex Anglorum*, king of the English. This seems to have been the papal chancery's way of rendering *brytenwealda*. Abbot Adomnon of Iona referred to Oswald of Northumbria as *imperator*. The *brytenwealda* had important ecclesiastical powers. Æthelberht was able to make or persuade (I suspect the terms overlap here) British bishops to attend a conference with the Roman mission, although he had no authority to do so as king of Kent. The conversion of the West Saxons meant they required a seat for their bishop, which was fixed at Dorchester on the Thames. The endowment was authorised by the then *brytenwealda*, Oswald of Northumbria, as well as by the king of the West Saxons. Oswald had no other title to act like this in Wessex. In the middle of the seventh century Oswald's brother, Oswiu, was both king of Northumbria and *brytenwealda*. The see of Canterbury fell vacant. The new archbishop was chosen by Oswiu in association with the king of Kent. He went off to Rome for his *pallium*, the symbol of his metropolitical authority. He died on the journey and the Pope, relying on ancient canon law, appointed his successor. He announced that he had done so to Oswiu, *rex Saxonum*, ignoring the king of Kent.

Although we should like to know in more detail just what being *brytenwealda* involved, how continuously the powers were exercised, and so on, clearly the office mattered. The most common title given to Anglo-Saxon rulers was *rex*, king, but that does not mean *brytenwealda*. The practice of the papal chancery shows that it knew that one Anglo-Saxon king stood above the others, who he was and where he could be found. The earlier holders of the office came from different kingdoms in turn and there was no apparent continuity. In the seventh century this situation changes. There were several Northumbrian overlords to be succeeded by Mercian ones. The Mercian overlords saw most of the century out. They placed a new interpretation on the powers of the overlordship and found new ways of expressing them, transforming English society in the process. The office of *brytenwealda*, when carefully studied, can throw light on the making of the kingdom of England and the kind of political society it was.[30]

NOTES

1 Fourth edition, revised by W. S. Maguiness and H. H. Scullard, London, 1961.
2 Nicholas Higham, *Rome, Britain and the Anglo-Saxons*, London, 1992.
3 Eric John, *Anglo-Saxon Archaeology and History*, 5 Oxford University Committee for Archaeology, 1992, pp. 5 *et seq.*
4 *HE*, v, 9. James Campbell, *Essays in Anglo-Saxon History*, London, 1986, pp. 123–4, suggests the possibility that an early literary source lies behind what Bede says here, 'for these names belong to a fifth rather than an eighth–century context'. I think this is very probably true but it does not affect my point.
5 H. M. Chadwick, *The Origins of the English Nation*, Cambridge, 1907.
6 Eric John, *Orbis Brittaniae*, Leicester, 1966, pp. 5 *et seq.*
7 *Translatio Sancti Alexandri*, ed. Pertz, M[onumenta] G[ermaniae] H[istorica], *Scriptores*, ii, pp. 637–81.There is what seems an independent version of the same story in Widukind of Corvei.
8 F. M. Stenton, *Anglo-Saxon England*, 3rd edition, Oxford, 1971.
9 Charles Thomas, *Christianity in Britain to AD 500*, London, 1981.
10 *Ibid.*
11 Now the subject of an important book by N. J. Higham, *The English Conquest*, Manchester, 1994.
12 Dr Higham, *English Conquest*, pp. 203 *et seq.*, dismisses Arthur as mythical. It has seemed to many of us that the matter–of–factness of the basic information, especially the fact that the relevant sources never call Arthur 'king', suggests there was a real Arthur somewhere. He could be accommodated without doing any harm to Dr Higham's general argument.
13 Edmund Leach, *Political Systems of Highland Burma*, London, 1964.
14 Stenton, *Anglo-Saxon England*.
15 Stenton, *Anglo-Saxon England*, p. 304. 'In general it would seem that the circumstances of the migration to Britain had disintegrated whatever forms of primitive aristocracy had existed amongst the continental English, leaving few representatives of a genuine aristocracy of birth apart from the king and his kinsmen.' Sir Frank modified this view considerably in *Latin Charters of the Anglo-Saxon Period*, Oxford, 1955, pp. 60–1. It is not until p. 304 that this disintegration is noticed and there is some evidence that Stenton held this view somewhat perfunctorily cf. his remarks on Hengest. He always thought the early Anglo-Saxons did have an aristocracy, although he does not make

it clear they were more than minor royals. (This is a perfectly possible view of a primitive aristocracy and bears some resemblance to the aristocracy of Saudi Arabia.)

16 J. M. Wallace-Hadrill, 'The Blood Feud of the Franks' in *The Long Haired Kings*, London, 1962.

17 Eduard Hlawitschka, *Lotharingien und das Reich. Schriften der MGH*, Bd 21, Stuttgart, 1968, discusses the scatter feuds that rent Lotharingia in the tenth century in some detail. I owe a good deal to discussions with Professor Laraine Baric of the University of Salford, who pointed out to me the limitations of the 'benign' view of the feud taken by Evans-Pritchard and Max Gluckman. (Professor Gluckman was the inspiration behind Michael Wallace-Hadrill's similar view of Frankish feuds in *The Long Haired Kings*.) She introduced me to the existence of scatter feuds, of which tenth-century Lotharingia gives such good examples.

18 I wonder if it is possible that there is any correlation between the extent of the prohibited degrees and the degrees of kinship liable to take part in the feud?

19 Hlawitschka, *Lotharingien*, pp. 27–30, for the succession problems to Charles III.

20 *The Battle of Maldon*, ed. Donald Scragg, Oxford and Manchester, 1991, l. 255.

21 To be fair to Sir Frank, in his last paper on the ceorl, 'The Thriving of the Anglo-Saxon Ceorl', *Preparatory to Anglo-Saxon England*, ed. D. M. Stenton, Oxford, 1970, pp. 383–93, he modified his views somewhat. He acknowledged that the ceorl was frequently if not always a slave–owner and depicted him as a richer, more complex, more diverse figure than would appear from *Anglo-Saxon England*. Dr Higham suggests, I think rightly, that the curious rejection of much of Chadwick's work, especially that in his *Anglo-Saxon Institutions*, by Stenton is explained by the fact that Chadwick depicted Anglo-Saxon society as more hierarchical than he found tolerable. My book is the first account known to me that has absorbed Chadwick's *Anglo-Saxon Institutions* into its structure.

22 G. W. S. Barrow, *The Kingdom of the Scots*, London, 1975, pp. 1–68. G. R. J. Jones, *The Agrarian History of England and Wales*, ed. H. P. R. Finberg, Cambridge, 1972, p. 265, n. 2. for references to Dr Jones's numerous articles, cf. especially 'Multiple estates and early settlement', in *Medieval Settlement*, ed. P. H. Sawyer, Chichester, 1972.

23 Barrow, *Kingdom*, pp. 1–68.

24 Peter Sawyer, 'The Royal *Tun* in pre-Conquest England', in C. P. Wormald (ed.), *Ideal and Reality in Frankish and Anglo-Saxon Society*, Oxford, 1983, p. 285, has some interesting remarks on the history of estates in the late Anglo-Saxon period. 'The compact estates of the Wiltshire Domesday may have once been the component parts of much larger units that had been broken up. That seems to have happened to the estate of Bedwyn ...' The royal estates of the eleventh century do therefore seem to reflect arrangements of great antiquity that survived centuries of alienation and illegal seizures.

25 See Bede, *The Ecclesiastical History of the English People*, ed. J. McClure and R. Collins, Oxford, 1994, pp. 341 *et seq.*

26 It has been suggested by Dr C. P. Wormald in his Jarrow Lecture for 1984, p. 22 that Bede was referring to extra incomes for gesiths. They had their inherited estates and the king supplied something extra: 'Bede may have described bookland as *ius hereditarium* but he can never have thought that inheritance was invented by the endowment of the Church. My own solution does, I think, cover all the evidence, including Bede's puzzling phrase. It derives from the distinction, very widespread in early legal systems, between *inherited* and acquired poperty. What one inherited from one's kin could not be alienated from one's kin; but what one acquired in any other way could

be distributed at one's pleasure.' I cannot for the life of me see the relevance of this distinction. The inherited property, if it existed, I can see must go to the man's kin. On this distinction the man could leave his acquired property – what the king gave him – to whom he liked. Bede makes it clear he could do no such thing: it went back eventually to the king. A second argument of Dr Wormald's is why, if the Anglo-Saxons did not know of legal rights of inheritance, 'They differed so much from their Germanic cousins as to know nothing of the rights of heirs memorably enshrined in the Frankish *Lex Salica* and the Lombard Edict of Rothari.' He then cites Dr Ernst Levy, whose book on the Vulgar Roman law opened up the whole discussion. But Dr Levy is clear and emphatic that neither these codes nor any of the others contained Germanic law. They were all Vulgar Roman law, some of them more vulgar than others. The Anglo-Saxons were the only Germanic people who issued vernacular codes containing authentic Germanic law. They do not touch on hereditary tenure. Where he most drastically fails, however, is that he does not deal with Bede's criticism of the new bookland, that it forces young warriors to seek service in other lands because they cannot get anything from the king, all the available land having been booked to magnates who claimed to have founded monasteries. But according to Dr Wormald they had their inherited land, which they must have abandoned. Stenton *Latin Charters of the Anglo-Saxon Period*, pp. 60–1, took the same view of Bede's letter as I do.

27 *Æthelweard's Chronicon*, ed. A. Campbell, London, 1962.

28 Stenton, *Anglo-Saxon England*, p. 123. It would be possible to minimise Eddius's remarks here but I follow Stenton in thinking Eddius meant to dismiss any suggestion of a real debate.

29 Carl Erdmann, *Forschungen zur politische Ideenwelt des Frümittelters*, Berlin, 1951.

30 Dr C. P. Wormald, 'Bede, *Bretwaldas*, and the Origin of the *Gens Anglorum*' in *Ideal and Reality in Frankish and Anglo-Saxon Society*, suggests a minimalist interpetation of the notion of the *brytenwealda/bretwalda*. 'In a nutshell, a king with great power might be hailed as *Bretwalda*; but a *Bretwalda* may not, as such, have had powers' (p. 117). '... the *Bretwalda* was less an objectively realized office than a subjectively perceived status' (p. 118). Dr Wormald thinks that Englishry was an example of Dr Wenskus's *Zusammengehörigkeitgefühl* and traces signs of it before Bede entitled his history in the way he did. He acutely points out that Boniface's letters written before he had discovered Bede show a wide sense of what being English meant, not all of it flattering. He observes, 'the Anglo-Saxons developed a sense of communal identity which inspired one of the world's great histories, and which drew its strength from spiritual ideals rather than political realities' (p. 128). But the political disunity in early Anglo-Saxon England that he stresses to belittle notions of the *brytenwealda* also emphasises the notional nature of that Englishness. From what I have said above the Roman *curia* recognised that the *brytenwealda* mattered in practical politics. The *curia* was well used to the political *machismo* of Germanic kings but did not treat that institution as an example. It seems to me that in discussing the problems of *Stammesbildung* one cannot oppose spiritual ideals and political realities. The politics are what make the ideals prevail. It was hegemony, overlordship, the resistance to the Vikings that did so in this case, and the notion of *brytenwealda* was part of it. None the less what Dr Wormald has to say about the creation of his spiritual ideals and where they came from is very important.

CHAPTER 2

Anglo-Saxon pagans, saints and sinners

THE ANGLO-SAXONS were pagans for almost the first two centuries of their time in England. What did this paganism amount to? It is almost impossible to say. We have a mid-ninth-century account that goes into some detail on the pagan practices of the Old (i.e. Continental) Saxons. It occurs somewhat improbably in a work by two monks of Fulda called the *Translatio Sancti Alexandri*. This work was commissioned by a Saxon nobleman, Count Waltbrecht, who had recently founded a great Saxon monastery. He was given the remains of one St Alexander – I should guess, the almost mythical early Pope, Alexander I. Waltbrecht was the grandson of Duke Widukind, the great opponent of Charlemagne and his Franks, who remained a pagan until late in life. Waltbrecht was only a second-generation Christian, and pagan traditions were likely to be still remembered in his day. Unfortunately for reasons given in the last chapter, the relations between Anglo-Saxons and Old Saxons are obscure. We cannot be sure how much resemblance there was between the two paganisms. Ibn Fadlan's account of the goings-on of the Muscovite Vikings[1] suggests they had something in common with the Old Saxons and both were a good deal more savage than the evidence suggests the Anglo-Saxons were. In the twelfth century much was written in saga form of the religion of the pagan north:[2] the sagas plainly represented much earlier traditions. What is said suggests that the religion of the north differs in some ways from either that of the Old Saxons or that of the Muscovite Vikings. (The sagas are vastly more entertaining, for one thing.) In the end, comparative study will not get us very far. We can only rely on insular sources and what is indubitably general and Germanic. But it can be said that no branch of Germanic paganism displays much sign of either piety or morality Bede explains the significance of the names of the months. Four of them were named after pagan festivals. Hredmonath was roughly our March: Eostermonath the month (April) when the cults of the goddesses Hretha and Eostre were celebrated. Eostre gained immortality by giving her name to the greatest Christian festival, Easter. Blodmonath, November, was when the cattle were slaughtered. This was not as extravagant as it sounds because men could not provide enough food for all but a handful of cattle through the winter. Four days of the week are still named for heathen deities, Tiea, Woden, Thor and Freya, who became Tuesday, Wednesday, Thursday and Friday. Place names attest to the importance of hills and mounds in Anglo-Saxon paganism. Harrow on the Hill comes from the Old English *hearn*, meaning 'sanctuary' and was plainly a cult centre of some importance, as in a way it still is. These sanctuaries seem to have housed the cults of more than one god. The prudent king of Essex, Redwald, even included an altar dedicated to Christ.

The chief Anglo-Saxon god was Woden, whose nature and the style of whose godliness have been brilliantly illuminated by Professor Turville-Petre.[3] Woden was the god of warriors, and his cult developed comparatively late, about the beginning of the Christian era.[4] His cult seems to reflect the change from an agricultural life style to one based on war. In a way he is the god who presided over the fall of the Roman empire. He was not himself a warrior, and he is sometimes made to look ridiculous – in Scandinavian tradition, at any rate. What characterised him was not military ability but what in New York is called *chutzpah*, a combination of hard-faced impudence and low cunning in getting out of awkward places. Richard Wagner, who had an extraordinary empathy with Germanic paganism, got Wotan (his spelling) right in *Das Rheingold* and *Die Walküre*. As in the *Ring*, Wotan had a special fortress called Valhalla, guarded by courageous warriors recruited after they had been killed in battle. He feasted them nightly and in the great battle that would be the end of the world he would lead them to defeat. The nearest parallel to Woden in the modern world would be a Premier League football manager. I am not merely being facetious but trying to indicate that there are traces of the kind of psychological imagination that produced the religion of Woden still with us. It is not surprising that the earliest generations of Anglo-Saxon Christians were drawn to the cult of Michael, whose place in Christian eschatology is not dissimilar, except that Michael is going to win. He was a popular patron of early churches, some of which are suspiciously close to former shrines of Woden.

Another well attested pagan cult in both English and Continental sources is what a Belgian scholar called *l'ivression sacré*. The Anglo-Saxons believed that getting high on alcohol was a passport to mystical experience. They held what were called byttfyllings round bonfires on high places. These events called for some organisation, and the groups responsible for that organisation were called gilds: the first examples of what was to become a characteristic feature of medieval economic life. Contemporary Christian writers called them *deoflumgylde*, devil's gilds. By the middle of the Anglo-Saxon period they had lost their pagan connotations but their other activities continued, as I suppose they still do.

The Pope at the turn of the sixth and seventh centuries was Gregory the Great and he sent a mission, made up of monks he had attracted to the monastery he had made out of his Roman town house, to the English. Its leader was a man later known as St Augustine of Canterbury. Why did Gregory do this? Many scholars have supposed he had quasi-political motives. It was thought Gregory was having trouble with the Irish, and weighing up the Irish has never been a strong point of English historiography. By this school the Irish were seen (or as many as were visible, which was not a lot) as charming and simple; ascetic, of course, but essentially anarchic. Anyone acquainted with modern American politics must conclude that they have changed over the ages more than somewhat. This same school saw Gregory as an ecclesiastical Justinian who sought to organise a highly centralised Church tightly controlled from Rome. The Irish were an obstacle to his plans. They entered Gregory's world in the person of an Irish monk called Columbanus, who was certainly born in Ireland but spent all his adult life in south-east Gaul and northern Italy.[5] He founded a number of monasteries, the last of which, Bobbio, near Milan, was perhaps the most famous. As far as we know Columbanus was the first to create a monastic empire by means of which his monks could be protected and moral standards promoted. His flagship monastery was Luxeuil, and from there he ran his monastic connexion, taking all major decisions himself. Like most Irish clergymen he calculated the date of Easter differently from the clergy of the Roman tradition – as did some Gaulish clerics, for that matter. The school of historians I am criticising blow this up to a major heresy but what was at issue was a method of calculation not easily, and certainly not permanently, resolvable owing to lack of mathematical and astronomical expertise. There could be no question of heresy here but it was thought that what was at issue was a clash between the Irish and Roman temperaments: that no contemporaries, least of all contemporary Romans, took the issue very seriously was ignored. Having said that, true though it is of the state of affairs looked at on a large scale, the point remains that in Northumbria the issue did matter. Wilfrid seems to have thought it important, and it made Bede's life uncomfortable on occasion. The trouble was, there was always a certain tension between Deira and Northumbria. In the middle of the seventh century it was accentuated when Bernicia stood for the 'Irish' Easter and Deira stood firmly for the Canterbury mode of calculation, thus adding liturgical to existing tensions. Columbanus's Irish monks, towards the end of Columbanus's life, penetrated Italy itself when Columbanus was forced to flee from Gaul to Bobbio. He thought little of the Gaulish bishops he and his monks had to deal with. A study of the agendas of the reforming synods of the time in the Gaulish provinces suggests that many of them were depraved men totally unfit for their office. If Columbanus called them rude names he spoke no more than the truth. But bishops are seen by many as the rock on which the papal notion of the Church rested. Even if the episcopate represented a holy whorehouse, to question its quality was anarchy. Columbanus and Gregory were not in fact far apart in their views of their contemporary bishops. But this school of thought was obsessed by Irish anarchy and supposed that Gregory had conceived a master stroke like a holy Bismarck: he would put an end to this anarchist nonsense by converting the English.[6]

The Columbanian monks are likely to have been mainly from Gaul and Italy and unlikely to have known anything about Ireland beyond what Columbanus told them. His writings do not suggest that Ireland played much part in his thought. How could the conversion of the English have affected Luxeuil or Bobbio? It is hard to see that, since the English had few, if any, contacts with the Irish, their conversion could have made much difference in Ireland anyway. Within two generations of the conversion of the English, Irish holy men were drawn into important links with the new Christians, especially those in the north of England. But the influence went from Ireland to England, not in the other direction.[7] In any case, none of this can have had the slightest effect on the structure of the Church.

If one looks at Columbanus' writings without preconceptions and at Gregory's policies without confusing them with those of Innocent III, a very different picture emerges. Columbanus left a small corpus of literary work.[8] His main book was a collection of miscellaneous comments on the monastic life called simply *Regulae*, 'Rules'. He also addressed letters to the Popes of the day, including one to Gregory the Great, whose reply, if there was one – and I shall later suggest there was – has not survived. Some of his letters are highly critical as earlier scholars did not hesitate to point out. But Columbanus does not suppose them delinquent like the Gaulish bishops. What he is critical of is their slackness in wielding the sword of Peter to cut heresy out of the Church.[9] In the early years of this century a French doctoral thesis pointed out, reinforced by the approbation of the famous

Duchesne in his widely circulated study *The Origins of Christian Worship*, that within ten years of Columbanus's death Luxeuil, his monastic capital, was professing the rule of St Columbanus and St Benedict. If we follow up the connexions between the three abbots, Benedict, Gregory and Columbanus, a rather more credible prehistory of the conversion of the English emerges.

Although Gregory never knew Benedict, who died about the time Gregory was born, their reputations remain for ever intertwined. Almost all we know of Benedict comes from the writings of Gregory.[10] He tells us that Benedict wrote a rule conspicuous for its discretion, and in the second book of his dialogues gives what purports to be a brief biography. It is hard to see how far Gregory meant to be taken literally and how far he was turning Benedict's biography into an allegorical account of the monastic life – an abbot called Exhilaratus is rather hard to take. Many now think that the story of Benedict's relationship with his sister Scholastica is meant, not literally, but as a personification of a spiritual experience. Gregory regarded monasticism as the foremost weapon of Church reform and he saw Benedict as a potential ally. This not to say that Gregory thought of himself as an ecclesiastical Justinian, with Benedict as his henchman. The true story is rather more interesting as well as more plausible.

Columbanus knew of Benedict and admired him. His successors at Luxeuil were doing nothing he would have disapproved of when they joined their two rules together. A few years ago Dom Adalbert de Vogüé, in his great edition of the *Rule of St Benedict*,[11] noticed for the first time that Columbanus wrote with the Rule at his side since he quotes from it twice. This seems to me to show that Gregory did reply to Columbanus. He could hardly not have replied: Columbanus was one of the most famous, if controversial, ecclesiastics of the Mediterranean world. Who else was likely to have been in a position to supply him with a copy of the *Rule* other than Gregory?

What was happening had to do with the very special ecclesiastical situation in Gaul. When Clovis and his Franks took over Gaul, unlike the other Germanic conquerors of the Roman empire, they became Catholics, not Arians. There were too few new, let alone literate, Christian Franks to be able to furnish bishops for the Gaulish Church, so that until the advent of the Carolingians most of the bishops came from the old Gallo-Roman establishment. Columbanus's solution – he was the first to try it on any scale – was to build a connexion of monasteries that could protect each other in times of persecution. The persecutors were usually the bishops. This was likely to appeal to Gregory, who was much criticised for appointing monks to central Italian dioceses even when, as was usual, they were not gentlemen. The earliest monks were not clergy. They worshipped at the parish church like everyone else. The respectable regarded them as a kind of hippy. The founding father of Western monasticism was St Martin, who eventually became bishop of Tours. His appointment was a true *exceptio probat regulam*. He was an ex-Roman legionary who, when released, became a monk and attracted a following. We have an account of his election to the see of Tours by his contemporary and biographer, Sulpicius Severus: it is hilarious. Martin was the last person the aristocratic clergy wanted, but his monks – dirty, unwashed, with unkempt hair – turned up in force and were so menacing none dared gainsay them. So Martin was elected: he was the outstanding Gaulish bishop of his time.

Gregory introduced this conflict into Rome itself. His own foundation did not follow the rule of St Benedict,[12] which has led scholars to question whether he had ever read it. But his monastery was an urban institution, whilst the *Rule* was for rural communities. In such a matter you cannot legislate for town and country in the same breath. Gregory used his community as a recruiting ground for the kind of higher clergy he wanted. He seems to have appointed a dozen monk–bishops,[13] most of whom were regarded with distaste by the predominantly aristocratic secular members of the papal *curia*. For about a generation monks and seculars alternate in the see of Peter. The relations in the curia between monk and secular were not harmonious, as we can see from the papal obituaries in the official collection, the *Liber Pontificalis*. Gregory's successor was a man called Sabinus, an enemy of the monks. In the first life of Gregory, written by a religious of the community of Whitby in Yorkshire, a peculiarly unpleasant miracle is ascribed to Gregory. He appears in the night to Sabinus and kicks him to death.

The last of the Popes associated with Gregory was Honorius I. He was a monk and very much prepared to use papal authority to promote the monastic party. He showed his sympathy for the Columbanian ideal and his acceptance of Columbanus's criticisms of the bishops by granting Columbanus's successors the privilege of exemption from episcopal authority, placing them directly under the authority of the Holy See. Columbanus's connexion did not endure but others persisted in attempting the same policy with the same means, with no permanent success until the creation of the Cluny connexion in the tenth century. Cluny's means were essentially the same as Columbanus's, the exemption from episcopal authority secured by papal privilege and a direct and immediate relationship with the Holy See. The impact of Cluny's success on both religious and secular society can hardly be overestimated.

Now the conversion of England was begun by Gregory the Great. This meant that the English were not just converted to a liturgy and a book but brought into a whole web of papal policy and faced with the consequences of Columbanus' view of monasticism. For example, a Northumbrian monk called Wilfrid encountered Columbanian monasticism in south-east Gaul. He was deeply influenced by the encounter and on his return to Northumbria set about replicating Columbanus's idea of monasticism in England. The consequences were what Northumbrian (and not only Northumbrian) politics were about for a generation.[14]

There is no mystery and not much politicking behind Gregory's motives for sending Augustine. The old empire had a great hold on men's imaginations still; Gregory was no exception. England was the only substantial part of that empire in pagan hands. The circumstances were favourable. The overlord of the English, Æthelberht, had a Christian wife with her own personal bishop. Conscience, imagination, desirability and feasibility are sufficient explanation.

It is hard to gauge how much residual Christianity there was left in England. It was certainly not equally distributed. The south had been in pagan hands for over a century. Even then, when Æthelberht accepted Christianity and gave the mission an old church for Christian use, Bede knew it had been dedicated to St Martin. (Mr Campbell has suggested to me that knowledge of this dedication was probably derived from the Queen's household.) This can have been known only from popular memory, and it sounds as if the building had not been put to other uses. The residual Christians had been cut off from resources financial and intellectual but is it likely that they would – or could – have embraced the religion of Woden? In the north Christianity had certainly not died, and much of the north was conquered by pagans only a generation before the arrival of the mission.[15]

Gregory had chosen a senior monk from his Roman community to head the mission. Augustine reached Kent and met Æthelberht for the first time on the Isle of Thanet in 597. Æthelberht insisted on meeting in the open air in case Augustine had some sinister magic up his sleeve. (It does not sound as if the Queen or her bishop had had much effect on his education.) There were good reasons why Æthelberht may have been minded to accept the new religion, and I think he must have been, to accept conversion from Rome rather than baptism at the hands of a Gaulish bishop. Had he done so the way would have been open for the see from which he had come to claim authority over the new Church, and that Æthelberht understandably did not want. (Perhaps he had learnt some things from his wife and her bishop after all.) It seems that Gregory understood this, and Augustine was consecrated bishop before he reached England. Gregory never meant Augustine's seat to remain at Canterbury indefinitely. Gregory had some knowledge, however imperfect, of the English situation. He knew that London was by far the largest and most populous English town, and he intended Augustine to move his see there as soon as possible. But London, then as now the most pagan centre in England, did not accept the new faith for another half-century, and by then tradition and reverence for Augustine had made it impossible to displace Canterbury.

There is little doubt that Gregory's drive and enthusiasm were the decisive force behind the mission's success, limited though it was in the first generation. James Campbell has written:

> Not the least remarkable thing about the mission was the number of missionaries; nearly forty, with others joining them in 601. To compare this number with the total of Italian clerics known to have to come to England in the four and a half centuries of Anglo-Saxon relationship with Rome which followed, namely five (all legates on brief visits), is to have a hint of the force of Gregory rightly called the Great.[16]

At first the mission seemed to have things all its own way. Canterbury was soon joined by the see of Rochester, always to some extent dependent on it. The king of the East Saxons was converted and a see established at London. The success was deceptive. When Æthelberht died in 616 his son was still a pagan. The first Christian king of the East Saxons died about the same time, and his sons drove the first bishop of London from his see. The new king of Kent soon converted to Christianity and King Redwald of East Anglia became a Christian on a visit to the Kentish court. Redwald had succeeded Æthelberht as *brytenwealda*, and that must have seemed a great triumph. But Redwald, returning home, found his wife and some of his senior *witan* opposed, so he sought a compromise. As Bede put it, 'in one and the same temple he had an altar for the sacrifice of Christ and another for the victims of demons'.[17] It is possible that Redwald was buried at Sutton Hoo.[18]

About the same time Redwald helped the head of the Deiran royal family, Edwin, drive his Bernician rival into exile at Iona. Edwin then became king of Northumbria. He was showing signs of seeking conversion. His patron and superior is unlikely to have looked with favour upon Edwin's entry into the orbit of the king of Kent, as his conversion must have entailed. It is usual to suppose that Edwin teetered on the brink for three years before committing himself to the new religion. It has recently been plausibly argued that Edwin waited nine years before conversion and that the Kentish princess he married, Æthelburga, along with the first Northumbrian bishop, Paulinus, went north in 619. Paulinus was not consecrated bishop of York until 625 and Edwin was at last baptised in 628.[19] In effect Edwin postponed his baptism, his public act of adherence to the Christian faith, until after the death of the *brytenwealda*, Redwald – another proof that the office must be taken seriously.

The Canterbury mission was not destined to convert Northumbria permanently. In 633 an alliance was forged between the pagan Mercians, now growing in power under their king, Penda, and the Christian British king, Cadwallon. They attacked Northumbria and won the battle of Heathfield: Edwin was killed. Paulinus fled from York, escorting the Queen and her daughter back to Kent. He never returned. The heroic figure was the one member of the mission who stayed, James the deacon. Only Bede tells us anything of him and he does not say very much.[20] He was, however, still working as a missionary when Christianity was reintroduced into Northumbria, this time for good. The source of this new conversion was the abbey of Iona. Iona is in what is now called Scotland but was then the ecclesiastical centre of the kingdom of Dalriada, whose inhabitants were called Scoti. They had invaded western Scotland from Ulster, and until the tenth century Scoti meant Irish, although it is the root of Scot and Scotland. The Bernician leader, Oswald, had taken refuge there when exiled by Edwin and become a Christian. Oswald defeated the pagan–Christian alliance, became king of Northumbria and turned to Iona for a bishop. The Irish, including Iona, determined the date of Easter by their own conventions – now, but not originally, special conventions. As has already been pointed out, the date of Easter became a problem from time to time because astronomical knowledge was insufficient to furnish a permanent solution. This meant that after a while the date of Easter became impossibly early or late. The resolution of the problem was early felt to be one of the functions of the Pope. The incursions of the English had cut off communication between most of Ireland and mainland Europe. Rome and Ireland were separated in this matter largely by circumstances and inconvenience. Another great issue of principle was at stake, or so it seemed, raised by the peculiar organisation of the Irish Church. The Roman principle, inherited from the days of the Christian empire, was for a Church based on urban centres presided over by a monarchical episcopate. The Irish, on the contrary, enjoyed an essentially rural organisation. They did not deny or disregard the traditional liturgical functions of the bishop, but their bishops lived in monasteries. If they were not themselves abbots they lived under the authority of the abbot of the monastery. This is supposed to have constituted a lack of respect by the Irish for the proper principles of hierarchy. Ireland had never been part of the Roman empire, and consequently there were no towns there. What alternative did they have? As we have seen, it was the Irish monk Columbanus who had plainly seen that in the sub-Roman world in which he lived the urban episcopate was the main source of corruption in the Church, and he convinced many, including some Popes, of the need to base the structure of the Church much more on the monastery and the countryside.

King Oswald established himself as *brytenwealda* and subjected the south of England to his hegemony if not his direct rule. He was killed at the battle of Heavenfield and succeeded by his brother Oswiu (642–71), who also ruled the southern English intermittently. It has been pointed out that at the height of his power Oswiu ruled more of Britain than any ruler before James I. Oswiu's main claim to fame is to have ended the dispute, in England at any rate, over the date of Easter. He ordered a synod to be held at Whitby in 664 to determine the question once and for all. In Northumbria the liturgical divisions were verging on the farcical. The queen, formerly a Kentish princess, followed the Roman Easter whilst Oswiu was faithful to the tradition of Iona, which meant that one was feasting for Easter whilst the other was fasting for Lent. But in Northumbria serious political complications had set in.

Oswiu had made his son under-king of Deira, with considerable personal power. Under the influence of the queen – she was not his mother – the young man had adopted the Roman Easter. It was presumably prevalent in Deira anyway. Under-kings tended to identify with the basic customs of their back yard and were not very successful if they did not. On the other hand their fathers expected them to obey their commands implicitly. Not surprisingly, under-kings frequently ended up in rebellion. The Easter question meant that a liturgical component had been added to the tension, always prevalent, between Bernicia and Deira.[21] But this added source of tension could be removed quite easily if Oswiu adopted the Roman Easter, and that is what he did. There was what appears, according to Bede, to have been a full debate in a synod held at the abbey of Whitby in 664. The Irish party was largely made up of the monks of Lindisfarne, the offshoot of Iona founded when Oswald became king of Northumbria. The Roman party was led by the bishop of an English see who was of Frankish origin and whose command of English was not adequate to present a case. The responsibility fell to a young Northumbrian monk, called Wilfrid, making his debut on the Northumbrian scene. Wilfrid is often presented as a pompous, pushing prelate by those who ignore his Columbanian background. The late Père Grosjean spoke of Wilfrid's *calcul* in achieving the position of spokesman for the Roman party in the synod. There was no scope for calculation on his part. He could not possibly have contrived that the senior bishop of the Roman party should be unable to speak English. If ever a man was pushed into the limelight on an occasion like this, that man was Wilfrid. The Celtic party defended their liturgical practice by an appeal to the tradition of Columba and Iona. (Columba was the founder of Iona.) By way of rebuttal Wilfrid cited the tradition of Peter and Rome. Oswiu then asked who was greater in the kingdom of Heaven, Columba or Peter. Celt and Roman alike cited Matthew xvi: 'Thou art Peter and on this rock [Peter's given name was, of course, Simon, and Jesus was renaming him] I will build my Church.' This is not a real debate: it is obvious that Oswiu had made up his mind from the start. If he had not, prudent politics would suggest that it was better not to have a synod at all than exacerbate relations with Northumbria by maintaining the *status quo*. Eddius, Wilfrid's first biographer, says Oswiu was smiling when he asked the question – in the circumstances, a decidedly leading question. Oswiu added that he would have no quarrel with the man who held the keys of the Kingdom of Heaven. Conformity was required or departure from Northumbria. Some of the liturgical conservatives withdrew to Ireland.

This left Wilfrid by default the leading Northumbrian ecclesiastic. He had been a monk of Lindisfarne but by favour of Alhfrith had been made abbot of Ripon, in Deira, which drew him into the Roman party. In the aftermath of the synod Oswiu made considerable concessions to the Roman party.[22] Soon after Whitby the Northumbrian see was moved to York, as Gregory the Great had wished, though its bishop was not immediately given metropolitan status. In fact the Northumbrian see was vacant. The bishop in 664 was Colman, who would not change his liturgical practice and withdrew to Ireland. His successor was a tactful and eirenic choice called Tuda. He was Irish but from southern Ireland, where contact with Gaul had persuaded the people to adopt the Roman Easter. He died of plague within the year and Wilfrid was chosen to succeed him. It is certain that, when he chose Wilfrid, Oswiu meant him to rule the whole Northumbrian see.[23] Wilfrid went to Gaul for consecration. He has been criticised for doing so and then staying on in Gaul for a long time. It seems that Wilfrid scarcely had much choice. He could not have gained an impeccably canonical consecration in England, and that was essential after an upheaval like Whitby. Wilfrid did not dally but was consecrated soon after his arrival in Gaul. The date of his arrival, probably by coincidence, fell just before a Gaulish synod, where he was consecrated. Inevitably, under the circumstances, it was a grander consecration than was usual. He did not return to Northumbria for months but it is unlikely that the delay was voluntary. It is evident from Bede that at some point Oswiu and his son quarrelled. The son rebelled and was never heard of again. This rebellion must have occurred after Whitby. Oswiu knew that Wilfrid was his son's protégé and was unlikely to have looked on him with much favour. It would seem that Wilfrid, out of favour at the Northumbrian court, was forced to stay in Gaul by the political situation.

In 667 the recently elected archbishop of Canterbury died on the way to Rome, so the choice of his successor, by ancient custom, lay with the Pope. Pope Vitalian had connexions and sympathies with the eastern Mediterranean. He made what looked like a completely mad choice, a sixty-seven-year-old monk from Tarsus, in what is now Turkey, called Theodore. Theodore knew both Greek and Latin. He may have been an insane choice but that choice certainly worked.[24] Theodore was completely exotic to the English: the only thing they knew about his place of birth was that St Paul came from there too, which is unlikely to have done him any harm. He was burdened with no local patriotism, had an acute political sense and a great deal of tact. In fact his pontificate lasted twenty-one years and he was able to accomplish much. He founded a school at Canterbury whose quality survived him. He wrote a penitential – a guide for confessors: it is now generally accepted that he was in fact its author and in consequence gained a reputation as a master of Christian morality. He was plainly the most popular bishop the English had so far encountered, and Bede said of him that he was the first pastor the English willingly obeyed.

He slowly – and caution here was inevitable – reconstructed the diocesan structure of the English Church. The first dioceses were tribal sees but English political geography was now in a state of change and the mode of the day was greater unification and a reduction in the power of the tribe. It meant that every political crisis entailed an ecclesiastical crisis every time a tribe lost territory. A good example is Lindsey, which had been a Northumbrian dependency but by Theodore's day was gradually slipping under Mercian control. A few years later Mercian dominance of Lindsey became permanent. Theodore made it a separate diocese so that its integrity did not ebb and flow with the vicissitudes of political control.

Theodore plainly favoured an increase in the number of dioceses and a consequent decrease in their size. It has been argued that he wanted to reconcile English and Irish ideals of Church government. The Irish had no towns and necessarily no dioceses in the conventional sense. There were towns in England, though they were small and in decay. This was not a situation that called for reconciliation. The fastest mode of transport was a horse: the larger the diocese the less often a bishop could visit his flock. Theodore was merely being realistic. He broke up dioceses but he never made diocesan boundaries straddle tribal ones. He also had to deal with the kind of situation that faced Wilfrid when he was made bishop of York. Canon law required three bishops for a licit consecration, and when Theodore arrived in England there were not always three bishops available at any one time. The ready acceptance by the English of Theodore's often radical changes is proof of the sense and tact with which he worked: it also suggests that his English contemporaries were not without sense, either.

One of Theodore's first problems was what to do about Wilfrid. Wilfrid had already returned to Northumbria, to find another Lindisfarne monk called Chad intruded into his see of York. It is impossible for Chad not to have known that his election was irregular. Wilfrid made no fuss and retired to his monastery of Ripon. But a serious breach of canon law had occurred, and Theodore had to do something about it on his arrival. He deposed Chad and restored Wilfrid. The Mercians had not been Christian long enough to be able to provide a bishop from among their own people. They had to have a 'foreign' bishop and, Chad being available, Chad was who they got. Wilfrid retained York until he was expelled by King Ecgfrith in 678. He was never to achieve real restoration to episcopal office. Theodore acquiesced in Ecgfrith's action and took the opportunity to subdivide the see of York. This, of course, not only made sense but could be justified by Gregory the Great's written instructions. Wilfrid, as a riposte, became the first Englishman to appeal to Rome. Restoration to his see was not his first consideration but the maintenance of his monastic connexion. Wilfrid was making a great monastic connexion in the manner of Columbanus and for the same reason, the good of the Church. He had been deprived of his monasteries, and he also complained that the new bishops were deliberately chosen to be objectionable to him. The Roman council obviously thought he had been treated badly but did not wish to disavow Theodore. They restored Wilfrid's Northumbrian monasteries and they restored Wilfrid to the see of York whilst maintaining Theodore's division of the diocese, giving Wilfrid the right to replace any objectionable bishop. When Wilfrid returned to Northumbria in 680 he produced the papal decision and was promptly thrown into prison by

Ecgfrith and kept there for nearly nine months in very harsh conditions. On release he went into exile. He was very uncomfortable first at the court of the Middle Angles and then at that of the West Saxons. He found refuge with Æthelwahl, the pagan king of the pagan South Saxons. Within five years he had converted them both and was given a great estate at Selsey on which he built the first Christian church of what was to become the diocese of Chichester. The West Saxon king, Cadwalla, attacked the Isle of Wight and in the process killed Æthelwahl. The Isle of Wight was still pagan, so Cadwalla gave Wilfrid another great estate and the mission of converting the islanders. Wilfrid had now to return to Northumbria, so he gave the estate and the mission to his nephew and the last stronghold of English paganism was converted in a generation.

In spite of his considerable achievements Wilfrid has had a bad press. Dr Mayr-Harting has put it succinctly:

> If there were popularity stakes for the story of the Anglo-Saxon Conversion to Christianity, they would not be won by Wilfrid. The discreet silences of Bede,[25] and the protestations of his own monk and biographer, Eddius, have both in their different ways helped to detract from the saint's reputation. In the *Realencyclopaedie* for Protestant Theology and Church (1908), not the obvious place to find a favourable verdict, Böhmer wrote that in truth Wilfrid did not fight for Right, nor for Rome, *sondern für sich selber* (but only for himself), Meissner pursued him with a relentless hatred through the pages of an acute book on the Celtic Church which reads like the fears of a paranoid Irish abbot. Even dispassionate historians, however, find the apparently self-centred litigiousness, the pomp and circumstance, and the crusading energy of the man [*sic*] unattractive.[26]

These strictures seem to miss the point entirely. Böhmer, who was a considerable historian and wrote what is still the best book on the Anglo-Norman Church, gives the game away when he poses, as the alternatives Wilfrid did not pursue, Right or Rome. Because Wilfrid pursued neither of these 'objectives' he is self-centred. Böhmer does not see that Wilfrid's right was not his and that Rome was not an issue, except for the nineteenth and twentieth-century historians of the kind who find the thin end of the Scarlet Woman under every bed. It is clear from Eddius that Wilfrid appealed to Rome not against the division of his diocese but to maintain the integrity of his monastic connexion. Wilfrid had spent years in Columbanian territory and had imbibed the Columbanian ethos to his fingertips.

Wilfrid saw clearly that this was the only policy capable of reforming the Church and deepening the conversion. I cannot see that there is any possibility of evading it. Wilfrid and Columbanus had only limited success with the policy. That did not prevent other, less well known men seeking to emulate them. The monastery of Peterborough (Medhamstede) was the head of such a connexion.[27] Dr Keynes has pointed out[28] that 'The association between Medhamstede and Breedon was perhaps the main axis in a Middle Anglian monastic "empire", which appears to have taken shape in the late seventh century, and which seems to have endured well into the ninth.' It is unlikely this 'empire' was entirely independent of Wilfrid's example at least.

The essential means were a great monastic connexion, sometimes protected from the bishops by charters of papal exemption, though not in Northumbria, where Wilfrid was both bishop and head of the connexion, but very much so in Columbanus's part of the world, where his great foundation, Bobbio, got the first such papal charter of exemption. It was not until the policy was given an enduring form in the early tenth century by the foundation of Cluny and the speedy formation of its connexion that the kind of reform of the Church based on the rural monastery that Wilfrid and Columbanus sought became possible. Neither of the two monks could have envisaged the tremendous consequences that success entailed. Unlike its predecessors, Cluny had the advantage of a favourable political ambience. Professor Joachim Wollasch, the greatest living authority on Cluny, once said to me that he did not think there was anywhere else in Europe where it would have worked. Cluny had the achievement but Wilfrid and Columbanus had the vision, none of which has been taken into account in the hostile verdicts quoted above.

The allegation of Wilfrid's lack of humility is remarkably imperceptive. We know in fact very little about his life style except that he rode with a retinue where missionaries of the Irish tradition would walk. The fact that people who talk like this usually have a Volvo in the garage is merely funny. In Wilfrid's day the horse was the fastest way of getting about. Wilfrid was not indulging in pomp and circumstance but choosing the means by which he could reach the most people in the time he had at his disposal. What Wilfrid can be criticised for is his lack of political nous. He was bishop of York, the chief Northumbrian prelate, and far too friendly with the Mercian king to be tolerable to the Northumbrian establishment. It is true he did it for the sake of enlarging his monastic connexion but he should have seen that he could not stand aloof from the everyday politics of Northumbrian–Mercian rivalry. The early abbots of Cluny never made the same mistake. If we pursue the popularity stakes metaphor a little further, Bede and Cuthbert would be strong contenders for the title of most loved early Anglo-Saxon saint. Nobody ever persecuted them, nor did they ever convert anybody that we know of. Wilfrid did in fact inaugurate successful missions to the Frisians and to the South Saxons, and he was imprisoned and exiled for what he thought – almost completely correctly – was right.

It used to be thought that Gregory the Great's monastery followed the rule of St Benedict and that Augustine was therefore a Benedictine monk who may be presumed to have brought the *Rule* with him. As has already been pointed out, it is now clear that Gregory did not use the *Rule*. It is clear that it was Wilfrid who first brought the *Rule* into England, although he did not use it exclusively in his monasteries: it is clear where he got his knowledge of it from.

We need to look a little deeper into what was special about Benedict, into why men should have wanted to erect connexions round his *Rule* and into why it was important for the English Church. Monasticism was founded by St Anthony of Egypt, and a version suitable for monks living in the harsher climate of western Europe was made by St Martin of Tours. What Anthony and Martin meant by monasteries were collections of hermits, subject to very little central control. St Jerome, writing about 400, could say, *monachus id est solus*, 'a monk, that is, a hermit'. Benedict deeply distrusted the eremitical life for all but the very few. He favoured what came to be called the cenobitic model for a monastery: a tight community of monks ruled by an authoritarian abbot. Benedict was not the first to think along these lines. About 500 a document was composed called the *Rule of the Master* because it is in the form of a dialogue between the Master and a disciple. Endless speculation has been devoted to identifying the author. One of the first candidates was Cassiodorus but he is a non-starter; it has even been suggested that it was an early work of Benedict himself. This is a case of trying to eat your cake and have it if ever there was one. The Master overlaps a good deal with Benedict and there is common wording. He was also more verbose than Benedict, and his rule was generally held to be a long-winded expansion of Benedict's until a French monk, Dom Genestout, on the eve of the War suggested that Benedict's rule was an abbreviation of the Master's. A telling point in favour of this is that the Master quotes from obscure fathers of the Church. The quotations are repeated by Benedict, but the Master knew he was quoting, Benedict did not. This is an equally telling point against the notion that the Master is really Benedict Mk I. The argument is still going on but the party of the Master is very much in the ascendant.[29]

The fact that Benedict modelled his rule on that of the Master in no way diminishes his importance. Benedict was an editor of genius. He cut out the Master's absurd, if picturesque, details, such as how bread arrived at mealtimes – in a little trolley suspended by a rope from the ceiling. This was meant to symbolise the ravens feeding Elijah. What would have been the reaction of a member of the community after twenty years of this palaver? Benedict drew up a rule that could be put into practice; the Master's never was. Benedict's additions were few but they transformed monasticism. Before Benedict monks were laymen who were expected to worship in the parish church – the Master permitted mass to be said in the monastery's chapel only twice a year. Under Benedict's rule it was usual for the monks to attend mass in the abbey church. Benedict made monasteries into spiritual republics, which meant that some of the monks had to be ordained to serve the communities' needs. Benedict opened the way for the monks to become part of the clergy. Gregory the Great carried the process a stage further. He made monks bishops, and there could no longer be any doubt as to the monks' clerical status. (It did not stop bishops trying to make monks pay tithes, like laymen, as late as the twelfth century.) Benedict did not create the whole tradition that bears his name. He was very anti-intellectual. He never speaks of a library. Apart from the Bible, the monks' reading was confined to a very few books carefully selected by Benedict. Even the Bible did not escape his censorship. Monks were forbidden to read the racier books of the Old Testament, such as the book of Kings, before bedtime in case they got too excited. On the other hand it is plain that Benedict expected monks to be able to read, though the language of his *Rule* was pretty low Latin.

This anti-intellectual stance could have done immense harm to the spread of literacy and Christianity if his disciples had done as he wished.[30] What prevented it was the work of another monk, less famous than Benedict but not less important, Cassiodorus, who retired from a successful career in politics to found a monastery, the Vivarium. His father was an immensely wealthy horse trader, said to be capable of supplying the entire Ostrogothic army with horses. Cassiodorus's idea of a monastic life was certainly a life of meditation on spiritual themes. But unlike Benedict he placed the highest value on literacy and literary work. He collected books and set his monks to copying them. When Columbanus and Wilfrid brought about the nearest thing then possible to Benedictine monasticism they added the tradition of Cassiodorus to that of Benedict. This was how the English were converted.

Obviously English monasticism was not perfect or all of a piece. What is startling is the speed with which the English produced works of art and

cultic objects of great splendour. The two most famous early insular manuscripts are the Lindisfarne Gospels and the *Codex Amiatinus*. The Lindisfarne Gospels were the work of one man, a Lindisfarne monk called
Eadfrith. He completed his work just before he became abbot of Lindisfarne in 698. The *Codex Amiatinus* was written at Bede's monastery,
Jarrow, in his lifetime. The scribes used as model Cassiodorus's great Bible
– very neat evidence that Cassiodorus had a direct influence on the young
English Church. The *Codex* was intended as a present for the Pope when
Abbot Ceolfrid retired in 716 and set out on a pilgrimage to Rome. I
imagine he did not intend to return but in the event he died on the journey and the book never reached Rome. It is in the Bibliotheca Lorenziana
in Florence. The Lindisfarne Gospels are the more beautiful to look at.
Eadfrith used Irish models for his ornamentation, using abstract and animal
motifs found on metal objects of Irish provenance. The *Codex*, however,
if less beautiful, was more significant for the future. For the first time English artists essayed what was an alien style to them: the representation of
recognisable human portraits. They did not do it very well but they began
the assimilation of a richly humane Mediterranean tradition of portraiture
into English pictorial style.

Perhaps the most significant feature of early English Christianity was the
speed with which the English monks mastered Latin sufficiently well not
only to copy texts but to undertake original literary composition. The first
notable author was the West Saxon monk, abbot and bishop St Aldhelm.
He was educated at the Anglo-Irish monastery at Malmesbury in the 660s.
He was then a student under Theodore of Tarsus at Canterbury. He was
abbot of Malmesbury for thirty years and then, in 705, bishop of Sherborne. His literary work came from the mind of a man of affairs who had
heavy non-literary commitments. Not surprisingly he wrote less than Bede
and, though his work had some influence here and in Frankish Gaul, it was
of less lasting importance than Bede's. His most famous work was the treatise on virginity written for the nuns of Barking about 686. It was much
copied and, if it contained sensible advice to nobly born nuns to shun pride
and avoid too rich clothes, it cannot be said that moralising on sexual matters brought out the best in the early English. It is interesting to see the
sources available to Aldhelm. He used Ambrose, the *Conferences* of Cassian, the African fathers, Cyprian, Tertullian and Augustine. He also used
Eusebius's *Ecclesiastical History* in Rufinus's Latin translation. It is unfortunately true at this period that such quotation did not mean the writer had
read the book he quotes. Lists of quotations were in circulation for those
who wished to display their learning and conceal their ignorance. In some

of his writings Aldhelm relied on the works of a polymath of a previous generation, Isidore, bishop of Seville. There can be no question that his knowledge of Isidore was both wide and deep. We do not know where Aldhelm got his knowledge of Isidore from. Aldhelm got his first education from an Irish abbot who would have been likely to know Isidore, but two manuscripts of Isidore survive from south-western Britain, and Aldhelm could have got his knowledge there.

What is striking is the speed with which the English received the Continental, Latin, tradition. Eadfrith had to have a Gospel text to copy for the Lindisfarne Gospels. What he used was a Neapolitan manuscript. This is easy to tell, because Eadfrith, following his model, prefaced each Gospel with a list of readings and the festivals to which the readings were appropriate. The readings are of a marked Neapolitan flavour. Among the cults indicated is that of St Januarius – he of the liquefying blood – then as now revered in Naples but in very few other places. The obvious source here would be Abbot Adrian, who left a Neapolitan monastery to accompany Archbishop Theodore to England. An alternative source would be the Northumbrian Benedict Biscop, who had visited Italy, though he penetrated no farther south than Rome. What is important is that less than century after the conversion of an illiterate population to Christianity there was sufficient knowledge of Latin for Englishmen to have significant literary contacts with the Mediterranean world and to make it necessary for modern historians to argue about who got what from where. It is not very important in itself to know where Eadfrith got his Neapolitan Gospels from or how Aldhelm came to know Isidore of Seville. What is important is that there was sufficient diversity of source material available to make scholarly dispute about origins and influences inevitable.

The new Christians did more than copy Latin texts. Towards the end of the seventh century some Anglo-Saxons were writing original books. Round about 700 appeared the first life of Gregory the Great written anywhere. It was written at the double monastery of Whitby, a monastery of which both men and women were members but which was always ruled by an abbess. No one knows quite how or why this odd form of cloister was invented (though the late Père Grosjean once told me he was convinced that the problem could be solved.) The origin is not in Ireland, as used to be thought, but must be in Francia, where such monasteries already existed and where many English noblewomen received their monastic training. It is therefore possible that the *Life* was written by a woman. As it is obvious that these double monasteries were not male-dominated, since the ruler was always a woman, it may even be thought probable. (Women authors were not unknown in the early Middle Ages.) The *Life* is in many ways a crude and superficial biography but the Latin is passable if not elegant. About the same time 'Eddius'[31] wrote his much maligned life of Wilfrid, and an anonymous life of Cuthbert, written from a very monastic viewpoint, appeared. Bede followed with another life of Cuthbert, written from a much wider perspective.

It is important not to dismiss these books as crude and unoriginal. The Whitby life of Gregory has what looks like a charming story but is in fact a theological point of the first order. Nearly three centuries earlier Christendom had been rent by a theological controversy between the greatest of the Latin fathers, Augustine, and a man whom Augustine called a porridge-sodden Briton named Pelagius. Pelagius offered a somewhat superficial view of Christian moral theology in which God's grace was played down and human moral striving played up. Augustine was the theologian of grace at its most transcendent but in the course of the dispute he advanced the view that no unbaptised person could go to heaven. He certainly meant physical baptism by water. It is likely that this thesis always had its opponents. Traces of opposition are found in Celtic sources, which has led some scholars to believe that there was always a residual Pelagianism among the Celts (and others to believe that there was a residual common sense that survived the Augustinian onslaught). It is possible there is some truth in this view but you do not have to be a Pelagian to see the rigidity of Augustine's view and to note the difficulties such rigidity creates. A little earlier than the life of Gregory, Abbot Adomnon of Iona wrote a biography of the founder of Iona, Columba. It is one of the greatest of the saints' lives of the Middle Ages. The death scene is incredibly powerful. Adomnon tells of a miracle of foresight performed by Columba. It is necessary to realise that such miracles were important to Adomnan because he was concerned to present Columba as a kind of Christian druid. The druids' followers apparently laid great stress on their foreknowledge of the future. Columba realised by intuition that a pagan of great moral virtue was dying unbaptised. He hastened to the side of the dying man, arriving just in time to baptise him. The line of thought is obvious but Adomnon saved his orthodoxy by having his man alive, if only just, at baptism.

The Whitby life of Gregory goes much further. We are told that Gregory was reading a book of Roman history – which one, we do not know. He found a passage in which the emperor Trajan was leading his army from Rome on a campaign. As he rode, an old woman, the widow of a former legionary, tugged at his bridle and told him she was not getting her pension. The emperor said he was too busy at the moment but to come and see him when he returned. She replied, 'I shall have starved to death by then', so Trajan got off his horse and settled her case on the spot. Gregory was so moved – and perhaps surprised – at finding a just secular ruler that he could not help praying for him. A stern angel – of the Augustinian school, no doubt – appeared and rebuked Gregory. Trajan died unbaptised: what is the point of praying for him? Gregory was unmoved and went on praying. Eventually the angel reappeared, looking pale and wan, with bags under its eyes, and said, 'We give in. You are such a holy man, no one in heaven can get any rest.' (I paraphrase, or rather the late Robert Bolt did.) The angel restored Trajan to life and Gregory baptised him. The Augustinian challenge had been met head-on and the first steps had been taken to broaden the doctrine of baptism. On one level a piece of superstitious nonsense; on another, a first-rate piece of theological thinking.

Most important of all, almost a century after the coming of Aidan to Northumbria, a native monk wrote the *Ecclesiastical History of the English People*. Bede wrote a good deal more than that: his biblical commentaries were perhaps more important to his contemporaries than the *History*. But the *History* retains its influence to this day, whilst the commentaries are almost forgotten. The *History* is in many ways a parochial book, reticent to the point of dishonesty. Bede is a master of the art of conveying a wholly misleading impression without actually telling a lie. I would offer as examples his account of the conversion of Edwin or his version of Chad's elevation to the see of York. The nearer he gets to his own time the more reticent he becomes. Bede was clearly a timid man: not for him the outspoken recklessness of Wilfrid. Since timidity is rather commoner than outspokenness in the groves of academe, this helps explain why Bede gets so much better a press than Wilfrid. But, when Bede wrote, Wilfrid had been dead for only a generation, and his career was still a live and controversial issue, which must explain much. Professor Walter Goffart has recently made a case that Bede was bitterly hostile to Wilfrid and meant to harm his reputation.[32] If so he certainly succeeded. It is evident that there was still a substantial element in the Northumbrian population of Romano-British descent, and some residual Christianity. Bede totally ignores them, though Wilfrid and his biographer did not. Within a generation of Bede's death his writings had been taken *en masse* to the Continent by the Anglo-Saxon missionaries, and his influence on what was to become Carolingian Francia was immense. In England Bede came into his own with the monastic revival of the tenth century: in the process he ceased to be a Northumbrian writer and became an English one. Freed from his Northumbrian parish, his overwhelming virtues obliterated his local and, let it be remembered, his temporal limitations.

It is interesting to shift our perspective, leave the world of learning and the learned, and look at *Beowulf*, an Anglo-Saxon poem that gives a unique insight into a half-Christian primitive society. It is the oldest epic poem in any Germanic language. It exceeds three thousand lines in length, and its date and origins are much disputed. Recently two German scholars[33] have revived the thesis, never quite abandoned in Germany, that it is a late poem of the same, or similar, date as the composition of the manuscript (the late tenth century). Their reasons seem to me of the *a priori* sort, such as the fact that texts are not transmitted over several generations without being deeply affected by the transmission. This is certainly true of a literate society, but to balance that we have several social anthropological studies of illiterate societies. There is no doubt that members of such societies have phenomenal powers of memory, making it plausible that quite lengthy texts could be transmitted intact by the power of memory alone. It has also been noted that, when literacy takes a society over, the phenomenal power of memory disappears. The argument from the necessarily corrupting fact of transmission has not the required force here. It seems to me that there is good evidence that *Beowulf* is basically an early poem. Although transmission has not left it entirely unaffected, the corruptions are relatively minor. It is, for instance, clear that the linguistic habits of King Ælfred's day have left their mark, but to no very serious extent. The poem reflects a much earlier time than the date of the manuscript. The form of land tenure and the concomitant inheritance rules that play an important part in the plot (the poem is surpassingly ill plotted) point to an era before bookland was introduced. Beowulf had to earn his 'inheritance' before he got it. The poem is set in Scandinavia and is decidedly pro-Danish in its sympathies. It refers to real events in Scandinavian history, and it uses motifs and episodes found in other Scandinavian poems. The poet was very much at home in this milieu, as were many other seventh-century Englishmen, to judge by archaeological finds, notably those at Sutton Hoo. It is not easy to feel that such feelings could have long survived the Viking invasions. It is true that Anglo-Viking relations were close in the nineth and tenth centuries but they were exceedingly hostile relations and do not seem to me conducive to the detached and sympathetic interest the poem shows. The majority of scholars have felt that the poem is eighth-century but there is a marked difference between those who think it is early eighth-century, the age of Bede and *Beowulf* (my own view) and those who think it belongs to the late eighth century and the age of Offa and the Mercian hegemony.[34]

It clearly hails from a time when Christian ceremonies and the Christian liturgy had taken root, because there is every indication that these were matters the poet took for granted. It can therefore hardly be earlier than the seventh century. In a generation inspired by the late J. R. R. Tolkien's lecture 'Beowulf and the Monsters'(written in between times from *The Lord of the Rings*) a school of English and American scholars have sought to argue that it is a deeply Christian poem full of allusions to the fathers of the Church. It is supposed to be a Christian allegory. No direct quotation from the fathers has been identified: it is all done by indirect allusions to patristic passages seldom recognisable to any but the ardent believer in the thesis. Where was the audience that could have appreciated that kind of poem? I doubt whether Bede could have recognised the allusions alleged, let alone the gesith who heard it sung 'at the mead bench'. Again, if the poem is a Christian allegory Beowulf would have to be a type of Christ, and no one has claimed that. Beowulf as Christ is completely implausible, as is the thesis of the whole school.[35]

Because the poem is set in Scandinavia it lacks local and topographical references that might have helped place it. But lines 1944–62 have been cited to argue for a Mercian context.[36] These lines form part of one of the digressions that are a feature of the poem, which can sometimes be explained and sometimes not. The digression drags in a much earlier Germanic king, Offa of Angeln. This has led some to believe that Offa of Mercia was seeking to cash in on the earlier Offa's legendary prestige: that some Mercian courtier knew it and included the digression to flatter the current Offa. If so it is a great insult to Offa's queen, whose reputation was in fact very high. Offa of Angeln is mentioned only in passing: the digression is about his wife, Thryth, who was in the habit of having warriors put in fetters or slaughtered if 'like the fascist bus conductor in Barcelona she misinterpreted a casual look'. To see this as an instance of the *topos* of the taming of the shrew is going rather too far. Offa of Angeln appears only as the husband of Thryth and gets only two and a half lines. It seems to me that if the poet intended an abstruse allusion to flatter Offa of Mercia he would have expanded Offa of Angeln's role considerably.[37]

The debate has had an unexpected consequence that leads us straight back to Northumbria. German scholars have discovered a new tool for understanding the early Middle Ages: it is called leading-name research. Aristocratic surnames do not occur until the middle Middle Ages. In this early period it is first names that often run in families and can disclose lineages and locations. Thus the early kings of Wessex, the descendants of

Cerdic, have names beginning with C until the late seventh century, when the last king with a C name was succeeded by a son called Ini. The Mercian kings are unusual in having only minimally discernible naming patterns at all. Offa's name points not to Mercia but to Northumbria. It is a characteristic name from the Bernician royal family. An Offa was brother to St Oswald and another was brother to Osred I. There is an Occa and a Boffa, both permissible variants in the leading-name game. How did the greatest Mercian king come to be called Offa? We shall never know. We do know that he was not closely related to his main predecessor, Æthelbald. Offa can have got Mercia only by fighting for it: he certainly had Northumbrian connexions of some sort and was a benefactor of the shrine of St Oswald at York. Once again the poem points back to Northumbria. It seems to me that the old thesis of the age of Bede and Beowulf still stands.

It will be apparent that *Beowulf* is a poem that requires deciphering rather than reading. But it is worth the effort. It throws important light on Anglo-Saxon religion a century or so after the conversion. It provides an alternative to the mainly hagiographical sources we have so far studied.

There is in the poem no evidence of hope of heaven or hell. There is no conception of personal sin or redemption. It is a poem imbued with an ethos much older than Christianity but an ethos undergoing evolution and in transition. If Wilfrid occasionally reminds one of Beowulf he was none the less deeply Christian. Early Anglo-Saxon theology was much more at home in the Old Testament than in the New – that is obvious from a reading of the first life of Wilfrid – but the book was firmly anchored in the Bible, all the same. Some of the poem is lost beyond recall. There are numerous words for what we must call a sword but they are unlikely to be synonyms. It is as if there were a language that had only one word for motor car, say automobile. Someone faced with an English text containing words like Jaguar, Porsche, Mini, 'banger', 'limo' and so on could not translate the text at all. The limitations of a person's language make for limitation of his thought. Now swords play a very great part in the poem. Beowulf's swords let him down with monotonous regularity. One senses that the sword motif and the failure of the swords were important to the poet. But we have never owed our life to a sword and can have no inkling what emotions such dependence induces.[38] We can see that the poem is suffused with what Virgil called 'a sense of the tears of things': that the relation between lord and retainer was intensely close but is presented almost entirely in economic terms. There is nothing in the least like the relationship between Achilles and Patroculus in the *Iliad*.

There was another aspect to early English religion than the scholarship, the libraries, the Mediterranean connexions. King Sigeberht of the East Saxons, a Christian convert, was murdered by his kinsmen because he would forgive his enemies. They were not being vindictive or anti-Christian. Forgiving one's enemies was a dangerous virtue in a society in which individuals depended on their kinsmen and, in the last resort, the feud for protection. We might here glance at St Guthlac, an excellent example of what early English Christianity was about. He was a Mercian nobleman who ran a gang of bandits and showed his Christianity by returning a third of what they stole to the victims. He renounced his wild life and founded a famous and austere monastery in the fens at Crowland. He is the perfect link between Bede and Beowulf: we know about him because he was the subject of an interesting Latin biography. We must not exaggerate but it is impossible to escape the feeling that, though there is much to puzzle us, the Anglo-Saxons had got a very long way in their first Christian century.

NOTES

1 P. G. Foote and D. M. Wilson, *The Viking Achievement*, London, 1970, p. 399.
2 G. N. Turville-Petre, *The Myth and Religion of the Pagan North*, London, 1964.
3 Turville-Petre, *Myth and Religion*.
4 The first person to notice this was Max Weber in his *Sociology of Religion*. This must be the most tedious work of genius ever written but it is a work of genius: it was travestied by most of the participants in the religion and the rise of capitalism debate, notably by Tawney.
5 Columbanus was more than an isolated individual with a few followers. He gave rise to what has been called the Hiberno-Frankish movement based on his flagship monastery, Luxeuil. See F. Prinz, *Frühes Mönchtum im Frankenreich*, Munich, 1965, chapter 4.
6 It is true this view has not found many defenders in the last fifty years but *Anglo-Saxon England* (3rd edition), p. 727, reads: 'There is a brief but masterly survey of the same field in S. J. Crawford's *Anglo-Saxon Influence on Western Christendom* (Oxford, 1933).' In its context this remark places Crawford's book on a par with Levison's masterpiece. Although Sir Frank praises Levison's book highly, in practice he either ignored or rejected it. One of the essays that comprise the Crawford book (the others are excellent) is the main begetter of the thesis that Gregory converted the English to dish the Irish. The thesis that Gregory aspired to be the Justinian of the canon law with the *Rule* of St Benedict as the mainspring of his policy is to be found in Dom John Chapman's *St Benedict and the Sixth Century*, London, 1929.
7 See Clare Stancliffe's interesting paper 'Kings who opted out' in C. P. Wormald (ed.), *Ideal and Reality in Frankish and Anglo-Saxon Society*. She points out that the habit of kings retiring to monasteries or going on pilgrimages from which they did not return was neither prompted nor encouraged by Rome or by the successors of St Augustine's original mission. She finds only two Continental examples, both probably influenced by Anglo-Saxon missionaries. The same idea was found in Ireland and she thinks it probably came from there to England rather than vice versa.

8 *Opera Omnia Columbani*, ed. G. S. M. Walker, *Scriptores Latini Hibernica*, 11, Dublin, 1957.

9 *Ibid.*: see the very long epistola v and especially p. 44.

10 Book 2 of the *Dialogues* in *Gregoire le Grand: Dialogues*, Sources Chrétiennes, ed. A. de Vögüé and P. Antin, Paris, 1978–9. There are numerous translations of Book 2.

11 *La Règle de Saint Benoit*, ed. A de Vögüé and J. Neufville, Sources Chrétiennes 181–6, Paris, 1971–2.

12 Dom Kassius Hallinger, 'Papst Gregor der Grosse und der heilige Benedikt', *Studia Anselmiana*, 42, 1957, pp. 231–319. This epoch-making article renders Dom Chapman's approach (see n. 5) totally untenable. Dom Hallinger shows conclusively that Gregory had no wish to impose any one rule on monks or to seek any uniformity of observance – that would have been impossible in his world, in any case. He was prepared to accept any honest rule as canonical. Dom Hallinger showed that Gregory did not impose the rule of St Benedict on his own Roman monastery, which means that St Augustine, the apostle of the English, was not a Benedictine and cannot be shown to have known the *Rule*.

13 Jeffrey Richards, *Consul of God*, London, 1980.

14 B. Colgrave, *Eddius Stephanus' Life of Wilfrid*, Cambridge, 1927, introduction, gives a résumé of Wilfrid's career.

15 Thomas, *Christianity in Britain*.

16 James Campbell, *The Anglo-Saxons*, ed. J. Campbell, Oxford, 1982, p. 45.

17 Bede, *HE*, ii, 15.

18 Stenton, *Anglo-Saxon England*, p. 51. It is equally possible that it was one of his successors buried there. Campbell, *The Anglo-Saxons*, pp. 32–3, has a brief and illuminating essay on Sutton Hoo. The late Michael Wallace-Hadrill had a paper, published only in a much diluted form, that questioned whether Sutton Hoo was a royal burial at all. It was the tomb of someone rich and important who is as likely to have been a king as not but the decisive evidence is the presence or absence of 'regalia'. Those who think Sutton Hoo is a royal burial place great importance on the whetstone. The whetstone is certainly a whetstone and differs from other whetstones in the British Museum only in its size (two feet against four inches) and the fact that it has never been used. If the whetstone was meant to be used by the deceased in Valhalla (this is what Michael Wallace-Hadrill suggested to me) it would naturally show no signs of wear. Against the claim that the whetsone is a sceptre is the absence of any decoration in the form of precious metals, although the other grave goods are rich and splendid.

19 D. P. Kirby, *The Making of Early England*, London, 1967.

20 Bede, *HE*, ii, 20.

21 The remarkable passage in *Anglo-Saxon England*, p. 91, cited in the essay on Stenton, shows clearly how serious the division over the date of Easter was potentially in Northumbria.

22 Eric John, 'Social and Economic Problems of the Early English Church', in *Land, Church and People*, ed. Joan Thirsk, *Agricultural History Review*, 18, supp., 1970, and Thomas, *Christianity*.

23 John, 'Social and Economic Problems'.

24 *Archbishop Theodore: Commemorative Studies on his Life and Influence*, ed. M. Lapidge, Cambridge Studies in Anglo-Saxon England, 11, Cambridge, 1995, appeared only when this book was being edited, so I am able only to notice it. It shows the enormous breadth of knowledge and contacts that Theodore brought with him: the importance of Theodore's Syriac background, in his day beginning to be swallowed

up by Islam; the importance of his stay in Rome; his influence on biblical study in England and above all his pentitential studies that unite the traditions of the Irish and that of St Basil. Mr Charles-Edwards, p. 170, writes: 'Theodore's Penitential is not, therefore to be summed up in terms of Theodore going Celtic. The contrast between insular and continental systems of penance has been exaggerated, and this exaggeration has created the problem. Theodore may be seen, in his penitential teaching, applying rules he had inherited from Basil, and applying them, moreover, to the conditions of a country in which feud was part of the fabric of society. Inevitably this meant that his approach came close to that of the Irish, for they faced a similar situation.' Mr Charles-Edwards is especially good on the effect the feud had on penitential practice.

25 Walter Goffart, *The Narrators of Barbarian History*, Princeton, 1988, chapter iv, 'Bede and the Ghost of Bishop Wilfrid', has important things to say about Bede's treatment of Wilfrid.

26 Henry Mayr-Harting, *The Coming of Christianity to Anglo-Saxon England*, London, 1972.

27 F. M. Stenton, *Preparatory to Anglo-Saxon England*, pp. 179–92, was the first to notice this. He was also the first to grasp the connexion between monasticism, loosely defined, and missionary activity. *Anglo-Saxon England*, pp. 148–9.

28 Simon Keynes, *The Councils of Cloveshoe*, eleventh Brixworth Lecture, Vaughan Papers in Adult Education, No. 38, University of Leicester, pp. 30 *et seq*. The quotation is found on p. 40.

29 M. D. Knowles, *Great Historical Enterprises*, London, 1963.

30 The late Dom Cuthbert Butler's *Benedictine Monasticism* is an unjustly neglected account of the subject. It deals very well with this aspect. For some reason Dom Cuthbert aroused the wrath of the late Dom David Knowles; see *The Historian and Character*, Cambridge, 1963. This is a classic instance of what E. M. Forster called the historian sitting in his professorial chair giving marks to men. The dismissive essay on Cuthbert Butler is the longest in the book although he was the least considerable of the men whose character Dom David studied.

31 On the identity of Eddius see Goffart, *Narrators*, pp. 281–3.

32 Goffart, *Narrators*. It is possible to argue that Goffart overstated his case but I am convinced it has a basis of truth.

33 W. G. Busse and R. Holtei, 'Beowulf and the Tenth Century', *Bulletin of the John Rylands Library*, 63, 1981. Since this article was published a number of other studies has appeared arguing for a late date for Beowulf.

34 At the moment opinion seems to be much more sympathetic to Busse and Holtei's view than to mine or Whitelock's. She is not here to say what she thinks, though it would not be difficult to guess: but for my part I would not budge an inch.

35 Eric John, 'Beowulf and the Margins of Literacy', *Bulletin of the John Rylands Library*, 56, 1973–74, pp. 388–422, *passim*.

36 Dorothy Whitelock, *The Audience of Beowulf*, 1951, Oxford.

37 Eric John, 'The Point of Woden' in *Anglo-Saxon Studies in Archaeology and History* 5, ed. W. Filmer-Sankey, pp. 131 *et seq*.

38 The paper that became 'Beowulf and the Margins of Literacy' was delivered to a seminar at Columbia University in New York. It was a lively seminar that owed much to Professor Bean and Professor Hanning and their students. One of the participants, a lady from the City system, objected strongly to my suggestion that the poet intended mild criticism of Beowulf for his behaviour towards the dragon, although I was not

the first to make the point. I also made the point that the words for sword, etc., were not synonyms but words whose meaning we had lost. I quoted Wittgenstein, though not by name: 'do not ask the meaning, ask the use'. The same lady asked: what is this nonsense about the distinction between meaning and use? There is only one kind of reply in this situation in which the point is important: quote an extreme example. So I said to her: the word 'fuck' and the word 'copulate' mean the same thing but they are not used in the same way. In her *Fiefs and Vassals* (Oxford, 1994), p. 13, Susan Reynolds expresses the same idea in more conventional terms: 'Discussions of terminology, moreover, generally start from the assumption, not only that certain words are particularly significant for feudalism, but that such words have core or technical meanings and these technical meanings were somehow more real and significant than the others. To do this is to ignore how language works. Words used in real life, especially abstract nouns, do not have core meanings which are more central or more right than others. Dictionary makers deduce meanings from usage. They do not control usage.' So far so good, but Bosworth and Toller, the compilers of the main Anglo-Saxon dictionary, do nothing of the kind. They impose meanings and admit exceptions only when the context forbids their choice of meaning. For example, their definition of *folc* is 'people': in some contexts *folc* cannot mean anything other than 'army', so 'army' goes to the end as a subsidiary meaning. But the cases where *folc* means unambiguously 'people' are no more frequent than cases where it means unambiguously 'army'. But all the ambiguous usages are classed with 'people', not 'army'. (The poem *The Battle of Maldon* uses *folc* eight times. Only two of the contexts allow it to mean 'people', the rest mean 'army'.) The practice of dictionary makers is not clear-cut: they often do control usage, or try to. In the case of *folc* the sensible thing to do would be to list the cases in which *folc* means unambiguously 'people', those in which it means 'army', and the neutral or ambiguous terms separately.

CHAPTER 3

Thought and action under the Mercian hegemony

THINKING AND TALKING as well as doing go to the making of political entities. It is worth while to follow up some of the the political and ideological themes that seemed important to the Anglo-Saxons themselves. I do not mean to imply that the early English had sophisticated abstract or philosophical notions at their disposal. They did not: but they did have a political vocabulary of a sort – and that not of a very English sort, into the bargain. They also had notions about their political community and what should, or should not, go on in it.

The obvious place to begin is the royal titles used in royal charters, the earliest considerable body of literary evidence. It seems that, with the partial exception of the kingdom of Kent, early kings thought of themselves as kings of their people, not of their countries. Just as Bede called his book *The Ecclesiastical History of the English People*, so early charters speak of the king of the West Saxons, etc. Apart from Kent no territorial titles are used in any charter with a reasonable claim to authenticity until the first half of the eighth century, when Æthelbald of Mercia uses one. It seems certain that the charter titles are significant. They are not simply evidence of the literary culture of the clerical *dictatores*. (*Dictator* is the usual term for the composer of a charter, as distinct from the scribe who wrote it.) We can assess the cash value, as it were, by marrying them with the political activity that accompanied them. We should be able to move tentatively from the minds of the clergy who wrote the charters to the minds of the kings whose wishes they were trying to express.

Most of the evidence comes from a narrow but exclusive circle, the religious and literary elite of the royal court. The evidence is deceptively varied in character: narrative sources, letters, royal charters. The early charters are generally taken to be local products: that is, the charter was written at the behest of the beneficiary, who must provide the labour and bear the cost. The early charters have a deceptively local and variable air about them. The charters were granted to the greatest men of the kingdom: the very early ones to churchmen, secular or monastic. Some of the communities they benefited had been lived in or ruled over by the saints who founded them and whose *Lives* provide what looks like a quite different type of source. In fact an identity of views on most matters, especially political, between the authors of the *Lives* and the dictators of the charters can usually be presumed. If we look at the careers of the early figures we know something about, we can see how narrow are the circles from which all our sources come. We have already seen that Aldhelm was an important literary figure, a monk, then an abbot and finally a bishop. In other words he was at home in the royal court as well as in the library. Abbot Adomnon of Iona wrote a life of Columba, who was not only the founding abbot of Iona but a kinsman too (they were both O'Neills, *recte* Uí Néill). Adomnon was also a much travelled man familiar with life in more than one cloister and more than one court. At first sight Bede seems a simple monk who never held important office. But his *History* was commissioned by the Northumbrian king and he was freely given information from all over England as well as from the papal archives. He shows intimate familiarity with the world of high politics – especially as regards what it was expedient to ignore.[1] These are the great names. The charters were mostly written by smaller men, but men sometimes familiar with the great names, and with their books often. What they say has to be taken seriously, even if it does sometimes read like nonsense on stilts.

It seems unlikely that, even if kings were content to let their literary men compose their charters, they took no interest in what went into them. Bede's king certainly took an interest into what went into his *History*: the sensitivity with which Bede treated political matters shows he had to be careful. The charters that survive in full were invariably witnessed by the King's *witan*, the greatest men in the kingdom, whose subscription implied recognition of royal authority as described in the charter. Since that authority could be and sometimes was disputed, the kings who claimed it could not be indifferent to how it was described. In any case the formulas of the charters match too neatly the political intentions of the kings who grant them for it to seem plausible that they represent only the whims of the churchmen who produced them.[2] This allows us a deeper insight into the nature of the Mercian hegemony. In the early eighth century King Æthelbald had to contend with the sharply expressed criticism of the great West Saxon missionary Boniface, then a metropolitan in West Germany. Boniface wrote a letter of complaint to Archbishop Cuthbert of Canterbury. Equal in rank they were, equal in stature they were not. Boniface complained that much was amiss in Cuthbert's province, which he took to be all England. He clearly thought Æthelbald was the villain of the piece: the king was obviously informed of the criticisms. What seems to have riled Boniface was the levying of the secular burdens of maintaining fortifications and bridge-building from the lands of the Church. Such was Boniface's prestige that, although he had not the slightest claim to jurisdiction in England, Æthelbald called a synod at Cloveshoe[3] in 747, the decrees of which show that a real attempt was made to meet some of Boniface's criticisms. A second, purely Mercian, synod was held at Gumley in 749 and from its decisions, and the fact that only two of the Mercian bishops attended, we can see what all the fuss was about.

For once there is little doubt that the saint was wrong and the king was right. We have already seen that the endowment of churches and the need to make it possible for them to support libraries, schools, scriptoria, as well as clergymen, created problems of land tenure and, above all, military service. The Church's needs were met by the creation of bookland, as was discussed above. I do not think we can make sense of Bede's letter to Ecgberht unless we suppose that bookland was originally exempt from military service. What Æthelbald proposed to do at Gumley was limit that exemption. He proposed to lay the burden of maintaining bridges and building fortifications on the holders of bookland. To Boniface this was pillaging the lands of the Church. Æthelbald pointed out that an adequate defence of the kingdom was as much in the interests of the Church as it was in the interests of secular society. It is hard to gainsay him, and he got his way, in any case.[4] Offa, his successor in every sense, added the further burden of supplying warriors for the *fyrd*. That meant the Church must use some of its land to endow the warriors who would perform the service. These three burdens used to be called the *trimoda necessitas* (or the meaningless *trinoda necessitas*) as though the phrase were an Anglo-Saxon technical term, which it is not. The sources speak of the common burdens or some equivalent phrase.

It was now possible, as has already been pointed out, for laymen to be given bookland with no loss of services, and the reign of Offa sees the first land books with lay beneficiaries. By the time of the triumph of Wessex in the tenth century bookland had become the common form of aristocratic land tenure.

The Mercian kings found other uses for bookland.[5] We find that Æthelbald was the first Anglo-Saxon ruler to intervene in kingdoms other than his own and supervise the granting of land books. He booked land in Wiltshire in the heart of Wessex; he confirmed the privileges of the Kentish Church; both the charters in question imply at least quasi-sovereignty.

What under Æthelbald had been occasional became frequent and brutal under Offa. One of Offa's first appearances in a charter is as a witness to a charter by which Eanberht, *regulus* of the Hwicce, granted privileges to Bishop Mildred of Worcester. For Bede the ruler of the Hwicce was *rex* without qualification, and *regulus* implies demotion. Creating bookland was a royal prerogative and Offa, however grudgingly, is recognising Eanberht's royal status. But his witness is stated in very high terms and amounts to overseeing the grant. In 767 Uhtred, again called *regulus* of the Hwicce, books land with the assent and permission of Offa, king of the Mercians. Soon after this, Offa booked land to 'my sub-king Ealdred namely the ealdorman of the Hwicce'. Offa was reducing the kingdom of the Hwicce to a mere province of Mercia. In 781 Offa annulled titles bestowed in the names of kings of the Hwicce at the synod of Brentford. He was mainly concerned with the title deeds of Worcester cathedral; he compelled the cathedral in the future to hold its property in the Mercian kings' name. There are no more charters given by the rulers of the Hwicce after Brentford, and the chief religious centre of the Hwicce was compelled to accept that it was now a Mercian diocese.

Offa repeated the process equally successfully with the South Saxons. They had had a long connexion with Mercia. When they were converted Wulfhere of Mercia stood as godfather to their king and gave him the Isle of Wight as a christening present. This did not necessarily imply subordination but, whatever the legal pretexts, if any, Offa made his annexation of Sussex utterly plain. In 770 a charter was granted in the name of Osmund, king of the South Saxons, to which Offa added one of his arrogant witnessing formulas. By 780 we have a document issued in the name of Oslac, ealdorman of the South Saxons, and that was the end of their independence and their charters.[6]

The most important field of Offa's colonial policy was the kingdom of Kent. Kent had a history of independence much older and stronger than the kingdoms so far discussed. It also housed the chief see of the English Church. The charters of the period imply that Offa's authority in Kent was very great, which is true, and unchallenged, which is not. The late Sir Frank Stenton showed that Offa probably lost control of Kent for some years and, although he succeeded in reasserting his authority, it was never secure and scarcely survived him. In 764 he made the first known grant of Kentish land by a Mercian king. The king of Kent and the archbishop of Canterbury were both witnesses and were both, in different ways, humiliated. The humbling of the king is obvious. Since even archbishops of Mercian provenance tended to dislike Mercian interference in Kent, and since this act of witness looked very like an admission that Canterbury was becoming a Mercian see, the humiliation of the archbishop may be inferred. About 770 Offa granted a Kentish estate to a Kentish abbot without reference to the Kentish king. The next stage was reached when Offa annulled a grant made by King Ecgberht of Kent because it was not lawful for him to grant estates in hereditary right. We do not know the date of this act but Ecgberht disappears from history after 780.

The East Angles kept their king, Æthelberht, but in 792 Offa had him beheaded, so he could scarcely have regarded him as an equal. Offa certainly booked estates in Wessex in his own name and although landbooks from this time survive in the name of West Saxon kings some of them have witness lists that reflect gatherings of Mercian *witan*. If they are authentic they must imply some supervision of the booking process but it may be they were originally in Offa's name and have been converted into West Saxon royal charters by scribal chauvinism. All this is summed up by Offa's decision from 774 onwards to call himself *Rex Anglorum*, king of the English. Offa would brook no other kings south of the Humber but he never used the traditional title of *brytenwealda*. He preferred to make southern and eastern England part of Mercia and to rename Mercia England whether their inhabitants liked it or not. It has been pointed out the Northumbrian kings at the height of their power ruled an area larger than any king before James I. This is true but it may be doubted whether any Northumbrian king, or James I either, possessed the power within his kingdom that Offa did in his. Something of this may be seen from one of Anglo-Saxon England's largest archaeological survivals, Offa's Dyke. The dyke runs from the mouth of the river Wye to the Irish Sea. Some, perhaps all, of it was surmounted by a stone wall. It seems common sense to suppose it was meant to keep the Welsh out. However, it could also have been used as base for what have been called punitive expeditions. The effort was immense and the expense in labour and resources must have been very great. It is unlikely that Offa paid for it himself. It seems probable that his subjects provided money or labour or both.

That Offa was a popular ruler seems unlikely but he was a powerful king and everyone knew it. Charlemagne, for instance, no mean authority on such matters, recognised Offa as the sole ruler of the southern English. The general tenor of Mercian policy at the time was expressed in a charter by one of Offa's successors, when he called himself *imperator*. He is not reviving the title *brytenwealda*. He calls himself Emperor of Mercia because all the English south of the Humber were deemed to be Mercian, whether willingly or not.

This changing conception of kingship, this concentration and deepening of royal power, found ideological expression too. If it is going too far to speak of English political thought at this time, it is even worse to speak of the English as ignorant savages who did not know what thinking was. Anthropologists have shown that primitive thought is often extremely acute: what makes it 'primitive' is its marked lack of structure. Something of this is true of the Anglo-Saxons. From early times their kings were reckoned to be descended from Woden. It is now certain that Woden descent was confined to royal families. No magnate, however powerful, could claim Woden as an ancestor. Nor did any member of a royal family other than a reigning king so far as we know. Woden descent was a validating concept, a mode of legitimation none the less powerful for being not very precise and not very historical.[7] It marked off the one family a king could come from. That this was important is shown by Alcuin's observation that the troubles of the Anglo-Saxons of his day – the late eighth century – were due to the way the old royal kindred groups were dying out.

Woden descent was recorded in royal genealogies. Genealogies occur as early as Bede. I have pointed out that the famous one in the *Historia Ecclesiastica*[8] tracing the Woden descent of the kings of Kent is not by Bede. I am sure Bede would never have admitted that a pagan deity could have any part in the Christian scheme of things. In the indubitably Bedan genealogies Woden finds no place. However the Kentish genealogy, whilst not by Bede, is still contemporary with him and early evidence that Woden descent mattered.

The most important collection of genealogies is that edited by David Dumville and dubbed the Anglian collection.[9] The pioneer of genealogical studies of this type was the late Kenneth Sisam,[10] who thought the collection was of Mercian origin, but Dr Dumville has shown that it is Northumbrian and hostile to the Mercian kings.

The collection was contemporary with Offa but attributes Woden descent to the Kentish royal family, whose royal status Offa would not accept. It includes the West Saxon royal genealogy: it is possible that Offa would not have cared for that, but it does not include either Hwiccean or South Saxon genealogies. The game to which the making of these genealogies belongs was a political game. The late R. W. Chambers first noticed that the West Saxon genealogy from Woden to Cerdic formed perfect alliterative verse. He wrote: 'These lines go back to times when a line of royal ancestors, both real and imaginary, were recorded by memory rather than by writing. They are pre-literary, and were doubtless chanted by the retainers of the West Saxon kings in heathen days.' It would be difficult now, let alone at a time when life-spans were so much shorter, to produce by natural means a pattern of names that formed perfect verse forms. I cannot believe that men in the eighth century were not as capable of perceiving this as we are, just as all of them, Christian or not, must have known who Woden was. By making them mean what seems to make sense to us we risk making the same mistake nineteenth-century social anthropologists made when they tried to explain the phenomenon of totemism, for instance by supposing that tribes revered totemic animals because they found them of economic importance.[11] In fact it has been shown that some tribes adopt as totems animals not known to them by direct experience. The French social anthropologist, Claude Lévy-Strauss, put it succinctly when he said that totemic animals were not good to eat but good to think about. It seems to me that these genealogies were likewise good to think about and were not literally believed, which is not to imply that they were arbitrary fabrications.

It seems to me that Woden descent was meant to legitimate a *stirps regia*, a royal family. If, as often enough, the succession was fought over, at least the number of contestants was limited. It seems to me that the original Germanic social groupings, of which the Anglo-Saxons are an example, were not really tribally organised. They were much more like Tacitus's *comitatus*. A *comitatus* was originally a voluntary band adhering to a leader and all bound together by an oath, with the object first of plunder then of settlement. In Anglo-Saxon times Beowulf in fiction and Guthlac in reality give us an insight into this kind of society. Naturally the early members of such groups were familiar with the bonds of tribal society and as they became more settled used the forms of tribal society as models.

By the eighth century these originally mobile bands were settling into stable kingdoms. When problems of continuity over generations were raised, as they were bound to be when a *comitatus* acquired a permanent locale, the Woden-based genealogies were the answer. But they could not go further and limit the succession to a single individual. That world could not contemplate an incompetent leader, not even a landowner who did not pull his weight. A family gave one expectations – limited expectations, it is true – and to turn expectations into reality the individual had to prove himself. To use the vocabulary invented by the late Michael Wallace-Hadrill, *fortuna*, i.e. luck, conferred *nobilitas* on members of a successful *comitatus*. It was necessary when a *comitatus* settled into a kingdom that for one family *nobilitas* must be further elevated into a *stirps regia*, a royal line. The effect of the Mercian revolution – for revolution it was – meant something more was necessary. In matters of royal succession the English were now ready to replace a free-for-all by the legitimation of a single heir. This was achieved, of course, by means of what Michael Wallace-Hadrill called 'the magic that was unction'. To explain what he meant and to understand its nature we must go back a little.

The first half of the eighth century was marked by a new kind of relationship between England and the Continent. The Anglo-Saxons began to repay the cultural debts they had incurred and repayment was channelled through missions to what are now the Benelux countries and western Germany. Those territories, still pagan, lay on the fringes of the Frankish world. Frankish rulers encouraged these missionary efforts, since the converts tended to end up their subjects. As in so much else the pioneer was Wilfrid, who started the conversion of the Frisians whilst staying there on his way to Rome. A disciple of his, Willibrord, left Northumbria for Frisia in 695, perhaps because he felt that, being so close to Wilfrid, he had no future in Northumbria. He completed the conversion of the Frisians and founded the see of Utrecht. But the greatest missionary was a West Saxon monk from Crediton called Wynfrith. He got a commission from the Pope in 719 to convert the Germans: the Pope gave him the new name of Boniface by which he has been known ever since. He stayed with Willibrord for a time and then went his own way. He knew and admired the *Rule* of St Benedict and spread knowledge of it in northern climes. He founded one of the greatest German monasteries, Fulda, and in 732 the premier German see of Mainz. He was martyred in 754 aged about eighty. Because there is a good early life of Boniface written by a close disciple and because his letters, unusually for the time, were collected, we know a good deal about him. He was a great exporter of texts from England to Germany, notably the works of Bede: he more than anyone else was responsible for Bede's great international reputation. He was on friendly terms with the Frankish rulers and was invited to assist in the reform of the Frankish Church.

The kings of Francia, anciently Roman Gaul, were a family called the Merovingians descended from Clovis, the first Christian and Frankish king of Gaul. For more than a century they had been *rois fainéants*, powerless puppets of a family later known as the Carolingians (correctly, if pedantically, at this time the Pippinides or Arnulfingers). The Carolingian mayors of the palace, not the titular Merovingian rulers, were Boniface's patrons. What kept the Merovingians going was their particular charisma, obviously of enormous importance, since it preserved their position, though long shorn of power. They were the only family allowed to wear their hair long, hence their usual title, the Long-haired Kings. It is likely that the

Carolingians too felt the power of this charisma but in 751 their current head, Pippin, decided, or was persuaded, to ask the Pope who should be the king of the Franks, the Merovingian titular king resting on tradition or himself, who actually did the job. The Pope gave the answer he was obviously expected to and said that he should be king who exercised the power. The Carolingians needed a counter-charisma to the Merovingians' long hair. They could not themselves credibly wear their hair long. They forced all surviving male Merovingians to enter monasteries, where they would be tonsured, or face execution. But they were provided with an alternative charisma, probably by Boniface.

The Frankish royal annals say that Boniface crowned Pippin. Admittedly they were written fifty years after the event but the probability that they were telling the truth is very great. It has already been pointed out that the Franks, unlike the other Germanic invaders of the Roman empire, became Catholics, not Arians. There was also a strong element of collaboration by the Gallo-Roman establishment, and in the event the Gaulish episcopate remained for the most part in the hands of the old Gallo-Roman families. The Carolingians came from Austrasia in eastern Francia. Thanks to men like Boniface, there was no shortage of candidates who could make as good or better bishops than the old establishment could furnish. Their political allegiance was likely to be to the Carolingians and certainly not to the Merovingians. The established bishops in 751 must have realised that if the Merovingians went their monopoly of office was likely to go too. It seems unlikely that any of their number would have wanted to crown Pippin and commit political suicide in the same ceremony. Equally Pippin needed the holiest and most charismatic man he could get to preside over a political revolution. If Boniface is to be believed, and I think he is, the late Merovingian episcopate was undistinguished. On all these counts Boniface was the man to crown Pippin. The contemporary bishops were not deposed *en masse* but replaced one by one as they died off. It was the Carolingian practice to choose members of their family or relatives of Austrasian magnates closest to them, and the result was a very impressive collection of bishops indeed.

A special ceremony was devised for the occasion and was plainly based on Old Testament precedent. Pippin was seen as replacing Chilperic as David had replaced Saul and the centre of the ceremony was the anointing of Pippin by Boniface as David had been anointed by Samuel. Most scholars think this was the origin of royal unction, which then spread throughout western Europe, including England. The notion is open to legitimate doubt. The difficulty is that the magic that was unction was meant in this wider application to achieve the exact opposite of what happened in 751. Anointing was meant to legitimate the dead king's heir, not to justify the replacement of one dynasty by another. There is some evidence that royal anointing was known and used on the periphery of western Europe long before 751. In Visigothic Spain kings were certainly anointed, and, in spite of the Moslem invasions that had destroyed Visigothic Spain, Visigothic legislation, especially ecclesiastical legislation, was widely known and influential in Francia. Another part of Europe where anointing was a familiar rite of passage was the Celtic kingdoms. Abbot Adomnon of Iona says Columba ordained Oswald emperor of Britain. He also speaks of an occasion when Columba tried to avoid ordaining a certain Aidan as king of Dalriada but was compelled to do so by angelic chastisement. Clearly a physical ceremony was meant, though we cannot be quite certain it included unction.

It seems to me that the ceremony of 751 was most probably of Boniface's devising. The evidence of Visigothic influence in Francia is most obvious a generation later. Boniface came from a family that lived on the fringe of the Celtic (as it did also on the Anglo-Saxon) world. He must have known Celtic men and Celtic customs. The first recorded case of an English royal anointing had to do with Offa. In 786 or 787 Offa received the first recorded papal legation since the days of Gregory the Great. They held a 'contentious' synod at Chelsea: contentious because Offa proposed, and the Pope accepted, that the chief Mercian see, Lichfield, should be given metropolitan status. This obviously reduced the importance of Canterbury and must have been part of Offa's policy of reducing Kent generally to subordinate status. Some of the recent archbishops of Canterbury had been Mercian churchmen but Offa seems to have despaired of ever dominating the see.[12] The elevation of Lichfield and the demotion of Canterbury were widely and intensely unpopular, and Offa's successor gained some popularity by undoing both policies. No one ever got something for nothing from the papacy but the Pope wanted nothing that Offa could not easily give. The legates therefore held a synod to reform the English Church. Among its proceedings Offa's son and heir, Ecgferth, was anointed king though his father was very much alive. The precedent was the consecration of Charlemagne's two sons by the Pope in 781. That seems to have been the first time an heir to a kingdom had been consecrated in his father's lifetime. It is noticeable how comparatively quickly Frankish custom became English custom too. In this case it is easy to explain. One of the legates was Alcuin, an ex-Northumbrian and now a chief adviser of Charlemagne as well as temporary papal legate. We know little about the circumstances of Offa's succession except that it was a very bloody affair, and Offa wished to avoid a repetition. The Church supplied what the religion of Woden could not, the anointing of an heir in his father's lifetime so that the heir began to reign the moment his father died: indeed, in a sense he was already reigning before his father died. What the consecration of Pippin had achieved was to deepen and broaden contemporary notions of kingship. Unction, whether it was previously known or not, marked an extension of Germanic notions of kingship beyond its traditional military parameters. Just how much difference that made can be seen from the rest of the legislation.

The legation, led by Alcuin, brought its proposed decrees with it. They were first taken to Northumbria and then shown to Offa and the southern bishops, who accepted them. The most important points pertained to the royal succession. Kings were to be chosen by the chief priests and magnates: they were not supposed to be nominated by the reigning king, in other words. So far as England was concerned this decree was a completely dead letter. Three centuries later both Edward the Confessor and William the Conqueror nominated their heirs. Only legitimate sons by lawful marriage were to be eligible for the succession. This was achieved in the long term, marked by the occasion in the twelfth century when Earl Robert of Gloucester, eminently suitable in every other way, was barred from succeeding his father, Henry I, by his illegitimacy. But in the eighth century contemporary views of marriage did not sit easily with the more extreme clerical views of legitimacy. In the traditionalist view legitimacy was a matter of social values. If a man got a low-born woman into trouble she was expected to fend for herself but if she were a lady the father was expected to recognise the offspring as his children and to provide for them. Sometimes these unions were treated as a form of marriage and everyone but clerical bossyboots would treat any offspring as legitimate. This is neatly illustrated by a Frankish crisis of about a century later. The emperor Charles III had only an illegitimate son by a 'concubine' of low birth and the Pope and the magnates, especially the bishops, would not accept him. Instead Charles was succeeded by his nephew, the emperor Arnulf, who was also the son of an irregular union. But his mother was a lady. This time neither Pope, bishops nor secular magnates raised any objection. In the end the clergy won this battle but not before the attempt to enforce canonical rules of legitimacy had created many political crises that sometimes redounded on the heads of the more radical reformers.

Most important among the conciliar decrees was a canon claiming that it was sacrilege to kill *christus domini*, the Lord's anointed. This has been taken by some scholars, including this one, to mean that anointing was already accepted practice in England. But, whether it was or not, the consecration of Pippin had given such anointing a new depth of meaning. From that time onwards kings are seldom assassinated. From the assassination of Edward the Martyr in 978 no English kings were murdered until Edward II in the early fourteenth century. When one considers that no one murdered Henry II, John or above all Henry III, whose monumental incompetence the English endured for half a century, it is evident that this theological development mattered.[13]

In 796–8 Kent again rebelled and it seems that Canterbury cathedral was sacked.[14] The archbishop, Æthelheard, was a Mercian, though not from the Mercian heartland. He came from the Lincolnshire monastery of Louth. He must have been appointed by Offa and was driven from his see during the uprising. The legate, Alcuin, suggested to him that he should reform his cathedral community so that there was zeal for study and reading. Then, when the time came, they could elect one of their number as his successor. Alcuin was trying to find a way of avoiding these dangerous and debilitating confrontations every time a new archbishop was needed. Æthelheard seems to have heeded his advice and when he died in 805 he was succeeded by a monk of Christ Church (i.e. the cathedral) called Wulfred. Before his death Æthelheard had begun the practice of demanding professions of faith from newly elected bishops. These are the earliest examples of what became a general practice, and some thirty survive from the ninth century. It has been suggested that the detested elevation of Lichfield was behind this policy.

We know nothing of Archbishop Wulfred from any narrative source: there is no biography, but a remarkable series of charters suggest he was committed to the reform of his cathedral community and was a conscientious archbishop in general.[15] The fact that he emerged from the community suggests that Æthelheard, too, had been an effective archbishop. Under Offa a number of councils of bishops were held where disputes, sometimes very secular-seeming disputes, could be settled and occasional ecclesiastical decrees promulgated. Offa's son died soon after his father and his successor, Coenwulf, who was not as powerful as Offa – no king simply inherited his predecessor's authority – set out to woo Kent and Canterbury. Kentish estates seized by Offa were returned: Kent was given its own sub-king (who was, however, Coenwulf's brother). In 803 he went further and in a great council at Cloveshoe the hated archbishopric of Lichfield was abolished and its incumbent deposed from the episcopate – presumably for his presumption.

There were still problems. The archbishops of Canterbury had been permitted to mint their own coins, though the king's name went on them as well as theirs. Coenwulf tolerated this practice, though neither his nor Wulfred's name appeared on the coins for six years. It is thought that he deposed Wulfred for a time during this period. The point at issue between prelate and monarch was that Wulfred, as an earnest reformer, wished to reduce the family's power over the monastery. He tried to reform two prestigious – and rich – communities, Reculver and Minster in Thanet, which had roots deep in the history of Kent and in that of the English Church. The object of the exercise was not simply the wealth of the monasteries but the implementation of a general and very Carolingian policy directed against secular control of monasteries, enunciated at the council of Chelsea in 816. The two monasteries shared the same abbess, Coenwulf's daughter, Cwenthryth. The dispute cost Wulfred dear, though some of what he lost at the time he later recovered from Cwenthryth. But the true significance of the dispute was that all the chief minsters in Kent were royal-family monasteries. Wulfred had the courage to try limiting royal rights against the king himself.

Wulfred was obviously a sincere and serious reformer. From the earliest days of Anglo-Saxon monasticism the communal element in these 'communities' was not strong. Monasteries tended to have monks who owned property and lived in their own separate houses. Lindisfarne was a house of this type, and Alcuin wrote to the monks there not to use their houses for gaming or holding parties but for prayer and study. Christ Church Canterbury, too, was in similar case. Wulfred speaks of its members as monks and as following a rule, though it cannot have been that of St Benedict. They were permitted, even by Wulfred, to have their own property but they must eat and sleep communally. They can leave their property by will but only to another member of the community. A generation later such a will survives. The testator was a kinsman of Wulfred, from whom he had inherited most of his property. He was pious as well as rich, and was in the habit of feeding thirty poor people a day out of his own pocket. He did as he was supposed to do and left his extensive property to the community, which is why his will has been preserved.[16] It need not be assumed that Wulfred thought the constitution of his cathedral community ideal. He did what he could: the times were not ripe for the imposition of full-scale Benedictine monasticism.

What is important is to avoid the idea that from time to time Benedictine monasticism was the norm and what the sources talk about are aberrations. The early history of the west European Church shows that some men did have ideals based on a genuine and fully communal monasticism, Wilfrid and Columbanus for two of them. But such ideals could never be realised except in a few locations and for relatively short periods of time. Wulfred's imperfect and inadequate reforms were not a lapse from traditional standards but a serious attempt to reform them. Why monasticism is so important is that right to the end of the period monasteries meant literacy, education and the handing on of civilised values, however outlandish their expression may sometimes seem to us. The test came with the appearance of the Vikings in force about a generation after Wulfred's reign as archbishop. If the Vikings attacked churches they went away again: they wanted movable, transportable, property. They might destroy buildings but they could not destroy the landed estates that produced the incomes on which it all rested. But under the earlier system, including Wulfred's style of reformed monasticism, if the Vikings could not carry off the estates the resident monks could. It was all too easy for the monk to privatise the former monastic property and slide into a way of life indistinguishable from that of his lay neighbours. By the last quarter of the tenth century there were a number of genuine full Benedictine communities. The Danes launched a new series of assaults on England but this time the monasteries coped and the sources of English civility held. That is why the story of the monks is so important a part of early English history.

Coenwulf never had the power in Kent that Offa sometimes enjoyed, though he was powerful enough to call a council of bishops not exclusively Mercian. Between 821 and 840 Mercia was governed by four kings who neither could nor did provide dynastic continuity. Mercian power in the south of England collapsed.

In the 820s a new power appeared in English history, the kingdom of Wessex, which had never counted for much before. From 823 three competing families fought over Mercia. This gave the West Saxons their chance. Their king, Ecgberht, had been the leader of the anti-Mercian party in Wessex during Offa's reign. He was driven into exile and sought refuge in Francia. First Ecgberht conquered the south-east, then in 829 he conquered Mercia and Essex and invaded Northumbria, which submitted to him. He issued coins as king of Mercia in London, some of which have survived. (In a largely illiterate society it needs to be remembered that coins represented the nearest thing to a mass medium that then existed.) Wiglaf of Mercia had revived Mercian independence and recovered London and its mint within a year. Ecgberht was never an Offa, and he never held great ecclesiastical synods – he probably could not. In 838 he held a council at Kingston in which he restored property to the archbishop of Canterbury. The charter by which he did so[17] is virtually a treaty between the king and the archbishop. Ecgberht made generous promises about the church of Canterbury's property and in return Canterbury became, to all intents and purposes, a West Saxon bishopric. The site of the synod, Kingston, had a special significance for the West Saxons, since it was the place where their king was crowned. Ecgberht died a few months later, and it seems likely that he held no power outside Wessex for the last nine years of his life. But his Kingston treaty held, and that mattered. His last policy was concerned with ensuring his son Æthelwulf an easy succession. He probably had him anointed at the same council. In the event Æthelwulf succeeded without difficulty, the first king of Wessex to succeed his father since 641. Possibly because Æthelwulf succeeded and managed to survive for several years, Ecgberht was successful in securing the West Saxon succession where Offa had failed in Mercia. This must have been a contributory cause to making Wessex's revival permanent.

I have attempted to present the early history of England and the English not as pre-ordained or evolutionary but to stress that England was a construct, England was made. The Mercian hegemony seems to have played a decisive part. A loose and shifting political scene had been tightened and made rigid, and the southern English were made to experience over several generations what political unity meant. Military skill and political nous had played a great part in all this but so too had feeling and imagination. The Mercian rulers drew upon echoes of Valhalla and aromas of the Old Testament and the resulting brew worked. What it meant to the men of the time we cannot tell. Were the peasantry, the thralls, the better or the worse off for what happened ? We cannot tell. But in general peace seems to have benefited most people, and life in southern England under the Mercian hegemony must have been easier and better than in the north, where *coups* and civil wars were almost the norm. The rise of Wessex was not inevitable. It was the Vikings who in the last resort turned Wessex into England, and a very painful process it was, but because Mercia lay between the Vikings and the West Saxons it was destroyed as a power in the land. But its achievement was none the less real and should not be overlooked. Unity became a habit and a new range of political skills developed: none of that was forgotten.

NOTES

1 Walter Goffart, 'Bede and the Ghost of Bishop Wilfrid', in Goffart, *The Narrators of Barbarian History*, Princeton, NJ, 1988.
2 Eric John, *Orbis Brittaniae*, Leicester, 1966, pp. 2–4.

3 Eric John, *Land Tenure in Early England*, Leicester, 1960, pp. 67–73. Nicholas Brooks, 'The Development of Military Obligations in Eighth and Ninth Century England', in *Essays presented to Dorothy Whitelock*, ed. P. Clemoes and K. Hughes, Cambridge, 1971, pp. 69–84 seeks to argue that the lands of the Church were subject to military service, only it was never levied. In my book this is the same as freedom from military service. Dr Brooks has some illuminating remarks on the point of bridgeworks in this context.

4 John, *Land Tenure*, pp. 71 *et seq.*

5 F. M. Stenton, 'The Supremacy of the Mercian Kings', *English Historical Review*, xxxiii, pp. 433–52, reprinted in *Preparatory to Anglo-Saxon England*, ed. D. M. Stenton, Oxford, 1970, pp. 48–66. This is the absolutely fundamental study of the Mercian hegemony.

6 Sir Frank Stenton has an interesting comment on this charter, *Anglo-Saxon England*, p. 211: 'One of the most instructive documents of the reign is a grant of land by Oslac, *dux* of the South Saxons, to which Offa at Irthlingborough, on the Nene, added a confirmatory endorsement. The contrast between the crude provincial script of the text and the practised, almost official, hand of the endorsement represents a real distinction between the primitive government of the local kingdoms and the beginnings of administrative routine in a court which had had become the political centre of England south of the Humber.'

7 John, 'The Point of Woden'.

8 John, 'The Point of Woden'.

9 David Dumville, 'The Anglian Collection of Royal Genealogies and Regnal Lists', *Anglo-Saxon England*, p. 5, pp. 23–50.

10 K. Sisam, 'Anglo-Saxon Royal Genealogies', *Proceedings of the British Academy*, 39, pp. 287–346.

11 E. E. Evans–Pritchard, *Theories of Primitive Religion*, Oxford, 1965, chapter on totemism.

12 Nicholas Brooks, *The Early History of the Church of Canterbury*, Leicester, 1984, pp. 118 *et seq.*

13 Clare Stancliffe, 'Kings who opted out', pp. 168 *et seq.*, illuminates another Christian contribution to early medieval kingship. Unexpectedly perhaps the importance of the theme of pilgrimage and monastic values in general is what she means and again her discussion points to the abiding importance of the 'Hiberno-Frankish' movement. Her paper is an important contribution to the understanding of early medieval thought.

14 Brooks, *Early History*, pp. 180 *et seq.*

15 Brooks, *Early History*.

16 Brooks, *Early History*, pp. 139 *et seq.* Dr Brooks's comments on the documents in question can sometimes be challenged. He seems to have an anachronistic view of what a monk was. He objects to a late eighth-century charter calling the community at Christ Church monks. But they did follow a *regula*, though it cannot have been that of St Benedict. Until the synod of Aachen in 817 the *Rule* of St Benedict had no legal force in either secular or canon law. This is the age of the *regula mixta* (which the late Margaret Deansley was the first to comment on, at least in Britain). The word 'monk' is quite appropriate.

17 Brooks, *Early History*, pp. 197–200.

CHAPTER 4

English politics in the ninth century: problems, solutions and more problems

THE MAIN ENGLISH PROBLEM in the ninth century was the Vikings. It is worth noting that the Vikings were the first 'English' problem. The problems hitherto had been wars between different groups of the English, which made them no less bitter and destructive. We know very little about the struggle for hegemony between the Mercians and West Saxons. We do know it was bloody and lengthy and very damaging in its cultural effects. When Ælfred said he did not know anyone who could read Latin south of the Humber, he has been taken to be blaming the Vikings, but Latin increasingly ceased to be the language of the charters before the Vikings reached Wessex on any scale.

Between 786 and 802 three shiploads of Vikings put into harbour at Portland and killed the reeve of Dorchester, who challenged them. In 793 Lindisfarne was attacked and Jarrow the following year. From that time until the third quarter of the tenth century there was constant war between the English and the Vikings. For some hundred and fifty years the Vikings dominated English politics and political thinking. Until recently the Vikings have been painted a deep black as destructive, barbaric and totally uncultivated villains. A few years ago Sir David Wilson mounted a great Viking exhibition at the British Museum and, faced with some splendid artefacts, not all of them looted, some scholars attempted a revision of opinion.[1] The new slogan proposed was 'Not raiders but traders'. It was pointed out that the Vikings were illiterate, so no one could state their side of the case. Their victims were literate, and could and did complain about being on the receiving end. The complaints were dismissed by the revisionists as biased. The Mafia owns laundrettes, hotels, restaurants and pizza parlours but that does not make them legitimate businessmen, i.e. traders. Their victims, if not dead, complain very much. Is that to be dismissed as bias? The Vikings certainly were sometimes traders, just as they certainly were, frequently, raiders. Their trading was on some scale, as the evidence from Dublin and York shows. It proves only they were prepared to turn an honest penny as well as steal a pound or two. Monasteries, which had been numerous before the Vikings came, suffered badly and it has already been pointed out that what there was of English culture depended on the monasteries. We know from Bede that there had once been Northumbrian royal charters aplenty: not a single one remains. In some cases whole diocesan structures collapsed and there were no bishops for generations. Western Scotland endured much destruction, and without the Vikings we should know a great deal more about early Scotland than we ever shall. It stands to reason that the Vikings risked death and discomfort over the years only if their raiding paid. But they persisted and must have made great profits mainly at English expense.

Having said this in rejection of much of the revisionist case for the Vikings, it is still true that the traditional picture is too black. The Vikings have been blamed for what were serious structural shortcomings in English society. If we take the monasteries, the Vikings could and did steal valuable portable goods, they could and did burn down buildings, but the buildings stayed burnt because the inmates or their families had stolen the endowment that had supported the monastery.

It may be said that the trading activities of the Vikings could be a mixed blessing. In Ireland the Vikings established a series of trading posts from Dublin to the Shannon. The result was the creation of much liquid wealth in the south of Ireland, which certainly helped to ruin the generations-old supremacy of the Uí Néill based on the north.[2] We cannot know whether the Uí Néill would have dealt better with the Normans when they came: I suspect they would not have. But, to sum up, this was a violent world and the Vikings had no monopoly of violence. It still remains that the revisionist school does not take the enormous difficulty of establishing a tradition of literacy seriously enough, or the threat to literacy that the Vikings represented.

Why did they come? Various answers have been suggested, ranging from population pressure to economics. It seems to me more profitable to see what drew them to leave home rather than what pressure forced them to go. Up to the 830s their incursions were sporadic. Sheppey was attacked in 835 and this raid coincides with four attacks on the Frankish port of Doresstadt in Frisia. At the same times there were raids on the West of England, and what amounted to permanent bases were established at Dublin and Noirmoutier at the mouth of the Loire. London, Portland, Southampton, Rochester and Rouen all suffered attacks in the early 840s. It is probable that some of these attacks were by the same raiding group. What drew the Vikings was the state of west European politics and the scope which those politics gave for immensely rewarding fishing in troubled waters. In modern jargon 'market forces' best explains the Viking raids.

After a successful beginning, Louis the Pious, son and successor of Charlemagne, had run into serious political trouble that has been variously accounted for. The best French medievalists of an earlier generation tended to be anticlerical and Louis's perfectly genuine piety was given heavy stick as well as landing him with a nickname. His main religious policy was to promote the *Rule* of St Benedict and in 817, for the first time anywhere, the rule was given legal force and made binding on all monks. Civil war in Francia prevented this policy from being implemented. If we compare Louis's scheme with Edgar's policy in England, which was implemented, the conversion to Benedictine monasticism did not just affect the character of monastic communities, it made for a considerable increase in royal and central power. It is not Louis's monastic policy that explains the distressing features of the latter part of his reign, of which the Vikings took advantage. Unusually for a Carolingian, Louis had three sons who survived into adulthood. Custom required the kingdom to be divided between them. It is clear this was not to Louis's liking, and, judging the empire itself not to be subject to Frankish customary law, he left the imperial title entire, with any special imperial functions, to his eldest son, Lothair. A division was agreed on but Louis remarried and produced another son, Charles, who also survived into adulthood. Louis had to provide for Charles but Charles's half-brothers would not agree to any satisfactory solution and the empire fell into a chronic and debilitating civil war. It was neither Louis's piety nor his incompetence that caused the civil war but his fecundity and the structure of Frankish society. In any case the Vikings did well out of it.

The structure of English society was not without its stresses either. The political problems of the early ninth century can be summed up in one word, Ecgberht. The confusion he had created in Mercia and Northumbria survived him. It is probable that Wessex continued to intervene in Mercia, now in a state of dynastic convulsion. Wessex did not have the power to conquer Mercia, although it seized Berkshire from Mercia before 848, since the future King Ælfred was born in that year at Wantage.[3] The late W. P. Ker once pointed out that the Vikings had a wonderful nose for sniffing out political divisions and some skill at exploiting them. From the 830s the attacks got worse.

There has been much discussion of the scale of the Viking invasion. It used to be treated as another folk migration. Folk migrations are no longer the historical currency they once were. P. H. Sawyer has suggested they were attacks of limited extent by quite small armies,[4] although he seems to couple this with settlement on quite a large scale. Most would follow Dr Brooks's argument[5] that, comparing sources from all over Western Europe, it looks as though before 850 raids were mounted by fleets of about fifty boats. (It should not be overlooked that some of these far-flung raids were made by the same fleet.) After 850 the sources speak of fleets six times that size. The looting of Francia and the British Isles could provide the capital to build more ships. Unfortunately we are not sure how many men each ship carried. The long-ranging ships probably had thirty oars. Some think they had one man to an oar, others three. That would suggest that the fleets disposed of somewhere between one thousand and three thousand men. By contemporary standards these are large armies. In the tenth century a battle in east Francia was decided by the absence of fifty knights. The discussion must be inconclusive: all we can hope for are very rough parameters within which to work. But what is clear is that at the height of the Viking invasions these armies must have been larger than the small groups Mr Sawyer contemplated. Equally, they must have inflicted more damage than he thought.

What of the Viking settlements? That the Vikings had sufficient numbers to do great damage is undeniable. Three dioceses disappeared, Hexham, Leicester and the see of the South Angles. In the north the succession in almost every diocese except York and Lindisfarne was interrupted for decades. There is evidence that books were copied and composed in Mercia in the pre-Viking period but virtually nothing survives. The preface to the vernacular translation of the *Regula Pastoralis* usually attributed to Ælfred the Great – I do not think he meant to claim authorship of the whole work but he certainly wrote the preface – says that learning was being neglected before everything was burnt. Things had got worse since. It was not all due to the Vikings but some of it was. It is one thing to neglect books that remain for use in more literate times but quite another to destroy them altogether. The Vikings certainly did damage, then, but did they settle? Evidence once used to prove a Viking folk migration is very dubious when examined at all closely. Narrative sources make it certain that the Vikings took land permanently in East Anglia, Mercia and Northumbria and shared it out. One might say, *mutatis mutandis*, exactly the same thing of the aftermath of the Norman Conquest. But there was no Norman folk migration.

The possibility exists – in my view it is a probability – of large estates being taken over by Viking warriors with English peasants to work them.

The warriors became aristocrats and rentiers at one blow. The main evidence is linguistic and the same difficulties I discussed in the first chapter apply, with the additional problem that it is much easier to distinguish Celtic linguistic usage from Old English than it is to distinguish Old English from Old Norse. There are numerous place names ending in the suffix '-by' and there are traces of Viking usage in the English language. The term for the highest rank after the king was ealdorman; it became the Anglo-Danish 'earl' (the Danish term is *jarl*). Except in Northumbria ealdorman remains current until the reign of Cnut. In Northumbria ealdorman had replaced 'earl' by Edgar's reign at the latest. Titles like earl and ealdorman are the common currency not of peasant talk but of the chat of aristocrats. There is, in fact, no compelling evidence of the large-scale immigration of Scandinavian peasants. Why should the Viking landholders have wanted them? The indigenous peasantry came from families that had worked the soil for generations and were likely to be more efficient than peasants used to a quite different terrain and in whose life fishing played a great part. In any case, were there enough spare peasants in Scandinavia to settle half of England?

Dr Alfred Smyth, in my opinion the most interesting of Viking scholars now working in English history, effected a revolution in Viking studies by showing that Vikings had a strategy that nearly subjugated all England.[6] In 865 and 871 there were Viking attacks the *Anglo-Saxon Chronicle* picked out as especially great. They took over Northumbria in 876 and Mercia the following year. They forced King Coenwulf of Mercia to give them half Mercia to divide among themselves. In all, there were three partitions of land that gave them about a third of eastern England. They could now winter in England and when the campaigning season began in the spring they had enormous mobility. The way was open for the conquest of the last English redoubt, the kingdom of Wessex. Dr Smyth has shown that the Viking strategy depended on the control of two key centres, York and Dublin. Why this should have been so is clear when we remember that the Vikings depended for everything on their ships. It is possible to sail from Dublin to the firth of Clyde. Then it was only a short haul to the firth of Forth and the open sea. One may object it was not all that short a haul but it seems to me it was within the Vikings' capacity. But the real point is that, short haul or not, the Dublin–York axis dominated English politics until well into the tenth century. There remain problems – the *Chronicle*'s emphasis on Danes and Northmen needs to be taken into account – but the point remains that Dr Smyth has provided not just the best explanation of the politics of the Viking incursions but the only plausible explanation anyone has so far offered. The ships could then hug the coast and by taking to the rivers sail to within twenty miles of York. Comparison of the English and Irish sources shows that is what they did, and neither the English nor the Irish found the nexus between the two cities easy to cope with. Two of the leaders of the 865 campaign in the English sources are called Ingmar and Healfdene; the latter is called king. They seem identical with the two Viking leaders the Irish knew as Imhar and Alband. (They were the sons of a formidable warrior called Ragnar Lothbrok.) The Irish annals reveals that Imhar – best known in history books as Ivar the Boneless – was king of the Norsemen in Britain and Ireland. It is evident that the Norwegians were the deadliest of the invaders, though it is likely many other Scandinavians, including Danes, joined them. But the leadership seems best called Norwegian. In these *comitatus* type operations the leadership set the style in every way. In the Anglo-Saxon invasions Hengest and Horsa probably came from Jutland, so their group were known as Jutes, but to judge by the archaeological finds many of them came from farther afield than that. When the groups came to settle it was presumably the mix of tribal customs familiar to the leaders that was imposed on the rest of the *comitatus*. It is evident that the Irish sources were aware of the Dublin–York axis and understood its significance. Healfdene was the junior partner and was probably killed in Ireland in 877 trying to maintain Ivar's 'empire'. Three English kings were killed in all this, two by sacrifice to Odin (or Woden, or Wotan) of a very repulsive nature. There is no reason to suppose that Ælfred would have escaped the same fate had he not defeated Guthrum, another descendant of Ragnar Lothbrok. Sir David Wilson drew attention[7] to one Ibn Rustan, writing some time after 992 about the Vikings in Muscovy. He describes a peculiarly nasty form of suttee practised there on the death of an important man. The Vikings, whether trading or raiding, were barbaric, unpleasant men with some horrid cultic practices.

Ecgberht's son and successor, Æthelwulf, now king of Wessex, had not stood idly by while all this had been going on. The Viking threat to Wessex must have been obvious before the great campaign of 865. In 854 Æthelwulf gave a tenth of all his lands in the kingdom to the Church. It was a typical means by which an early medieval king would try to get God on his side. It is certain that this decimation, as it was known, took place, even though all the charters in which it is recorded can be suspected,[8] since Bishop Asser, Ælfred's biographer, confirms that it did. The magnitude of the grant is neat evidence of the magnitude of the West Saxon's fear. We do not know what *quid pro quo* he expected, beyond victory in war, but a lifetime of medieval studies teaches one that an early medieval king was never so political as when he was on his knees. About the same time, and perhaps not unconnected, Æthelwulf attempted to solve a disastrous weakness in early Germanic social structure. It seems that in Wessex, as in Francia,[9] when a king died his kingdom had to be divided between his surviving sons. We have already seen that this custom had played a great part in the ruin of the Carolingian empire and how the Vikings profited as a result. It is hard to see that Wessex could have survived at all if Æthelwulf had not challenged law and custom. To change such a custom was not easy and in normal times would have been impossible. The solution was obviously to move to a system of primogeniture. The disinherited would not have taken the change lying down. Outside the royal family any younger son with expectations would realise that if the king made such a change every magnate in the country would follow suit, which is exactly what happened. It needed a great external threat – and that the Vikings provided – to make such a change even thinkable. In this situation every heir must face the possibility that if the Vikings were not stopped he would be likely to lose everything.[10] Æthelwulf therefore managed to change the law and defy custom, though he did it in rather an unexpected way.

He had a rather elegant solution[11] and we are fortunate in having adequate documentation. He did it by will. His will has not survived but it is summarised in that of his youngest son, Ælfred, which has.[12] Æthelwulf bequeathed his property to his sons Æthelbald, Æthelred and Ælfred in turn. He obviously expected them to reign in turn too. It is an early example of a seventeenth-century form of insurance called a tontine and now, for obvious reasons, illegal. Æthelwulf's second son, Æthelberht (the name is certainly significant), was excluded, probably because he was to be king of Kent when his father died, and his name suggests this was in Æthelwulf's mind when his son was christened. He did become king of Kent in 858. Æthelwulf was prepared to accept the separation of Kent (not to be confused with the modern county of Kent; it also included modern Essex and Sussex). He was not going to make Offa's mistake all over again. The main loser would be his first son, Æthelbald, whose sons, should he have any, would be disinherited. It is suggested by the name he bestowed on his second son that the idea of all this had been long in Æthelwulf's mind. Æthelwulf made a pilgrimage to Rome, almost certainly in connexion with his ideas over the succession, and Æthelbald rebelled in his absence. On Æthelwulf's return in 856 he left his son to rule Wessex undisturbed whilst he took Kent. This was due not to weakness, I believe, but to a desire to help his abolition of partibility. He also brought back a Carolingian wife, the granddaughter of Louis the Pious, Judith. Altogether a very Frankish situation. Æthelwulf's seeking out the Pope over a major change in the succession law has more than a hint of Pippin's dealings with the Pope in 751, and the changes he wanted would have gladdened the heart of his grandfather-in-law. His decision to leave Æthelbald undisturbed was a wise one and it avoided a disastrous civil war. In the event Æthelbald, having first married his stepmother, Judith (she was certainly much younger than Æthelwulf and certainly younger than Æthelbald), died young, without issue, so far as we know. In the way of this world Judith, twice widowed, turned east and married the count of Flanders. Ælfred was only eleven, Æthelred not much older and too young to succeed, although it was his turn. So Æthelberht took over Wessex as well as Kent.

All this must be considered with one of the most curious episodes in Anglo-Saxon history. In 853 Æthelwulf's youngest son, Ælfred, was sent to Rome to see the Pope, Leo IV. The *Chronicle, sub anno* 853, records: 'the Lord Leo was then Pope in Rome, he hallowed him [Ælfred] as king and accepted him as his godson.' Ælfred was then only four years old and had three elder brothers living. The episode makes sense only as part of Æthelwulf's plans for the succession. The annal was probably written down in its present form about 890 and it is plain that Ælfred's papal consecration was believed in the highest circles, not least by Ælfred himself, since it is mentioned in Asser's biography. It has been suggested that the Pope confirmed Ælfred and the Chronicler confused consecration with confirmation, since both involved unction. It seems to me incredible that a four-year-old boy should have been sent on a perilous journey to Rome only for confirmation.

Pope Leo wrote Æthelwulf a letter about all this that has survived. He said he had received Ælfred as his spiritual son and decorated him with the sword, honour and vestments of a Roman consul, which included a crown. This hallowing made the Pope claim Ælfred as his spiritual son. Confirmation could not have done that. It was all very Carolingian. An earlier Pope had consecrated two sons of Charlemagne as kings in their father's lifetime and the Pope clearly assumed this made him spiritual co-father, with Charlemagne, of the two young men. Another source, not hitherto cited in this connexion, is the *Annals of St Neots*.[13] The editor, Dr Dumville, points out that they are a Latin translation of an exceptionally good text of the *Anglo-Saxon Chronicle*. The annals say that the Pope confirmed and consecrated Ælfred. The case seems as complete as it could be: two chronicle sources, a papal letter, Carolingian precedents. (The Pope, contrary to what some English scholars seem to believe, did not operate one system of canon law for the English and a different one for everybody else.) The consecration of Ælfred by the Pope seems one of the best attested facts of Anglo-Saxon history but English scholars have been reluctant – rather more than reluctant – to accept it. The evidence has been ignored or explained away.[14]

All this bears witness to the value of the papacy in the early Middle Ages. The consecration of Pippin and that of Ælfred both involved difficult situations where some interests were bound to be injured but the greater interest was needed to prevail. The traditional way of cutting these Gordian knots was to fight it out. The papacy offered a bloodless alternative. In Francia the consecration of Pippin adversely affected the descendants of the old Frankish aristocracy as represented by the Frankish episcopate: but bishops are powerless against the Pope, and the revolution was consequently bloodless. The consecration of Ælfred again meant hardship for some for the utility of many (and had the process not been brought to a successful conclusion there would not have been much even for the some). The English in the event were fortunate. Neither Æthelwulf nor Leo could have been sure the plan would work had not nature lent a hand. The integrity of Wessex was preserved by the deaths of Æthelbald and Æthelberht childless. The third son, Æthelred I (not to be confused with Æthelred the Unready) succeeded without trouble: by now both he and Ælfred were married and had sons. Ælfred tells us in his will that he and his brother renewed their father's arrangements. Provision was made, not very generous provision, for the disinherited sons: the situation vis-à-vis the Vikings was approaching its worst moments, with the extinction of Wessex a strong possibility.

Æthelwulf had one other achievement. In 851 he was the first English king to defeat a major Viking army. We do not know the site of the battle but some three hundred and fifty shipfuls of Vikings were involved and they had already taken London and Canterbury and driven the king of Mercia into exile. It was shortly after this that he sent Ælfred to Rome: everyone must have known the Vikings would be back, and that helped to make his plan stick.

Æthelred I succeeded to the kingship in 865. Wessex was invaded by an army almost certainly led by Ivar the Boneless. The Vikings no longer depended on water for their communications but instead seized convenient defensible positions, sometimes near the coast, sometimes near navigable rivers. There they could easily protect their ships with fortifications and small garrisons. As an army they were now a full standing army, and a disciplined one at that. For the next ten years the initiative was always theirs. They could throw their whole weight against Wessex. Owing to the chance survival of an account by a man with local knowledge we know something of the tactics they followed. They found a convenient site for a fortification near Reading where the Kennet flows into the Thames. Æthelred and Ælfred attempted but failed to drive them out. The Vikings in consequence left their fortress and deployed a great part of their army on the chalk ridge in the middle of Berkshire then called Ashdown. The West Saxons attacked them and won a notable victory but the discipline and experience of the Vikings prevented them from following it up. In the next few months the West Saxons were defeated twice and in 871, at the beginning of the campaigning season, Æthelred I died. One of the new king, Ælfred's, first actions was to buy peace from the Vikings. It needs to be remembered that buying peace from the Vikings was not a policy invented by Æthelred II (the Unready), nor was it necessarily cowardly or foolish.

In 871 the Vikings left Wessex and took up quarters in London. They set up a mint there and minted coins. They must, then, have been interested in trade but with whom or for what we do not know. It is probable that a Viking army, though not the main force, stayed in London for some years. They lost control of Northumbria but took eastern Mercia into their power. The later shires of Lincoln, Derby, Nottingham and Leicester were certainly included. Loot was becoming scarcer and the Vikings were turning into settlers: reaping their profits by reaping their fields. In 878 the Vikings renewed their attack on Wessex, led by Guthrum. A large part of Wessex submitted. Ælfred retreated to the marshes round Athelney, and the conquest of England was nearly complete. But just before Ælfred's retreat a Viking leader, believed to have been a brother of Ivar the Boneless (who is thought to have died in 873), crossed into Devon from South Wales with twenty-three ships and about eight hundred men. The Viking leader, with most of his men, was killed by a company of local kings' thegns. The men of Wessex began to regain heart. Ælfred had not been idle and had made a series of raids from his fortified camp. A few weeks later the men of Somerset, Hampshire and Wiltshire rallied to him. Ælfred led them to an attack on the main Vikings' army, then based at Chippenham. He caught them at Edington and won the decisive battle of the war but was prepared to make peace. He behaved very differently with Guthrum from the way Ivar had dealt with St Edmund. He did not have Guthrum's power, for one thing, nor was Guthrum his prisoner. Guthrum agreed to accept baptism, leave Wessex and retire to Chippenham, then reckoned to be in Mercia. A year later the Vikings abandoned their attempt to conquer southern England and turned their attention to the exploitation of East Anglia. In 884 a Viking fleet from the Continent besieged Rochester but could not take it. Ælfred appeared and most of them fled to sea. Ælfred now had the reputation of a man to be reckoned with.

Ælfred realised that the main threat to Wessex came from East Anglia. He therefore attacked London in 886 and took it. Guthrum was now king of most of eastern England, and he decided that Ælfred could not be con-quered, so he made permanent peace. Ælfred did not claim, nor did Guthrum concede, an overall West Saxon supremacy – East Anglia and most of Guthrum's kingdom had never been part of Wessex and it is still Wessex, not England, that we are talking about – but the terms of the treaty were very much in Ælfred's favour. The West Saxon conquest of England had begun.

It will be apparent that the political skills of the house of Cerdic played an important part in the salvation of Wessex, and it will be apparent when Ælfred's military reforms are considered that the house of Cerdic deployed considerable military skills too. Ælfred's achievement was greater than may at first sight appear. From a later English perspective it might appear that his sole achievement was the conquest of London; most of England remained outside his grasp. But Ælfred was king of Wessex and for most of his life can have hoped for little more than the salvation of his kingdom and the preservation of his kingship. Both he triumphantly achieved. It is unlikely that Ælfred or anyone else saw him as the leader of the English until the recapture of London and the end of his life when, the *Chronicle* says, he was accepted as king by all those not under the sway of the Vikings. That meant Essex, western Mercia, i.e. the old kingdom of the Hwicce and present diocese of Worcester and the newly conquered London area.

In 883 appeared for the first time an Ealdorman Æthelred, the ruler of what was left of Mercia, who had married Ælfred's daughter before 889. But the old antagonism between Wessex and Mercia cannot have vanished overnight, and many Mercians must have believed that the defence of Wessex was achieved at their expense. There is not much, but a little, evi-dence that some Mercians preferred the Vikings to the West Saxons. Again Ælfred's achievements can be put into perspective by comparison with those of his East Frankish contemporary, the emperor Arnulf. The emperor's name seldom occurs in English history books because tradition-ally English historians mean by medieval Europe northern France with

Rome thrown in. This is certainly a mistake. Ælfred's contemporaries were very interested in Arnulf, and the reason is obvious. His main problem, too, was the Vikings. He came to power in a *coup* which overthrew his uncle, the emperor Charles III. (When English historians know of him they usually call him Charles the Fat.) Charles's power base was Swabia, and like most Swabian rulers he looked to Italy as his natural sphere of activity. Frisia and much of what is now northern Germany were harassed by the Vikings as much as the West Saxons were. Charles took this philosophically and was prepared to conclude treaties with them. But it did worry the north Germans, and Arnulf, though also a south German, was prepared to back them. (It is anachronistic and misleading to talk of Germany and 'German' at this time but I cannot talk about northern east Francia or southern east Francia without being confusing and pedantic.) Arnulf got enough support to mount a *coup* against Charles only a few weeks before Charles died. The principal East Frankish sources are two recensions of the Frankish royal annals, a northern recension from Mainz and a southern one from Regensburg. Mainz is strongly hostile to Charles, Regensburg understanding and rather pro. The best and most balanced source is the *Annals of St Neots*. The English were interested in Continental opponents of the Vikings (the author of the annals seems to have been a monk from Bury St Edmunds, a venue not without significance) and we need to be, too. Arnulf defeated the Vikings decisively in one campaign and that meant that the British Isles were the one lucrative field of action left to them.

Ælfred made important innovations in the manner of the defence of his kingdom but they need to be studied for the way they were developed by his daughter, son and grandson, so it makes sense to leave them to the next chapter. Ælfred's literary legacy does need to be studied here, although the Ælfredian revival, as it is often called, was not altogether due to him either.

A Welsh priest from St Davids called Asser became bishop of Sherborne and a member of the king's intimate circle. He wrote a life of Ælfred. It has been suggested he wrote it in Flanders with the intention of recruiting scholars to Ælfred's service with a little self-advertisement thrown in.[15] Asser used as his model Einhard's life of Charlemagne, itself based on Suetonius's *Lives of the Twelve Caesars*. It is not known whether Asser knew Suetonius directly. It was from Suetonius that Einhard learnt that it was proper to include intimate details of his subject's life, sometimes of a scabrous nature. Most people read Suetonius in Robert Graves's malicious and very funny Penguin translation.[16] Michael Grant's revision of Graves gets the tone of Suetonius very much more accurately. Suetonius was not a bitchy gossip columnist but an author aware of his subject's achievements and aware that his public knew as much about his subject's peccadilloes as he did. I do not think Einhard liked Charlemagne very much and he rather anticipates the Robert Graves school. There is no malice in Asser. He gives a quite unconsciously hilarious account of Ælfred's early struggles with piles but it isn't meant to be funny. (For someone like Ælfred who had to spend a lot of time in the saddle piles were the reverse of funny.)

Ælfred was associated with the translation of five Latin works between 892 and 899, the year of his death. Three are frequently said to be his actual work. The strongest candidate is the translation of Gregory the Great's *Regula Pastoralis*, the treatise Gregory wrote for the guidance of bishops. Ælfred wanted an educated priesthood, though young lay persons were not overlooked. It used to be said he wanted a system of compulsory education but if he did, which I doubt, nothing was done. The resources in teachers and the money to pay them were simply not there. So far as Gregory's book is concerned I do not think Ælfred was its author, nor do I understand him as claiming to be. In the preface, which he certainly wrote, he says he was taught the meaning, passage by passage, by three of his literary men, none of whom was a native West Saxon speaker. I think Ælfred is telling us that they translated it and he made the translation idiomatic. The other two works in which Ælfred may have had a hand interestingly reflect his own spirituality. They are Augustine's *Soliloquies* and Boethius's *Consolations of Philosophy*. The *Soliloquies* are too sophisticated for a man of Ælfred's generation to get to the bottom of but they taught him that the remedy for the arrogance kingly power inevitably creates is contemplation. Boethius's *Consolations* was early regarded as a Christian classic. This is because we know from other works that Boethius was a Christian. But this was his last work, written just before his execution for treason which a later generation took to be martyrdom. But he was executed for a political crime of which he may well have been guilty. Professor Mommigliano has argued that in the face of death Boethius's Christianity collapsed and he reverted to the traditional paganism of his youth.[17] Indeed, to have written a spiritual testament in such circumstances without a trace of Christian sentiment or a single Christian reference makes this argument hard to refute. That was not how Ælfred saw it. Most of Boethius's once pagan pessimism had been assimilated into Christian thought. For Ælfred it was a meditation on the transitoriness of life and the need to face up to a death by misfortune if necessary. If he did get consolation from it he deserved it.

Two other works not directly connected with Ælfred deserve comment. An abbreviated version of Bede's *History* throws some light on the way the Anglo-Saxon world had changed since Bede's day. It is an important stage in the book's elevation to English classic from parochial Northumbrian tract. Also important is the vernacular version of Orosius's *History*. This is important because it is peppered with asides that could be authentically Ælfredian. It is in some ways an account of how the ancient world looked to ninth-century eyes but it also contains the first real piece of geographical research since the classical empire.

Two other works survive from the reign. The first is the largest and most important English code of law to date. It is an elaborate confection owing something to the Carolingian capitulary style of legislation. It quotes the ten commandments, claims to quote Offa's law code and also gives in full the laws of Ælfred's predecessor, Ini. We should not know of the existence of Offa's or Ini's legislation without Ælfred. It is plainly meant to be an English code but drawing on predominantly West Saxon and biblical authority. Dr Wormald, who knows more about Anglo-Saxon laws than most, suggests that by Offa's laws Ælfred meant the synodical decrees of a Mercian council held in 786. Ælfred was claiming to legislate by the deepest Christian convictions, reinforced by a very high idea of his right to translate such convictions into laws. He compelled his subjects to take an oath of fealty: this was clearly imitating Carolingian example, was enforced and mattered, since a certain Ealdorman Wulfhere was deprived of an estate in 901 because he had betrayed the king in spite of the oath he had sworn.

The last literary work I wish to deal with in this chapter is not Ælfredian but traditionally associated with the king. It is the *Anglo-Saxon Chronicle*, which has been mentioned in passing already. It is not one chronicle but several, all related and overlapping, sometimes presenting differing and conflicting versions of the same events. They all seem to descend from a single text of which a very early copy has survived, known now as the A text or the Parker Chronicle, after Matthew Parker, who once owned it. The subject matter goes back to a remote period of Anglo-Saxon history and there has been unending debate about the historicity of the early portion, harmless and sometimes useful provided the debaters understand there is never ever going to be a permanent solution to the debate. About the middle of the ninth century it becomes an indubitably historical account of the first importance. It is at first a history of the house of Cerdic but as Wessex became England various recensions were made which, though containing common information, interpreted that information from different points of view. All the texts, and some related ones, are now the subject of a new and what ought to be definitive edition by a group of Cambridge scholars. In the meantime it will be best here to discuss the variant versions as they become relevant.

The Ælfredian literary work is evidence of something wider than literary culture, the momentous achievements of Æthelwulf and his two younger sons. I once heard Sir Richard Southern say in a radio talk that if Ælfred had lost he doubted whether the outcome would have been more important than that we should now pride ourselves on our Danish ancestry. But this struggling, feeble, but real, literary culture would have been extinguished. How many more generations of barbarism would that have meant? By the end of the reign, according to his charters, Ælfred was claiming to rule all of the English. In charters – by no means all of certain authenticity but from half a dozen different religious houses, so the titles must have been familiar – Ælfred had himself called King of the English or King of the Anglo-Saxons. His biographer gives him the same title, so it is certainly authentic, but there was still some way to go before it became true.

NOTES

1 Most notably P. H. Sawyer, *The Age of the Vikings*, London, 1971.

2 F. X. Lynch, *The Irish High Kingship*,

3 Professor Smyth's remarkable book *King Alfred the Great*, Oxford, 1995, came into my hands three weeks before my manuscript had to go to press. I cannot undertake an examination of his main thesis that Asser is a later forgery (scholars are going to be discussing it for a very long time) but I have seized on incidental points. At pp. 3 *et seq.* Dr Smyth devotes five pages to proving that Ælfred cannot have been born at Wantage, a fact for which Asser is the sole authority. I do not think he gets the situation in Berkshire quite right. At the time of Ælfred's birth Berkshire had or was soon to become part of Wessex. As Dr Smyth points out, the ealdorman of Berkshire, the Mercian one, fought for Ælfred. He seems to have been a transitional figure between the days of Mercian Berkshire and West Saxon Berkshire. Dr Smyth has not noticed *Anglo-Saxon England* (3rd edition), p. 245 n. 1, where one of the numismatist revisers points to a coin with Ælfred on one side and Burgred of Mercia on the other. They date it by reference to Asser's date for Ælfred's birth. What this coin does seem to suggest is that Berkshire did not pass to Wessex by conquest but by some kind of friendly agreement, hence the ealdorman's role as Ælfred's man in the Viking wars. Dr Smyth thinks the West Saxon hold on Berkshire must have been precarious, which it may well have been, so that it was too dangerous for Ælfred's mother to have been brought to labour at Wantage. Æthelwulf had several mature sons: Ælfred was expendable. There was good political sense behind such a venue for the young prince's birth. The obvious parallel is Edward the Elder's decision to send Æthelstan to be educated among the Mercians.

4 Sawyer, *Age*.

5 N. P. Brooks, 'Ninth-century England, the Crucible of Defeat', *Transactions of the*

Royal Historical Society, 5th series, 29, pp. 1–20.

6 Dr A. P. Smyth developed his views on this matter in three books covering the whole of the first Viking period. It will be convenient to group them together here: *Scandinavian York and Dublin*, 2 vols, Dublin, 1975, 1979. *Scandinavian Kings in the British Isles*, Oxford, 1977.

7 Foote and Wilson, *Viking Achievement*.

8 Simon Keynes, 'The West Saxon Charters of King Æthelwulf and his Sons', *English Historical Review*, cix, pp. 1114 *et seq.*

9 Stenton, *Anglo-Saxon England*, p. 66. Smyth, *King Alfred the Great*, has at its heart a massive indictment of what Dr Smyth calls the pseudo-Asser, that is, he thinks Asser's life of Ælfred is a total forgery. This involves a discussion of Ælfred's papal consecration, which Dr Smyth rejects entirely. He rejects my arguments in favour of that conscecration for reasons I find totally unconvincing. Basically he never mentions the ending of the partibility of the kingdom but that is the point at issue. Ælfred's consecration makes sense, and then it does make sense, only if one supposes that the ending of partible inheritance was why Ælfred was sent to Rome. This is why, in my opinion, the arguments of those who discuss Ælfred's papal consecration without discussing the issue of *die Unteilbarkeit des Reiches*, notably Whitelock, Nelson and Smyth, are worthless. Stenton was the first and, so far as I know, is the only person to point out that Wessex was a kingdom subject to partible inheritance, and by implication somebody must have abolished this custom at some point in time. I am afraid that for Dr Smyth's argument to be taken seriously he must face this issue. I obviously cannot produce a serious critique of Dr Smyth's book in the few weeks before my book goes to press. But there will be time – later.

10 The first man to recognise the importance, and the danger, to Germanic peoples of partible inheritance was Gerd Tellenbach, 'Die Unteilbarkeit des Reiches' in *Die Entstehung des Deutschen Reiches*, and cf. H. Kämpf, *Wege der Forschung*, WBG, Darmstadt, 1956.

11 John, *Orbis Brittaniae*, pp. 37–42. S. Keynes and M. Lapidge, *Alfred the Great*, London, 1983, pp. 173–8 and notes.

12 The text is printed in the original with translation by F. E. Harmer, *Selected English Historical Documents*, No. xi, Cambridge, 1914. Keynes and Lapidge, *Alfred the Great*, give a translation.

13 D. Dumville, *The Annals of St Neots*, Cambridge, 1985, p. 44.

14 Janet Nelson, 'The Problem of King Alfred's Royal Anointing', *Journal of Ecclesiastical History*, 18, 1967, now conveniently reprinted in her most distinguished collection of essays, *Politics and Ritual in Early Medieval Europe*, London, 1986. She does not take into account Ælfred's will or his father's intention to end partible inheritance in the kingdom, which gave Æthelwulf a powerful motive to send his youngest son to the Pope for royal consecration. This also meant that once Ælfred had succeeded to the crown he had no motive for distorting what had occurred in Rome. She wishes to dismiss the papal letter allegedly sent by Leo IV to King Æthelwulf alluding to the matter. She points out that several forged papal letters pretend to be sent in the name of Leo IV. Of what important Pope could this be not said ? Leo IV was the Pope when the letter was sent. Had it been in the name of any other Pope it must have been instantly dismissed as a forgery. On Dr Nelson's Catch 22 diplomatic it must still be dismissed as a forgery because it bears the name of the right Pope. However, this is the earliest paper published in her collection and my own comments were written before I had read Tellenbach and fully understood what was at issue.

15 Mrs Rosalind Lavington in an unpublished M.A. thesis (Manchester) has some illuminating points about Asser's connexions with the Continent. She argues that Asser
directed his book to east Francia and may have, at least partly, written it there. She
supposes that Asser was acting as Ælfred's ambassador to Baldwin of Flanders, since
Ælfred wished to form an alliance against the Vikings. In the event Baldwin married
Ælfred's daughter and Mrs Lavington thinks that in part Asser's *Life* was meant to reas-
sure Baldwin that Ælfred was suitable father-in-law material and in part as proof of
Ælfred's *bona fides*. She also argues that an important part of Asser's sources, even insular ones, stemmed from Frankish centres. Dr Smyth, in his *King Alfred the Great*, did
not know of Mrs Lavington's thesis but it needs to be taken into consideration before
we follow Dr Smyth and accept the pseudo-Asser. I am persuaded by Dr Smyth that
Asser as we have him was forged by Byrhtferth of Ramsey but I think there are a few
traces, very few, of a genuine ninth-century life of Ælfred behind him. I did not share
Stenton's high opinion of Asser as a source and I have made little use of him in this
book. Mrs Lavington, thirty years ago, grasped that Ramsey was an important and
neglected source, though that does not form part of her thesis.

16 It is useful here to refer to Gore Vidal's brilliant review of the Graves translation. It is
printed in the *Oxford Collection of Literary Essays*, ed. John Gross, Oxford, 1991.

17 A. Mommigliano, *Studies in Historiography*, London, 1966, pp. 187–8.

CHAPTER 5

The West Saxon conquest of England

IT USED TO BE THE CASE that scholars spoke of the reigns of Edward the Elder and of Æthelstan, Ælfred's son and grandson, as the reconquest of England. Except perhaps in Essex it was nothing of the kind. Only in the reign of Ecgberht, and then only for a very short time, was the West Saxon king acknowledged as the ruler of England. (The *Chronicle* calls him *bretwalda*, the only occasion that term is known to have been used.) What happened in the tenth century was a transformation of English politics by which political power was centralised, concentrated in the hands of the king of Wessex. To put it another way, England ceased to be a highly diversified set of political entities but became an increasingly tightly defined one. The sole ruling family was the house of Cerdic, the sole centre, as far as there was one, the city of Winchester. Until the middle Middle Ages the English court, and with it English government, were largely peripatetic. The see of Canterbury retained its traditional primacy over the English Church but it was an increasingly West Saxon see. It is not without significance that, when these things can be costed, Canterbury and Winchester were not only the richest sees in England but among the richest in the Church. All this began with Ælfred, as we have seen: he laid the foundations.

Ælfred's most famous innovation was the founding of the 'royal navy', or at any rate the creation of a fleet. He probably did this towards the end of his life, as it is mentioned for the first time in 896. The *Chronicle* says he had specially long ships of sixty oars 'built neither on the Frisian nor on the Danish pattern, but as it seemed to him that could be most useful.' This implies some nautical knowledge on the part of the chronicler and also that Ælfred had given the matter some thought. It seems from later events that larger ships were more effective than smaller ones on the rare occasions when fleets joined in pitched battle. The Vikings did not build very big ships because they frequently had to cross the North Sea and avoided pitched battles: for them mobility was what mattered. The English fleet was defensive and would have loved to draw the Vikings into sea battles. We are not told how or when the vessels were used but they cannot be dismissed. It is under Edgar that we learn something of how these ships were used but Ælfred was the pioneer.

Sub anno 893 the *Chronicle* speaks of another innovation with approval. Ælfred divided his *fyrd* into two. (The English army is always called the *fyrd* until late in the period and in effect the name never disappeared from the vernacular. The Viking army was the *here*, which implies bandits, although by the late tenth century Viking success had removed the sting from the term.) As the campaigning season was six months, it meant that English warriors were on duty three months of the year. When it is remembered that William the Conqueror got only forty days of service out of his knights, this is pretty impressive. Most historians have thought the ceorl was the backbone of the *fyrd*. There are strong objections to this view, not the least that it rests not on evidence – there is very little – but on the constant repetition by historians.[1]

There is only one mention of a ceorl fighting and that is in the late tenth-century poem called the *Battle of Maldon*.[2] The ceorl was called Dunnere, he was Ealdorman Byrhtnoth's personal vassal and behaved like the rest of Byrhtnoth's retainers, none of whom was a ceorl. *Maldon* is a poem and 'ceorl' can mean a high-born warrior in poetic vocabulary, as it also means a husband of whatever social class.

The greatest of Ælfred's innovations was the *burh*.[3] The word is the Anglo-Saxon term for a garrison but in the course of time lost its military meaning and became the borough. The question is how and when this happened. Maitland was the first to tackle the problem seriously. He grasped the basic fact that a *burh* was a garrison and propounded a theory, usually called the garrison theory, of how it became a borough in the civilian sense.[4] The late James Tait attacked this theory and argued that the *burh* was always a unit of local government – he did not mean in the sense of a unit of local military organisation.[5] It is true that Maitland's thesis now seems too simple but it is essentially an inadequate answer to the right question. There is no 'garrison theory': the *burh* was a garrison as a matter of fact. Maitland's contemptuous dismissal of Tait's argument is justified, in my opinion. It would be worth while to go over the ground again and trace the development of *burh* into borough. I am sure this could be done but I would observe that I have seen no source which uses the term in an unequivocally civilian sense before 1066. Even after 1066 there are unequivocal uses of the word in its military sense. Let me be clear here. There are several occasions on which *burh* may mean 'borough' and its garrison, the *burhwaru*, may mean 'citizens' but they are all ambiguous, and in my opinion ambiguous only to those scholars who wish to find local democracy in Anglo-Saxon England.

The fortresses are recorded in one of the earliest administrative documents to have survived, the Burghal Hidage. It is known principally from a late transcript of a much earlier Winchester document. It survives also in a number of post-Conquest versions. No two texts tell exactly the same story but they are nevertheless in substantial agreement. The first point to note is that the burhs did not pass away with the Vikings. Since in those days no one copied documents out of antiquarian interest: the number of surviving copies proves that they must still have been useful. (In Rufus's reign extensive damage to the fortifications of London required the efforts of several shires to repair them. It sounds as though it was the obligations of the *burh* that were invoked to achieve this.) Thirty-three burhs are listed and to each is assigned a round number of hides, patterned in such a way as to suggest that the new burhs were based on the old hundredal system. The burhs surrounded Wessex and by the time of Ælfred's son, Edward the Elder, no West Saxon village was distant from a *burh* by more than twenty miles. The document can be dated approximately from some of its inclusions and exclusions. London is excluded, though there is plenty of evidence that there was a *burh* at London. This is usually explained by the fact that when London was recaptured from the Vikings it was handed back to Ælfred's son-in-law, the ealdorman of Mercia. Many Mercian boroughs were not included, most of them the creation of Ælfred's daughter, the Lady of the Mercians. Oxford is included but only came into West Saxon hands in 911, when Ealdorman Æthelred of the Mercians died. In 919 Edward's sister, the Lady of the Mercians, died and he seized the whole of Mercia, including its burhs. Thus it seems certain that the original document can be dated between 911 and 919. Malmesbury was built in 914 and that is included, enabling us to date the document even more precisely. It would seem that the document dates from the reign of Edward the Elder – but the system did not.

We can be certain that Ælfred devised the policy and started to implement it because Asser talks of the towns and cities he restored and the others he constructed where none had been before. Asser also tells us he replaced wooden buildings with stone ones.[6] Worcester, though not a West Saxon *burh*, was the first we know to have been built. It certainly belongs to Ælfred's reign because, unusually, it was the only one whose foundation was recorded in a charter.[7] The hidage assigns twelve hundred hides to Worcester. The medieval shire of Worcester contained exactly that number, so it seems possible, even probable, that the *burh* engendered the shire. The transcript of the Winchester version of the hidage has an important addition the others lack. It says that if every hide is represented by one man, then every pole of wall can be manned by four men. Thus for twenty poles of wall eighty men are needed, and every furlong needs one hundred and twenty men. The other manuscripts abbreviate these calculations and say that in all twenty-seven thousand hides plus twenty-seven were needed. If, as we surely can, we suppose that these numbers refer to Wessex alone, twenty-seven thousand men were assigned to maintain the fortresses.[8] We do not know how they were garrisoned: that duty lay outside the *fyrd* service. This gives us an insight into the magnitude of the Viking threat and the extraordinary energy with which Ælfred countered it.

The actual constructions were very pragmatically planned. Archaeologists have shown that where the perimeters of the burhs are known they tally with the figures given in the hidage. We have arrived at the moment of the creation of an English bureaucracy, and a very efficient one at that. The study of individual burhs shows a remarkably intelligent use of what was there already. The *burh* of Southampton (then called Hamwih) was not in the town at all but was a renovated Roman fort a short distance away. At a number of places – Bath, Winchester, Chichester and Exeter – burhs were based on what could be usefully employed of the remains of Roman walls. Iron Age forts (or possibly Roman ruins) were used at Porchester and Chisbury. Natural features, e.g. promontories, were used at Malmesbury and Lydford but some like Ealing, were built from scratch. It used to be thought that military necessity alone dictated the shape of a *burh* but it is unlikely. The best excavated *burh* is Winchester.[9] The town plan within the walls owes nothing to its Roman predecessor. The town can be dated to about 900 and seems to have been an Ælfredian conception, although it could be earlier even if his son completed it. It was the nearest thing Wessex had to a capital and from the beginning was meant to be more than a fortress. With a few exceptions towns were regarded as part of the royal demesne. The peasants of the royal demesne could be taxed at will (in later times it was called 'tallaging') and, by analogy – an analogy kings did not fail to draw – so could the inhabitants of the towns. When we get a detailed account of the royal revenues, in the middle of the twelfth century, we find that the king got more revenue from the towns than from all the barons put together.

More light is thrown on this by drawing comparisons with what was going on in East Francia. We have already seen evidence that Anglo-

Saxons took a serious interest in Carolingian politics when we considered the *coup d'état* that overthrew Charles III and brought the emperor Arnulf to power. Arnulf left only a child to succeed him who died young. The crown of the East Franks went to Conrad, duke of Franconia. Most historians regard Conrad as the first non-Carolingian king in East Francia. I do not think Conrad would have agreed with them. He was closely related to the Carolingians on his mother's side and he tried to rule East Francia in the high Carolingian style as though nothing had happened. But quite a lot had happened and Conrad's reign was an unmitigated disaster. Conrad, at the end of his life, accepted failure and established the most powerful of what German scholars call the stem dukes, Henry the Fowler, duke of Saxony, as his heir.

Henry was certainly not a Carolingian and he inherited a problem as bad as, if not worse than, the Vikings: the Hungarians. They were rather like medieval Red Indians in their mode of warfare. They lived in tented camps that sound like collections of wigwams. They used bows and arrows on horseback, deadly weapons when faced with swords and spears rather than Winchester rifles. They even had an efficient system of disseminating military intelligence by smoke signals. They did not attack East Francia by the direct route through southern Germany because it involved terrain quite unsuited to their tactics, covered by mountains and forests. It was much easier to sweep over the plain that is now Poland but was then divided among weak tribal groups who dared not gainsay them. This meant that Saxony and Thuringia were willy-nilly gateways to East Francia. After a heavy defeat early in his reign Henry I was lucky enough to capture one of the more prominent Hungarian leaders and used him to gain a ten years' truce. He used the truce to follow Ælfred's example and surround Saxony, and perhaps Thuringia, with *Burgen*. Maitland was the first to notice that the *Burg* was based on the *burh* and that on the German evidence the administrative aspects of the fortifications have a remarkable family resemblance. Henry imitated Æthelwulf and made his kingdom impartible.[10] The English connexion was stressed even more when Henry married his son and intended heir Otto (later known as the Great) to Edward the Elder's daughter Eadgifu (sometimes called Edith).

Marriages between members of different royal families, the dynastic marriages of a later age, were very unusual at this time. But in the early tenth century the decline of the Carolingians into a condition of *pourriture noble* led to the creation of a number of succession states ruled by new royal families chronically short on pedigree. The importance of pedigree was part of the Carolingian heritage. The house of Cerdic was conveniently there to supply it. The family claimed to be contemporaries of the Merovingians and may have been so: they were certainly royal before the Carolingians were. Further, the current head of the house was well supplied with nubile daughters. Between *c.* 916 and *c.* 930 five of Edward's daughters married into Continental royal or semi-royal families. Apart from Otto the Great, their husbands included Hugh the Great, head of the family that under the name of Capetian were to become kings of West Francia and turn it into France. Even the head of what was left of the Carolingians, Charles, called the Simple, married one. When Charles was imprisoned by his enemies in due course, his son Louis l'Outre Mer found refuge with his uncle, King Æthelstan, who played a part in his eventual restoration as king of West Francia. Sihtric, the Viking king of York, married another. At the end of the century an English magnate and member of the house of Cerdic, Ealdorman Æthelweard, wrote – or had written – a Latin version of the chronicle. He sent a copy to his kinswoman, Matilda, abbess of Essen, the granddaughter of Otto the Great and great-granddaughter of Edward the Elder. In a passage of quite extraordinary arrogance that tells something of the effect all this had on the West Saxon establishment, he lists such of their royal kindred as he can remember. He remarks that there was another king of somewhere but his name and that of his kingdom have slipped his mind. It was actually Conrad, king of Burgundy. Æthelweard was right; he didn't matter much.[11]

It needs to be remembered that such weddings meant the exchange of gifts, sometimes splendid works of art. We can identify these gifts only occasionally because, like gift exchanges in the twentieth-century primitive world, they were taken for granted. By the year 1000 the Carolingian Utrecht Psalter was at Canterbury, where it had great influence on English figurative art. Rather later than the period I am dealing with, but typical enough to be relevant here, Earl Ælfgar of Mercia sent a splendid set of Gospels to Rheims. They were sent to commemorate his son, Burchard (very much a Frankish name), who had died and been buried there on his return from a pilgrimage to Rome. As a by-product of a mission from Æthelstan to the East Frankish court (Otto the Great was his brother-in-law) St Ursula and the eleven thousand virgin companions martyred with her migrated to Cologne. (The late Professor Galbraith remarked witheringly to me that he didn't believe there were eleven thousand virgins in Europe at the time.)

One of Ælfred's scholarly imports was Grimbald, who had been educated at Rheims. From 845 to 882 the archbishop of Rheims was Hincmar, certainly the greatest intellectual of the ninth century. Nor did his learning die with him, and his tradition was to matter very much to the Anglo-Saxons. It may be that Grimbald had some influence on the *Anglo-Saxon Chronicle*, and it has been suggested he was one of the men behind Ælfred's laws. It is becoming clearer how important Carolingian influence was on the numerous English law codes of the tenth century. We shall see, when we come to the Benedictine reformation in England, how much the English monks owed to Frankish churches and Frankish churchmen.

It has recently become possible to see how an intelligent Englishman viewed all this at the time. I have mentioned the *Annals of St Neots* before and pointed out that it is the best informed and most balanced of the commentaries on the deposition of Charles III. It seems to have been written at Bury St Edmunds, in my opinion in the last quarter of the tenth century.[12] It is a compilation, with only a little local matter, which may have been contributed by the compiler. Its main sources are a very good text of the *Chronicle*, Asser's *Life of Ælfred*, Frankish annals now preserved only in later Norman chronicles, Flodoard of Rheims, of whom we shall hear more, the story of Ælfred and the cakes from the first life of St Neot, Abbo of Fleury's passion of Edmund, king and martyr (of East Anglia), and some Frankish vision literature, including the *Visio Caroli*, which was a probable consequence of the deposition of Charles III. It was written by, or perhaps for, Hincmar's successor at Rheims, Fulk, who represented a reactionary because nostalgic view of the Carolingian world, probably shared by the compiler. The main theme of the annalist is the defeat of the Vikings, viewed not from an insular standpoint but with an intelligent and informed commentary that takes in both sides of the Channel. He was extraordinarily knowledgeable about Carolingian politics, in which he took a deep and sympathetic interest. In the annal for 879 he records the death of Charles the Bald and of Louis, king of the West Franks, who he knew was Æthelwulf's brother-in-law. He also knew the difference in rank and position between Charles and Louis. Then we turn to activities of 'the pagans' around Chippenham and Cirencester, then to goings-on in Bavaria via Fulham. There is nothing quite like it in any other Anglo-Saxon source, and it was written long after the events it records. It seems to me unlikely that the compiler was an isolated case and that among the establishment at least in tenth-century England there was interest in, and knowledge of, Frankish society and politics.

That the Vikings were no longer the threat they had been to the English at the time of Ælfred's succession was apparent by the time of his death. The last big attack on Wessex, in 892, was less impressive than it looked. The Vikings built fortifications at Milton Regis (near Sittingbourne) and Appledore, on the edge of the marshes. The next year they built a fortress at Beanfleet. *The Annals of St Neots* shrewdly point out the importance of the river Thames in all this. The fortifications were essentially to protect their ships and store their loot safely. The army was the remnant of a large force that had been decisively defeated the year before in East Francia. Ælfred summoned his forces from the burhs and the Vikings were heavily defeated. In 895 one of the greatest nuisances, the Viking leader Haesten, was forced to retreat overseas 'without profit and without honour but having lost many of his companions', as the *Annals of St Neots* put it. The Viking armies were disintegrating into small groups. It is possible that the army that had retired beaten across the seas was the same one that founded the French Danelaw, known to history as Normandy and ruled by men indifferently called count or duke. The written sources for the history of Normandy are very dubious indeed. Stenton thought that Normandy was created by enrolling Vikings into the service of the West Frankish king. The *Annals of St Neots*, which was interested in the formation of Normandy, and indeed ends with the treaty signed by Rollo and Charles the Simple that legitimated, if it did not create, the duchy of Normandy, leaves little doubt that Normandy was created by force of arms. It is probable that the Vikings were established in the area early in the tenth century and soon added the peninsula of the Cotentin to their domains. The West Saxons seem to have regarded this development with indifference – mistakenly. The Normans were to have a great influence on English history and in the last years of the tenth century to be accessories before the fact in inflicting great damage on the English.

When Edward the Elder succeeded his father in 899 eastern England from the Tees to the Thames estuary was controlled by Viking armies. They derived from the great partitions that marked the apogee of their power in 865. They were not politically united and acted in concert only occasionally. But they had a useful ally in Edward's disinherited cousin, Æthelwold, the son of Æthelred I. He joined the Vikings and persuaded them to ravage western Mercia and northern Wessex. This suggests that he thought he could revive the Vikings' fortunes and make himself their leader. But after the raid he had incited he could not expect to be remotely acceptable in the kingdom of his forebears. Edward replied by ravaging East Anglia: he had no traditional supporters there to offend. But he decided to be prudent and gave the order to withdraw. The men of Kent refused. They lost the battle but won the war. They killed the Viking king of East Anglia and obliged Edward by killing his troublesome cousin.

Edward embarked on a policy which suggests that the hostility between men of Viking descent and Englishmen was declining. We know of cases where Edward deliberately encouraged English magnates to buy land in areas where the Vikings were in control. None the less war began again in earnest when Edward embarked on a punitive expedition against the Northumbrian Vikings. They retaliated with an attack that reached the Avon and then sought to ravage the Midlands. They seem to have been misled by bogus intelligence into believing that the main English army was in Kent. The English army caught them at Tettenhall in Staffordshire. The Vikings were virtually destroyed and lost three of their kings. The English had learnt to play dirty too. Viking Northumbria was no longer capable of any large-scale action against the south: the Midland Vikings, with their customary allies, could have resisted West Saxon pressure for a long time. Now they had lost that support.

In 911, the year of Tettenhall, Ealdorman Æthelred of Mercia died. He was succeeded by his extremely competent widow, Æthelfleda, under the title of the Lady of the Mercians. Edward took control of Oxford and London. The move does not seem to have been resented. Æthelfleda did what no Anglo-Saxon lady had done before: she fought campaigns and won them. She was a kind of tenth-century Boudicca but she was successful. She kept the Mercians loyal, and there is no doubt she planned and led campaigns in the Midlands. She built burhs. We know little of them but they must explain how Edward was able to bottle the Vikings up in Colchester and make London impregnable.

Edward's success in the north created its problems. It made it easier for the Norwegian Vikings to renew their efforts to revive the Dublin–York axis. The death of Ragnall, son of Ivar the Boneless, allowed his son Sihtric (I shall use the English form of his name because the original, Syggtrygr, is as difficult to spell as it is to pronounce for those of us ignorant of Old Norse) to succeed peacefully as king of Dublin. Sihtric left Dublin in 920 and a kinsman, Gothfrith, replaced him. For the next seven years Sihtric, apparently without a rival, ruled York. His comparative inactivity must be explained by his respect for the power of the West Saxons. Edward sought to keep him in his place by fortifying Manchester and Thelwall in the same year. (I understand that Thelwall remains intact but so far the owner of the land has kept archaeologists at bay.) The Mercians do not seem to have liked Edward much, and relations deteriorated with the death of Æthelfleda in 919. Her daughter and heiress was virtually kidnapped and removed from Mercia. It seems likely that Æthelfleda had an inkling of her brother's plan and she is known to have been intriguing with the Vikings of York before her death.

Edward the Elder died in 924. On the surface a powerful and successful king, he was treated with contempt by the York Vikings, and one suspects that much of 'his' success was due to his sister. His son and successor, Æthelstan, was a very different man. He had from an early age a high reputation as a soldier. We do not know how he acquired it but his opponents treated him warily and they must have had reason. He was reputed to be educated and he may have been literate. He had been brought up in Mercia though no doubt imbued with West Saxon traditions.

On the initiative of Sihtric negotiations were opened at Tamworth, one of the great centres of Mercian power that had been fortified by Æthelfleda. The meeting was historic. For the grandsons of the two greatest warriors of their time, Ælfred and Ivar the Boneless, were the first two members of their families to meet face to face. The meeting was friendly and Æthelstan married his sister Eadgyth to Sihtric. History does not record her feelings on the occasion, or her opinion of her new husband, although it must have been a little like marrying the grandson of Count Dracula. Sihtric was required to become a Christian. Neither his new wife nor his new religion was acceptable to the York Vikings, so he repudiated both. These are the only two things agreed at Tamworth that we know about and both had collapsed. Whether owing to Tamworth or not, Sihtric had authority over Lincoln but he died young in 927 and Gothfrith, who had been ruling Dublin, came over to claim York. Æthelstan sent him scuttling back to Dublin and put in his own claim. He was probably the first Englishman of any account who had set foot in York for sixty-one years. He was now king of 'England' but his England was only Wessex plus appendages.

Gothfrith, driven back to Dublin, was a nuisance for years to come. He was a power in the land, and kept alive in himself and his family ambitions of restoring their lost position in the Midlands and the north of England. He allowed a rival city to Dublin, Limerick, to be set up, which suggests that he was not popular in Dublin. He conducted a series of mostly unsuccessful but very bloody campaigns all over Ireland. The Irish sources are clear about the harm he did and the slaughter he caused. If Æthelstan had not been able to expel him from York, that would have been the fate of England too. The Irish sources show us what the English were spared.

In 934 Gothfrith died. He was succeeded by his son, Olaf, who was accepted as ruler of all the foreigners in Ireland. In 937, only three years later, Olaf, who had more sense than his appalling father, destroyed the city of Limerick in a campaign of great daring. Olaf was now the undoubted heir of Ivar the Boneless and trouble was certain for the

English. His mind, not surprisingly, turned once again to York.

It needs to be remembered that Æthelstan's control of York was superficial and recent. Olaf's family had been in power there, off and on, for generations and he could expect powerful local support if there was visible hope of success. Most of the English knew that Olaf was an able soldier whose destruction of Limerick had been a master-stroke. The English massed against him were led by Æthelstan and his younger brother and eventual successor, Edmund. The Irish sources make it clear that the English won a great victory but the casualties were heavy on both sides. Two grandsons of Ælfred and three bishops were among the English dead.

Where did this battle take place? There is no doubt that it was fought at a place called Brunnanburh by contemporaries but there is much dispute over where it was. This is important because the farther south the battle was fought the greater the danger the English were faced with. Because historians have underestimated the difficulty with which the Vikings were contained and just how much of a 'damned close-run thing' it was, it has been usual to suppose that Brunnanburh was on the Scottish border. This idea was based on strategic calculations of a very dubious nature. Olaf's army was composed of Irish Norwegians, Scotsmen and so on, and men tend to fight as far from their homeland as they can. The English casualties show that the battle was a close one and suggests that the English choice of strategy was limited. Their enemies would never have fought so far north from choice. The most convincing arguments about the site of the battle seem to me those of Dr Alf Smyth.[13] He points out that three years later Olaf tried again, this time with at least temporary success. On both occasions Olaf seized York and attacked Mercia. Brunnanburh, Dr Smyth thinks, was on the frontier Edward had established between English and Viking Mercia, on Watling Street, that is. He thinks it was probably very near Northampton. The West Saxon conquest of England was again in very great danger and Brunnanburh was perhaps the most important battle in English history before the battle of Hastings. A case could be made out that Hastings was possible only because the English won at Brunnanburh.

It is impossible to overestimate the acumen of Olaf. He made no further move against York until he had routed his Irish enemies. He clearly meant to try again in York but waited three years until the adolescent Edmund had succeeded Æthelstan, who died in 940. Olaf then reappeared and without a battle seized the whole of England north of Watling Street. He held it all until his death two years later, when his less competent and untried successor, Olaf Cuaran, lost it as easily. The new Olaf's career was just beginning. He did not fight at Brunnanburh. His rival, Edmund, was also young but a little more experienced and he made a successful attempt to regain the five burhs that had once formed the eastern part of Mercia.

This greatly weakened Olaf's hold on York, and what is more there is evidence that the York locals were tiring of their Norwegian masters. I think Stenton was going too far when he suggested that the men of York had come to regard the West Saxon king as their rightful lord but unquestionably the family of Ivar the Boneless were no longer the congenial lords they had once been. Edmund, who was no Æthelstan, failed to follow up his capture of the five burhs with an attack on York. In 943 he concluded a treaty with Olaf, who agreed to accept Christianity, and took Edmund as his godfather. This implied real if undefined subordination. Olaf, however, could rule York only with the support of local men of Viking descent, and they wanted no truck with Christianity or with Wessex. Olaf courted them by reneging on his conversion but they still expelled him from York in favour of his cousin Ragnall. It may be that Olaf was expelled as a result of local resentment but there are sources – and they explain much that the local resentment theory cannot – which suggest that it was Edmund, with a combination of power and intrigue, who put Ragnall in power. Olaf returned to Dublin and followed his families' policy of raiding and looting until, after a devastating defeat – symbolically, we may think – at Tara, he returned to the Christian faith and died a penitent at Iona.

Ragnall did not last long and he too was driven from York and Northumbria. But Scotland was independent of the English and hostile to them. Scotland was not a coherent political entity at the time but a medley of small states, some of them of Norwegian extraction. These states were invaluable recruiting grounds for military service for the Dublin powers. Edmund did little about them, probably because he could not, but his younger son could and did, as we shall see. No Dublin king, although they all believed implicitly that York was rightfully theirs – and, of course, the English pickings that could be harvested from there were richer than Ireland as a poorer country could offer – ever dared risk Dublin for the sake of York. When out of power in York they could, and frequently did, bounce back from their Dublin base. Had they lost Dublin they must have disappeared from history.

In 946, on 26 May, Edmund was assassinated at Pucklechurch in Gloucestershire. According to the traditional view he was killed by a returned criminal whilst defending his steward. But the best evidence is the first life of Dunstan, whose author was present when the king was murdered. The life has not been given the attention it deserves. The author, whose name is not known, used to be thought German. It now seems he was an Englishman long resident in East Francia who had known Dunstan well in his earlier days[14] but who had had spent most of his mature life in Germany. He assumes that people can read between his lines. Dunstan was in the company of the greatest man in England, after the king: Ealdorman Æthelstan of East Anglia, nicknamed 'half-king'. He was an intimate of the royal family and a considerable landholder in Wessex. Dunstan saw a *nigellus*, which could mean a black imp or simply a very swarthy man. He asked Æthelstan whether he could see him too. The ealdorman's reply smacks more of the political than the supernatural. He said he saw only what it behoved him to see. The occasion was a political one too. Some sort of treaty was in the offing, and an important letter. But the author does not tell us any more details and we cannot know what really happened. It seems that Edmund was assassinated for political reasons and even fifty years later it was prudent to be circumspect.

Edmund himself is something of an enigma. He did restore the kingdom his brother had left but one cannot help but feel he had an easier task and performed it in a more laboured manner. It must have been obvious that the way to deal with the legacy of Ivar the Boneless was to attack Dublin. This seems to have been understood by his younger son, Edgar, who seems to have perambulated the British Isles annually with a fleet. He seems to have made his presence felt to the many Viking, or Viking-style, princelings in the Western Isles and there is evidence he included Dublin in his tours. It is no coincidence that England was entirely free of Viking activity during his reign.

We are not done with the Irish problem yet. On the event of Edmund's murder, leaving two boys too young to rule, his sickly younger brother, Eadred, succeeded him. In 947 Eadred went to Tanshelf in what used to be called the West Riding and received the submission of the Northumbrians. The real leader of the anti-West Saxon Northumbrians was not a pagan Viking but the archbishop of York. He, no doubt, saw that a complete West Saxon victory would mean that the king of Wessex–England would want a single archbishopric and that see would not be York. But on this occasion he led the Northumbrian magnates to offer their submission to Eadred. In 948 they repudiated the allegiance and invited a Norwegian, Eric Bloodaxe, to be their king. (A bloodaxe is a dirk or dagger, not a battle axe.) Eric was not one of the usual Dublin Norwegians but out of the topmost drawer in the northern world. He was the son of Harold Fairhair, the first king of Norway, and had succeeded his father on the latter's death. Seemingly too brutal even for the Norwegians, he was driven out in favour of his younger brother. The English sources have something to say about him, naturally, but he made a much greater impression on the authors of the sagas. Eric was exiled, available, charismatic and apparently just the man for York. Eadred invaded the north but Eric stayed put in York and Eadred did not care to try and get him out. Eadred had, however, put up an impressive show of force and the Northumbrians began to have second thoughts. They had also had first-hand experience of Eric by now, and that may have helped. In 949 Olaf Cuaran reappeared and was accepted as king of York until 952. Until the appearance of Eric Bloodaxe the Dublin Norwegians had provided all the candidates for the rule of Viking York, but now there was an actual – if ex-Norwegian – king in contention.

Olaf had shown some political skill. He represented a tradition of a sort. The Northumbrians must have realised that Eric would be likely to pursue what would nowadays be called an adventurist policy and expelled him. It was at this point that Olaf reappeared and was again made king of York. Eadred did nothing about this second apostasy. It seems likely that he knew his real enemies were Archbishop Wulfstan and his supporters and that Olaf might come in useful as an ally. It also seems as if Eadred did not think he could win an outright victory in the north without allies. The Northumbrians recalled Eric once again in 952. Eadred now felt he had to act and he managed to arrest Archbishop Wulfstan. Those were not the days for the niceties of canon law, and he stayed in prison until the Northumbrians expelled Eric once again in 954. Eric's problem was that he had no estates in Northumbria and little means of rewarding his followers unless he raided and robbed his neighbours. He could not move far from York, and he seems to have been especially active in northern Northumbria, where the wealthier people were mostly of English descent. Eric had many enemies. According to the sagas, which may well be informed here, he was very insecure in York, not daring to trust anybody. His position in York was very much of Archbishop Wulfstan's making. and without him Eric could not long sustain his power there.

He set out for Carlisle but was intercepted in a remote place called Stainmore and killed. Sir Frank Stenton in the *Oxford History* thought some kind of battle took place. It seems more likely that the leader of the English Northumbrians, Oswulf of Bamburgh, who had particular reason to hate Eric, had him ambushed and murdered. Eric was an impossible candidate for the rule of York. He had neither the traditions nor the resources the Dublin Norwegians could command. He was a blessing in disguise to the West Saxons, and his career suggests that Archbishop Wulf-stan was very shortsighted.

In 954 Wulfstan was released from prison but he was never allowed to return to the north. He was given the see of Dorchester, the see that extended from the Thames to the Humber, and after 1066 was moved to Lincoln. At that time it was full of men of Viking descent. He was the last Northumbrian-born Archbishop of York until after the Norman Conquest, although later in the tenth century there were two archbishops of Viking descent, both from East Anglia. They were both most loyal to the West Saxon connexion. It is not too much to say that from now until 1066 the archbishop of York was the representative of the West Saxon royal house, which had gained and never relinquished control of elections to York.

Northumbria now achieved remarkable unity in view of its horrible history. Men of English and Viking descent lived in tolerable amity. Before he died Eadred appointed an East Anglian of Viking descent, Oskytel, archbishop of York. Oskytel's appointment was a landmark in the formation of a united England. Not a Northumbrian, but not a West Saxon either, he had Viking connexions and was unswervingly committed to the West Saxon king. The kingdom had now one king to rule it and one royal family to provide him. It had two archbishops, both appointed by that king. The kingdom had to be governed with a certain tact: the West Saxons were no more lovable to the men of the north and the Midlands than are the modern inhabitants of Wessex today. To judge by the titles to his charters, Eadred liked to see himself as the conqueror of the north. He was really more of a skilful operator than a conquering soldier, which, perhaps was what the times needed. The men of York played their cards particularly badly. Eric Bloodaxe was never going to give them anything but trouble, and perhaps their biggest trouble was that they had only straws to clutch at. The kingdom of Dublin dragged on but no longer had any influence on English affairs. For a century there had been a possibility, sometimes a strong possibility, that a large part of England, perhaps all of it, would form a united kingdom based on Dublin. With hindsight we can see it could not have been a very stable kingdom, and we can see that the Dublin Norwegians constantly overplayed their hand. They were *surexcité par Emporheben*, as T. S. Eliot said in a different connexion. They had a narrow view of their self-interest which made them difficult to make friends with and impossible to trust. The West Saxons were also deeply distrusted, sometimes with reason, but they could form alliances and they did have a sense of limitation. The Norwegian saga literature is very enjoyable to read and more extensive than anyone else's, but it presents a self-image of the age. The Vikings saw themselves like that – they could even make Eric Bloodaxe a sympathetic hero. The West Saxons also valued heroic action but they tempered heroism with a sense of reality. If they enjoyed *Beowulf* and no doubt other epic poems now lost, they did not use them as guides to life. In any case *Beowulf* has a hard core of common sense to it.

NOTES

1 The classic statement of the peasant army thesis is that of Stenton in *Anglo-Saxon England*. 'In all the recorded fighting of Anglo-Saxon history the typical warrior is the man of noble birth, fitted to be a king's companion, with far more than the equipment of an ordinary peasant, and dismounting only for battle. The peasant contingents in the host move very dimly behind the aristocratic foreground' (pp. 290–1). His reasons for thinking they were part of the *fyrd* were not much more than that they had swords and other weapons. Surely the times would require this of any man who wished to survive in that world? In another place he mentions an account of an expedition that sounds as though it consisted entirely of aristocratic warriors. In his posthumous collection of essays, *Preparatory to Anglo-Saxon England*, his last word on the ceorl is to be found. He still thought the ceorl important but the ceorl had moved decidely upmarket. Since he is often cited as the last word on the problem of the ceorls it is worth pointing out that he left the problem quite open.

2 Ed. Donald Scragg, Oxford and Manchester, 1991.

3 Dr Smyth, *King Alfred the Great*, pp. 138 *et seq.*, has some important comments on the Carolingian influence on the West Saxon fortification policy that have been overlooked.

4 *Township and Borough*, Cambridge, 1898.

5 *The Medieval English Borough*, Manchester, 1936.

6 Asser, *Life of King Alfred*, c. 91.

7 Harmer, *Selected English Historical Documents*, pp. 22–3.

8 James Campbell, 'Stenton's *Anglo-Saxon England* with special reference to the early period' in *Stenton's Anglo-Saxon England Fifty years On*, Reading, 1994, p. 51.

9 Martin Biddle, *Winchester Studies*, i, 1975, Oxford.

10 Tellenbach, 'Die Unteilbarkeit des Reiches'.

11 *Chronicon*, ed. A. Campbell, Oxford, 1962, introduction.

12 The editor, David Dumville, thinks it was probably composed in the early twelfth century. I have set out my arguments for supposing it to be pre-Conquest in a forthcoming article, 'The Annals of St Neots and the Defeat of the Vikings'.

13 A. Smyth, *Scandinavian Kings in the British Isles*, 2, Winchester Studies i, Oxford, 1975.

14 Michael Lapidge, *St Dunstan, his Life, Times and Cult*, Woodbridge, 1992, p. 247. Professor Lapidge has not convinced everyone of his claim that B. was an Englishman but he has convinced me.

CHAPTER 6

Holiness and hubris

EADRED'S ACHIEVEMENTS were the more remarkable in that he never seems to have enjoyed good health, and he died in 955. Although he left England in the hands of the West Saxons and had a fair claim to be king of England in fact as well as in name, his will does not suggest he was very confident that it would last. It was drawn up late in life: he left a large sum to buy peace from the Vikings should it prove necessary. These buying-off operations are usually called Danegeld and are associated with Æthelred II (the Unready). It has already been pointed out that Ælfred bought the Vikings off on occasion. The term 'Danegeld' is not found until after the Conquest.[1] The pre-Conquest term was *heregeld*, and the money was meant for a quite different purpose. Eadred's successor, Eadwig, was left nothing, but he got what was now the royal demesne. The amount of land he granted by charter during his short reign shows that he was very rich indeed. Æthelwulf's farsighted move to make the kingdom and the royal property impartible was paying off. I have suggested that the Church bore some of the burden in that it would have had to provide benefices for dis-inherited younger sons and brothers, but we need also to remember the high death rate, which would have limited the problem. If we take the English royal family, only one younger son founded a line that lasted a hundred years, Henry III's younger son, Edmund, earl of Lancaster. It was not until the eighteenth century that one of George III's younger sons, the duke of Cumberland, founded a line that is still in place (the former kingdom of Hanover).

When Eadred died he was succeeded by his elder nephew, Eadwig. He was probably fifteen and his brother Edgar seems to have been two years younger. Eadwig seems to have been regarded as a disaster waiting to happen. It is difficult to see why. His reign was very short but there was no Viking invasion and no onerous taxation. By Christian, now conventional, standards he behaved very badly indeed at his coronation. He disappeared and Dunstan was sent to fetch him and found him in bed with the girl he later married and her mother as well. On the one hand this was not likely to have been an age of sexual puritanism; on the other a coronation was not just another ceremony. It was a real seeking of God's grace by men convinced of the existence of God's grace and its power to do them a great deal of good. They thought there was a real connexion between the sacrament of consecration and the prosperity of the country. The English had had their fill of the wrath of God over the last few generations. There must have been real shock and fear over Eadwig's behaviour.

Eadwig had almost from the beginning of his reign to buy support. Within the first year Eadwig issued a series of landbooks, almost all with lay beneficiaries. This points to a very early loss of confidence in the king and it is hard to see what but scandal over his behaviour at the coronation could have caused it. These land grants must have seriously depleted the royal demesne. That Dunstan was involved in whatever was amiss from the start is apparent, since Eadwig exiled him to Flanders. The movement to reform the English Church by introducing genuine Benedictine monasticism was in its infancy and Dunstan was its undisputed leader. The habits of political obedience, even in reforming monks, were very deep-rooted. Æthelwold, though Dunstan's right-hand man by now, did not accompany him into exile. Nor, in 957, when the Mercians and Northumbrians rejected Eadwig and replaced him with Edgar, did Æthelwold join Edgar, although he had been his tutor. Eadwig continued as king of Wessex until his death. Edgar never held Æthelwold's steadfastness in supporting Eadwig against him, nor was there the slightest rift between Æthelwold and Dunstan. There was an assumed connexion between an abbot's office and his political loyalty even when the abbot and the king were on strained terms. When the kingdom split in 957 it is obvious something very serious was at stake, since the situation was an open invitation to the Vikings to intervene. If we could penetrate the reasons for Eadwig's unpopularity we should be very near a deep understanding of how the tenth-century mind worked. I can get no farther than that.

Fortunately Eadwig survived for only two years and the kingdom was reunited under Edgar. The unification of England made possible, even necessary, some developments in government. The history of institutions, Bishop Stubbs observed, is generally regarded as dull and unrewarding. (I don't think he really believed it and in any case the history of institutions elicited some first-class historical prose from him.) The Vikings could not have been held and then repulsed without the sophisticated deployment of institutions. We have seen that Ælfred was very keen on promoting literacy, and it is relevant to ask why. He ordered his senior men to learn to read English or forfeit their jobs. For those who could not yet read – it is difficult enough in the twentieth century, let alone the ninth, to teach illiterate adults to read – he insisted they should have at hand by night and day someone, preferably a kinsman, who could. It is unlikely he expected them to console themselves with Boethius or soliloquise with St Augustine as part of their duties as ealdormen. Why then did he insist? The late Dr Harmer was the editor of one of the great editions of Anglo-Saxon source material, *Anglo-Saxon Writs.*[2] (It took her a lifetime of scholarship and it is a melancholy reflexion on the times that it would no longer be possible for a contemporary scholar to emulate her.) She noticed that in Ælfred's preamble to the *Regula Pastoralis* there were unmistakable traces of the standard protocol for vernacular writs. This was the first indication of the existence of the writ. Compared with the formal diploma, writs are casual to a degree. They are in the vernacular and are sealed, which diplomas never were. The king greets the recipient in the third person, using both his or her names. After the greeting the body of the letter – for writs are always in epistolary form – moves to the first person singular, always 'I', never 'we'. The letter is sealed so that it cannot be read without breaking the seal: the seal contains an effigy of the king, more what we would call a logo than a portrait. Only one writ survives from the tenth century, and from the very late tenth century at that. The pre-Conquest writs that survive were all meant to serve as title deeds, but the very peremptory tone of the writs shows that such was not their original purpose. By 1066 their popularity had rendered the cumbersome Latin diplomas obsolete. The peremptory tone I mentioned suggests that there were other ephemeral writs that have not survived because they were of no interest once the circumstances that prompted them had passed. It seems to me that it was his writs that Ælfred wanted his ealdormen to read, in bed if necessary. This must mean that the king wanted to communicate information about Viking movements and commands about coping with those movements. The *burh* must have been the destination of these writs as often as not: the seal identified the command completely with the royal will. To disobey a writ was to disobey the king. The situation at Ælfred's death shows that it worked.

This must suggest that the king had a royal writing office, and we are fortunate that thanks to Simon Keynes we know he had. A few years ago Dr Keynes wrote a solid book that showed beyond doubt that the charters of Æthelred II were produced by a royal chancery and not by their recipients.[3] Recently he has taken the origin of the royal writing office much further back.[4] He has found evidence that from Æthelwulf onwards charters seem to smack of central authority and that the charters of Ælfred and Edward the Elder cannot have been produced at the two major West Saxon ecclesiastical centres, Winchester and Sherborne. He argues, to my mind convincingly, that there was a small group of royal clerks at court who produced the royal diplomas. This means that Ælfred was imitating the Carolingian *Hofkapelle*.[5] It also means that when circumstances demanded a quick and efficient method of communicating intelligence about a highly mobile enemy the bureaucracy was already in place. It seems highly probable that the same office continued to produce diplomas, and the ease and speed with which all writs were issued prompted the invention of the writ charter. It seems clear from Dr Keynes that diplomas were still the most popular form of title deed in Æthelred's reign but it is also clear that the first title deeds in writ form (what after the Conquest were called writ charters) date from that reign too. All this means that the king's service demanded a supply of literate, educated men. In a seminal essay[6] on the making of Æthelstan's empire Michael Wood thought that something like the Ottonian *Hofkapelle* obtained in England. It is now clear such was indeed the case and that it was not new in Æthelstan's day. From Ottonian example it would seem that *capellani* accompanied their royal masters on their peregrinations and used their literary skills as they were directed. They also performed some religious duties and might collect relics. They could undertake, if required to, diplomatic missions. It does look from Michael Wood's article as though the English royal chapel was not very different. As an interesting and, as it happens, enormously portentous English example, Æthelstan sent the bishop of Ramsbury to Western Francia to escort his Carolingian nephew, who had just been chosen King. The Ottonian *capellani* could hear lawsuits. We have not much evidence here but Dunstan did it at least once. Asser seems to imply something similar was going on in Ælfred's day. This time unquestionably the English were borrowing from essentially Carolingian tradition. This enormously important activity was likely to have been understood by some of the establishment figures. It becomes easy to understand why Asser and the compiler of the *Annals of St Neots* were so interested in Francia and what went on there.

The education system that underpinned the royal chapel seems Ælfredian too. Ælfred proposed to allot a fourth part of his revenues to pay for a school that would teach young men to read the vernacular at least; for those who mastered Latin there is promise of high office. Æthelstan continued his grandfather's work. He may himself have been a pupil in the royal school: he was claimed to be learned by credible witnesses. But, even so, in Æthelstan's day there was a chronic shortage of suitable, educated, clergy. He followed Ælfred again in recruiting suitable clergymen from the Continent. In his day, as in his grandfather's, to Englishmen Francia meant East Francia. We have only to look at Asser and the St Neots compiler to see that. The latter, recording the deposition of Charles III, the succession of Arnulf and the splitting of Charles III's united empire into five separate parts, makes it clear that it was Arnulf's East Francia that mattered: he is dismissive of the western kingdoms even though one of them had a real Carolingian king.

There is some evidence that the traffic was not one-way. We know there were Englishmen working in East Francia, though not famous or prominent ones. Æthelstan recruited on some scale and went for bigger fish. He put an East Frank called Godescalc in charge of the newly restored church at Abingdon. There were at least three East Franks in the community at New Minster before 933. There was another at Christchurch who wrote a poem in praise of Æthelstan. But it is in London and East Anglia that the greatest concentration may be found. The bishop of London was one Theodred, and the name is German. He was surrounded by clergy also with German names. Most of this detail has been dug up by Michael Wood in his important article.[7] Wood also gives an impressive list of magnificent artefacts that came into England at this time, mainly from East Francia. The size of Æthelstan's writing office was still small. In that world it took time to establish a literary tradition, and such traditions were necessarily fragile for a long time to come. This should be remembered by those tempted to whitewash the Vikings. We know that when Æthelstan was crowned he was attended by Ælfheah, Beornstan, Ælfheah priest and monk, Oda and Cenwald. They sound like his writing office staff, and it seems certain that these men became bishops of Wells, Winchester, Winchester again, Ramsbury (later translated to Canterbury and the ambassador to West Francia) and Worcester. Apart from their court activities several of them were concerned with the creation of a reformed monasticism. Ælfheah (the second Ælfheah) played a key role in the conversion of Dunstan and Æthelwold to Benedictine monasticism. These two young men were court clerics who must have earned high office in any case, and at first their monastic status was a hindrance to the advancement of their influence at court. They were, of course, the men who really got monasticism on the move in Edgar's reign. (Æthelstan was Edgar's uncle.) But the two key figures encountered the new reform movement at the royal court and dedicated themselves to it, with the encouragement of the king's most important counsellors. The third key monk was Oswald. He was an East Anglian of Viking extraction and not a man of the court so far as we know. But his uncle, Bishop Oda of Ramsbury, later archbishop of Canterbury, was very definitely a leading member of Æthelstan's trusted circle. He was entrusted with an important diplomatic mission – to accompany the king's nephew, Louis l'Outre Mer, to take up the West Frankish crown. Bishop Oda took the opportunity to visit the reformed and reforming daughter of Cluny, Fleury. This was widely believed to hold the bones of St Benedict, whose remains had been brought there from Monte Cassino to escape barbarian vandals. (It is fair to say that the Cassinese monks always denied this and that Fleury's claims are not backed by very strong evidence.) Whether Fleury's claim is true or false is beside the point: in what was to be the *patria* of Benedictine monasticism, Francia, East and West, and England, it was implicitly believed that Fleury was the *aristerium sancti Benedicti*, the citadel of St Benedict, because it had the relics. Bishop Oda asked to become a member of the community and was tonsured. There was no question of his remaining there. He had made a grand gesture and returned to England to try and further the monastic cause in a small, but enormously important, circle. He recruited his nephew Oswald. By money and influence he got Oswald elected to a community in Winchester, perhaps even New Minster. This was not really backsliding. Oda had to accept the rules of the old monasticism before he could reform them. Even as abbot Oswald had not the authority over the community to change anything. He resigned in disgust and withdrew to Fleury, where he was a simple monk for several years. He was the only one of the three original monks who had extensive first-hand experience of Benedictine monasticism in an established Benedictine monastery.

With the appearance of Fleury in English history we meet a subtle change in Anglo-Saxon perceptions of Francia. Interest shifts from East to West Francia and influence with it. We must not make the disastrous mistake of supposing that this was due to the declining influence of East Francia, politically or intellectually. East Francia remained the leading political and intellectual power until the death of Henry III in the middle of the eleventh century. What had happened was that influence was now channelled through and from monastic communities where once it had been by means of talented individuals. The talented individuals did not disappear, exactly, but henceforth they were members of communities and their influence did not depend on face-to-face encounters. They wrote things; what they wrote was read and transmitted. Where an important political crisis enabled a Byrhtferth to encounter an Abbo things followed, but in the next generation a literate monk could encounter an Abbo and many more such in the library. But let us look at some of the implications of what I have just described. Clearly news of the new monasticism stemming from Cluny had reached the small but influential circle of Æthelstan's counsellors and must have come via the East Frankish recruits to Æthelstan's service. Cluny's fame had already reached East Francia and that abbey was to be as influential there as it was everywhere else. There were other reform movements in East Francia: that of the Flemish reformer Gerard of Brogne had some influence in England. Attempts have been made to build an opposition between these movements and the influence of Cluny,[8] without a great deal of success. The influence of Cluny and its original connexion, Fleury and Bourg-Dieu – the Cluny connexion was something quite other than the Cluniac order – was overwhelming and it drew English interest westwards.

The monastic party at court was at first small and there was bitter opposition. Dunstan was bullied and seriously ill-treated by men some of whom must have been clerical placemen, but the king was certainly of the monastic party, though he was aware of the need for circumspection. He authorised the tonsuring of both Dunstan and Æthelwold. According to Æthelwold's biographer, Ælfric,[9] Æthelwold 'learned from the King's counsellors many things useful to him ... and at length was tonsured by the King's orders and consecrated by Ælfheah, bishop of Winchester, whom he zealously served for some time'.

Now we know something of the government of England at the very top level and who the men were who ran it, where they came from and how they got their expertise. We need to look at what it was they ran. In the ninth century it seems that each West Saxon shire had its own ealdorman. Essex retained its pre-Viking organisation; England north of the Thames for the most part did not. It looks as if Æthelstan increased the size of the territories ealdormen were expected to govern. A law of Æthelstan's nephew, Edgar, makes it certain that three ealdormen overtopped the rest.[10] Mercia seems to have been divided into two. Eastern Mercia, as East Anglia is occasionally called, was run by the family of Aethelstan Half King, by origin West Saxon landholders, for most of the tenth century. Western Mercia, traditional Mercia, was run by Ealdorman Ælfhere. He, Ealdorman Æthelstan and the earl of Northumbria (the Anglo-Danish hybrid 'earl' had lodged itself in the north in Edgar's day and replaced 'ealdorman' everywhere in Cnut's) were equally half-kings or vice-gerents of their regions. Edgar's law does not imply he invented the system; it sounds like a customary arrangement now taken for granted and made use of. Wittingly or not, this system greatly distorted the balance of power. The ealdorman of Mercia inherited all the traditional problems the rulers of Mercia had always had to cope with. In the east it was perhaps expected that the Vikings would resume their raids and provide the ealdorman with problems enough, but Edgar's policies meant there were no problems at all with the Vikings. This must have augmented the resources of the Eastern landholders because they did not have to use them for war. Of course the balance was reversed in the next reign, when East Anglia was under constant attack from the Danes and Mercia was more or less immune until 1016.

Such was the devastation of the Viking wars that the Midlands had to be re-shired, and this was done some time between 900 and 1016. All shires were subdivided into hundreds except in the Danelaw (that is, the area in which Scandinavian law and custom prevailed), where the smaller units were known as wapentakes. The names of the hundreds are frequently the names of the places the hundred met at. Sometimes the names are very ancient, probably pagan, and the same is true of the Mercian hundreds. This suggests that, although the Mercian shire organisation had collapsed during the Viking wars, the hundredal system may not have. There is thus room for further research here.

The reorganisation did not stop there. It seems certain that Edgar added a new tier to local government and gave a new dimension to local military arrangements. We know from a compilation called the *Laws of Henry I* – not an official code of laws but a nostalgic account of the 'good old law' in the process of subversion in Henry I's day by the researches of 'malignant professors', according to its author – that hundreds were grouped into triple hundreds called shipsokes. The *Chronicle*, *sub anno* 1008, speaks of a *sea fyrd* levied that year. This annal implies that each three hundreds had to provide a ship. Since the word 'ship soke' means 'shipful' they must have had to provide a crew to man the ship, too. Ships like those of Ælfred held sixty men. By simple arithmetic this means that one crew member served for each five hides. By the time of the Domesday survey, 1086, it was the rule that the ordinary warrior, called a thegn, from Edgar's day, served for each five-hide unit. We know this meant development, because under Æthelstan a warrior had to serve for each two hides. What seems to have been a serious relaxation under Edgar may have been more apparent than real, since the five-hide units had to combine with others to furnish a ship. It looks as though the shipsokes and the five-hide units were created together. It seems certain that this was done by Edgar. In the early years of the eleventh century Bishop Æthelric of Sherborne wrote a letter complaining he had lost some of the three hundred hides his see had been endowed with[11] but implying he still had to fulfil the obligations. He makes it clear that his predecessors, in the plural, had held such a shipsoke. Taking a minimal interpretation of his words, this implies at least two predecessors and takes us back to the reign of Edward the Martyr at the latest. It is impossible that such a reorganisation could have taken place in that disordered reign, so the bishop's letter does point to Edgar. The chronicle attributed to Florence of Worcester, a post-Conquest source but responsible for much of what we know about the late tenth and early eleventh centuries, says Edgar made an annual perambulation of the British Isles with his fleet. This is likely to have been true, since a corollary of Edgar's coronation ceremonies was having a number of kings – from the Western Isles where we can identify them – row him on the Dee at Chester. A spectacular but apposite form of homage and presumably the fruit of Edgar's invention of the sea *fyrd*.

There exists a large charter, the *Altitonantis* charter, which purports to authorise the creation of the shipsoke of the bishop of Worcester and to name it Oswaldslow, after the ruling bishop. It is certainly a Worcester product. It is equally certainly partly doctored. No other centre purports to offer a parallel document, but then, no other *scriptorium* except Worcester produced a charter creating a *burh*. The false interpolations in the charter stick out like a sore thumb. They have to do with a quarrel between the monks and their bishop that turned on the date of the election of the first prior of Worcester. The charter refers to Edgar's nautical peregrinations and says specifically that they include Dublin. Until Dr Smyth wrote, this sounded too improbable to be credible. Now we can see that the peregrination would have had little point if it had not included Dublin, the power that enabled the kingdoms of the Western Isles to make a nuisance of themselves. The charter gains much more credibility in consequence. The charter purports to create a shipsoke, to which it offers alternative names, *naucupletio* and *scypfylleth*. All three are synonyms.

England was nearly unique in having cathedrals whose chapters were monastic. Three of the greatest cathedrals, Canterbury, Worcester and Winchester, were among their number. This seems to have been the result of a policy of Edgar's, who probably meant that all cathedrals should eventually become monastic, but it never happened. Once the reformed monastery cathedrals came into being, as is the way in the world of institutions, new forms of tension and new forms of fiddling came with them. The cause the forged portions of the Oswaldslow charter were designed to promote is an early, perhaps the earliest example, of this.

It has been pointed out that in earlier English monasteries the property of the monastery was divided up into individual prebends, held by individual monks who lived off the proceeds. Even in a reformed monastery such as Christ Church Canterbury, before the reign of Edgar, these monks could bequeath their prebends by will, subject to some restrictions on the choice of beneficiary. The policy of the new reformers was stated bluntly in the first life of Odo of Cluny: that monks should be celibate, refrain from eating meat and hold all their property in common.[12] These aims were harshly enforced by the English reformers too. The property of the monastery was communalised and, in the first generation of the English reform, disposal of the income was at the will of the abbot. But, at some point in the early eleventh century, so far as we can tell, the monks, having accepted the communalisation of the property and the abolition of the prebends, began to claim rights as a community to some of the property. Again the precocious Worcester *scriptorium* provides the first evidence. The Oswaldslow charter was doctored to prove that the first prior, Wynsige, was appointed in 964, the date of the charter and the probable date of the conversion of the cathedral into a monastery. Inspection of the archives of Oswald's great fenland foundation, Ramsey, where Wynsige was sent to learn to be a monk, new style, showed that Wynsige could not have been prior in 964. Some time in the first half of the eleventh century Worcester assembled its records into a permanent file, called a cartulary. (Worcester was the first monastery to have a cartulary in England. The next important one was Winchester but not until the early years of Stephen's reign.) The late Herbert Finberg christened the pre-Conquest portion of the cartulary *Liber Wigorniensis*, the Book of Worcester. It contains two, obviously very early, doctored charters that try to prove that Wynsige was 'Dean', i.e. prior, of Worcester in 969. Thus the forged portions of the Oswaldslow charter were out of date by the reign of Cnut. The intention behind this forgery is revealed by a writ of Edward the Confessor granting the prior and community of Worcester full rights over their share of the property. It would seem that control over the second most important church in Worcester, St Helen's, was the main point at issue. This type of dispute, this issue of jurisdiction, this concern for the rights of the community independent of the bishop–abbot, was to be repeated many times in the early post-Conquest period, but Worcester seems to have been the pioneer, as it certainly was in documentation. The dispute went on until 1092 when the then bishop, St Wulfstan, on his deathbed, reached a compromise with the monks.[13]

The bits and pieces of evidence, the sifting of narrative sources and the criticism of dubious charters are worth while because they are the only means of revealing the Anglo-Saxon monarchy at the height of its power. Edgar completed the removal of the power once wielded by the Norwegian Vikings by making their minor satellite kingdoms publicly acknowledge their status as his vassals. He appeared at Dublin itself, although he did not conquer it as Ivar the Boneless did. An Ely charter says Cumbrians, Britons and Scoti were set by God under his sceptre. A generation later we could be sure that Scotland meant what it means to us but before then *Scoti* means Irish. The heritage of Ivar the Boneless was destroyed for ever.

The burhs were still there and important. Their *raison d'être* was, of course, military but they did have a court that met three times a year alongside the shire court that met twice. We know that the *Burhgemot*, like the shire court, was sometimes attended by very important people. By, or soon after, 1066 the two courts had merged and met every six months. From Æthelstan's laws it is obvious that *burh* had become a synonym for port. In the tenth century a port was any trading centre, whether on the coast or not. The port–*burh* played a key role in the minting of coins. The Vikings soon learnt that a personal coinage was an important sign of independence and legitimacy. Ivar the Boneless murdered Edmund of East Anglia and subjugated the former kingdom. Edmund's former subjects continued to mint coins in his name with the epithet 'Saint' for some time. Every time such a coin changed hands it recalled East Anglia's former independence and the manner in which that independence had been lost. From Æthelstan's day efforts were made to confine mints to certain burhs only. No king could prevent the archbishop of Canterbury from minting his own coins, though he could set conditions. The coins of York are fascinating: they combine pagan and Christian symbolism. One York coin combines a reference to the cathedral's patron saint, Peter, with an image of Thor's hammer.

Uniformity was achieved in 973, by King Edgar, as one might expect. He prescribed that coins should be re-minted regularly, at first every six years. There were at least sixty burhs in England with mints. The moneyers were named on the coins and could be presumably be brought to book if they debased the coins and pocketed the proceeds. Old coins were no longer legal tender and had to be brought in for re-minting. The coins circulated throughout England and it is certain that silver pennies, the only actual coins – the larger denominations were simply units of account – were minted by the million. This can be determined by metallurgical examination of the coins. In the eleventh century the re-minting was accelerated to every two or three years and the quantity still ran into millions. This was done in the reigns of Harold I and his half-brother Harthacnut, neither of whom had the power of Edgar. Both were short-lived and Harthacnut was very unpopular. It is obvious that a powerful bureaucracy based on the *burh* was capable of sustaining, perhaps generating, a routine. It has been suggested[14] that eleventh-century governments were sophisticated enough to attempt to control the economy by determining the quality of the silver that went into the pennies – in other words, what most books call debasing the coinage was much more like what we call devaluation or its reverse. Governments certainly had the means to do this but had they the economic knowledge? I should not care to claim they had not. The minting was always closely supervised and highly disciplined. Cnut was so impressed by the English system that he exported English moneyers to Denmark but the subsequent collapse of quality shows how essential bureaucratic control was to the system. The Normans in their turn took over the system as it stood.

Another sign of the new times was the royal interest in law and order, a very practical not a theoretical interest. There is a fascinating account of a lawsuit from the time of Edward the Elder that shows why some people did not think much of him. His wife, Eadgifu, Edgar's grandmother, claimed an estate in Kent from one Goda. There seems no reason to doubt the queen's claim that Goda had been given the estate as surety for a debt and that Eadgifu had repaid the debt. It took six years for her to get a hearing from her husband and his *witan*, who then found for her. The judgment was not enforced until her friends, no doubt suitably bribed, persuaded Edward to proceed against Goda. When Eadwig succeeded, Goda seized the estate again. It was left to Edgar to restore the estate to the old queen and put paid to Goda. She gave it to Christ Church Canterbury, which is why its history has been preserved.[15] When a great lady like Eadgifu had such trouble in getting her rights respected it is obvious how powerful the local establishment was, and at the same time the power of Edgar is put into high relief. Local interests clashed with royal interests in Edgar's reign because the king savagely attacked them but when they did local interests lost. But the key period in the history of English law and order before the Conquest is the reign of Æthelstan. What Æthelstan attempted and achieved shows again that he was a much bigger man than his father.

The main problem seems to have been cattle rustling. Cattle and horses were very big business in that world. Edward the Elder tried to confine all cattle sales to a *burh* with the witness of a port reeve. This proved too ambitious and Æthelstan relaxed the law so that only property worth twenty pence or more had to be 'vouched for warranty', as the system was called. We have no evidence how well the system worked. Not the least importance of the coin evidence is that it shows that in the one category of legislation we can test against independent criteria the laws were obeyed. I think it probable that the legislation about vouching to warranty worked too. We have another piece of legal evidence to bear this out.

The second code of Æthelstan was promulgated at the council of Grately. It contains the essence of his law-and-order campaign, and its enactments were repeated more than once. One legal document meant to further the Grately programme is what is usually called Æthelstan's sixth code, although apart from two provisions it is not a royal code at all. It is important because it was meant to put one aspect of Æthelstan's programme into practice in one specially important part of the country. The inspiration behind Æthelstan's legislation is Carolingian. The capitulary of Servais (853), issued by Charles the Bald, is almost certainly behind VI Æthelstan, as the edict of Pîtres (June 864) lies behind the tenth-century coinage legislation. VI Æthelstan is also known as *Judicia Civitatis Lundonie* and this title seems to be contemporary. Since the contents have a positively Wild West flavour – cattle rustling and posses to pursue rustlers – the *civitatis Lundonie* must be the *burh*, not the city of London. Several bishops and magnates were involved and it is assumed they were normally resident in the *civitas*. Their task was to form posses and chase cattle rustlers. They also had to flush out families and friends who harboured rustlers. It was expected this would mean a big effort, involving important landholders and bishops. Since some of these delinquent kindred groups were ceorlish, we need to be careful in dismissing ceorls as merely free peasants.

Æthelstan went further. All freemen had to form groups of nine, with a tenth man in charge, known as tithing groups. They had to man the posses and do the policing. There is an element of a simple insurance policy in all this, since no one knew in advance when his cattle were going to be rustled. They also held a monthly business meeting at which business was transacted, food consumed and bytts were emptied. There is no reason to think VI Æthelstan was unique. London was the greatest of the burhs and its law-and-order regulations were as good a model as any.

There was another social aspect of all this not mentioned in Æthelstan's legislation but made brutally plain in the laws of his brother Edmund. It is evident that the lowest class in Anglo-Saxon society, the thralls, had been running away and joining the Vikings, as they were to do again in the reign of Æthelred II. From what Archbishop Wulfstan says of the later period, some at least became full Viking warriors. In Edmund's day this option was not really open to the thralls in most parts of the country but some of them banded together and took to robbery and plunder. Edmund ordered the posses to round them up. When caught the ringleaders were to be hanged and the rest punished but not so as to impair their economic usefulness. They were to be flogged, their little fingers were to be cut off and they were to be scalped. Again Carolingian legislation was the model Edmund or his counsellors followed. Some scholars have balked at this evidence of how nasty our Anglo-Saxon forebears could be and have translated the law as though it prescribed a haircut, short back and sides. The law exists only in a Latin translation and the word I render as 'scalped' is *extoppere*, 'topped off', and would be taken to mean beheading if the context did not make it clear they were to live. In Cnut's day scalping was used as a punishment for men of much higher social class than Edmund's revolting thralls.

It is plain that 'government at a distance' was becoming a reality in England. Even if the laws were not always obeyed – and we have the coinage legislation to warn us not to make too much of this – it is plain they made a substantial difference to society. The kindred and the feud were no longer the only means of protecting an individual from harassment. Edmund actually tried to outlaw feuds. But still the feuds were there. Sir Frank Stenton drew attention to an important one in the eleventh century:

> The *Chronicle* states that Uhtred was killed by the advice of Eadric Streona [Æthelred II's notorious and treacherous ealdorman of Mercia]. This statement is made improbable by northern sources of the Norman Age which show that the chief agent in the murder was a nobleman, known, from his rank, as Thurbrand the Hold. The most detailed of these accounts state that Uhtred and forty companions who had come with him to treat with Cnut for peace were killed by Cnut's soldiers through Thurbrand's guile. Thurbrand's part in the crime set in motion the most remarkable private feud in English history. Thurbrand was killed by Ealdred, earl of Northumbria, Uhtred's son, Ealdred, was killed by Carl, Thurbrand's son, and a number of Carl's sons were killed by Waltheof, son of Earl Siward, whose mother was Ealdred's daughter.[16]

This proves that feuds were still a reality and it shows that a man might be involved in a feud through his maternal kindred – what social anthropologists call a scatter feud, which could destroy the whole social fabric. Feuds were still a part of political reality, and we need to remember this when we come to look at the reign of the Confessor and his feud with the house of Godwin. To sum up, there is an unmistakable sense that the

wearer of the crown was intervening, constantly intervening, very persua-
sively and very deeply, in English society.

For generations official documents had assumed that the two main
classes of English society were the *twyhyndemen*, that is, the ceorls, whose
wergeld was two hundred shillings, and the *twelfhyndemen*, whose wergeld
was twelve hundred shillings. In Edgar's day the latter word becomes
obsolete and is replaced by 'thegn'. Thegns had existed from the earliest
days of Anglo-Saxon history but the word did not have its Edgarian sense.
These traditional thegns were not a social class but a power elite called
king's thegns. They had been high servants of the king, normally related
to the ealdormen and sometimes to the king, and were the group the ealdormen were recruited from. It needs to be pointed out that they cannot
be identified before the earliest charters but it is hard to see that as they
come into the light of day in the late seventh century they were in any
sense a new creation. From Edgar's reign 'thegn' became the name for an
ordinary warrior, who, I have suggested, served for five hides of land. In a
way the new name reflects a rise in status for the ordinary warrior but it is
doubtful if that was the reason for the change. The thegn, whatever he was
in his own neighbourhood, was the king's man, a royal servant. The term
rapidly gained general currency and again it is usage in royal documents
that achieves this.

There is another of Edgar's policies that illustrates his power – and his
ruthless use of it – to intervene in the localities. This is, at first sight curiously, his plans to revive English monasticism and to give that monasticism
a new and more severely disciplined character. I propose to reserve the
religious and cultural aspects of the revival until the next chapter. Here I
want to deal with the politics of the revival, and I shall not conceal that the
reformers had a less than agreeable side to their characters.

I pointed out earlier that St Wilfrid probably introduced the *Rule* of St
Benedict into England. For a long time it had little influence: although
there is an important Anglo-Saxon manuscript of it in the Bodleian Library
there is little evidence it was much read. The best the Anglo-Saxons seem
to have been able to do was the monastic life at Christ Church Canterbury, as reformed by Archbishop Wulfred, and discussed above. I shall
speak of Benedictine monasticism not as Benedict himself saw it but as it
had developed as described in the second chapter. That is, the monasticism
of Benedict tempered with that of Cassiodorus, which is what Edgar's
monks wanted. They admired and emulated, very successfully, Benedict's
authoritarian abbot but they placed a very different value on literary and
intellectual pursuits very different from his. The reformers were also aware

of the political aspects of their policies, even if they saw them as holy politics it was sinful to oppose.

Æthelwold, whom we have encountered in Æthelstan's service, left a contemporary account of the reasons for the decay of the monasteries as he saw it.[17] I have already pointed out that he puts no blame on the Vikings but is clear that the cause of the decline is something he calls *secularium prioratus,*[18] secular domination. He complains that abbesses – the document was written for nuns but there is no reason to suppose that male religious were in any better case – had alienated their community's land to kinsfolk and that grants of Church land had been made to local magnates to curry favour.

The reform may be said to have begun when King Edmund made the leader of the monastic party, Dunstan, abbot of Glastonbury, the most prestigious West Saxon monastery and the closest to the royal family. Edmund did so from motives of superstition, not piety or conviction. Like Æthelwold, Dunstan had been tonsured and thus committed himself to the monastic party in the reign of Æthelstan, and we have already seen that the royal court contained a Frankish and reforming element. The first monk we know of was Ælfheah, priest and monk, whom the king ordered to tonsure Dunstan and Æthelwold, who thus became monks without monasteries. Ælfheah was made bishop of Winchester, but further than that Æthelstan was not prepared to go, although it is obvious his sympathies were with the monastic party from the counsellors he surrounded himself with. His successor Edmund showed no sympathy for the monks and indeed, seems to have disliked Dunstan and sent him into exile. But almost immediately he had a narrow escape from death whilst out hunting. He interpreted the cause of the accident to Dunstan's banishment and attributed his escape to the intention he immediately formed of recalling him and making him abbot of Glastonbury. Æthelwold entered the abbey with Dunstan and said it was the only true monastery in England. Edmund had no real sympathy with the new monks and when some clerics, fleeing from a Flemish abbey reformed by the reforming local saint, Gerard of Brogne, sought his favour he gave them the abbey of Bath.[19]

It is unlikely that Dunstan had an entirely free hand at Glastonbury or that he could have imposed a real Benedictine discipline in spite of Æthelwold's verdict because Æthelwold proposed to leave Glastonbury and seek a stricter community; he probably had Fleury in mind. Eadred was now king and much more sympathetic to the monks than his brother had been. Dunstan persuaded him to keep Æthelwold in England by giving him the derelict abbey of Abingdon to revive and reform. The estates were in his hand. It is to be noted that Eadred parted only with his own property: he did nothing to make the men who had embezzled monastic property disgorge it. What the reform movement required was a swingeing attack on those of the landed gentry who held what had formerly been the lands of the Church. To recall Werhard, the Canterbury monk with the very considerable landed property he left to the cathedral community, what reform tenth-century style meant was that his property would become forthwith the property of Christ Church. It was his intention that it should happen after his death. Whether he would have welcomed a reduction to absolute monastic property *instanter* may be doubted. Eadwig had now succeeded his uncle, Eadred. He had no sympathy with the monks and he detested Dunstan, so he sent him into exile, and this time Dunstan went.

Exile was a common experience for reforming monks in the tenth century. So much so that a German scholar labelled it *Heimatlösigkeit*, homelessness, and drew attention to its importance.[20] Foreign travel was a rare experience in the tenth century but the reformed monks were the first group to have plenty of experience of it, sometimes willingly, usually not. Dunstan and Oswald both spent time in Frankish monasteries and so did some of their disciples, the monks of the next generation. Abbo, abbot of Fleury, who must have known Oswald at Fleury, was forced into exile by the bishop of Orleans and spent his exile at Oswald's great Fenland monastery, Ramsey. He was a much better educated man than his English contemporaries and he is known to have taught at Ramsey. Byrhtferth of Ramsey, the first biographer of Oswald and author of much else, was almost certainly a pupil. At Dunstan's request Abbo wrote a life of Edmund king and martyr of East Anglia. Dunstan provided him with the 'story' but Abbo made the 'story' into an important anticipation of the ideology of the crusade.[21]

In Eadwig's time Dunstan could find refuge in a Flemish reformed monastery. As I have already pointed out, Oswald could spend some years at Fleury, where his uncle, as bishop of Ramsbury, had received the tonsure. This was important because it meant that when the reform movement in England really got under way, with the accession of Edgar, and Oswald was naturally summoned back to England to become one of the trio of monk bishops who were to reform the English Church, he had a firm basis in knowledge and experience of what modern Benedictine monasticism meant.

Edgar had been a pupil of Æthelwold and it is the life of Oswald, not of Æthelwold, that tells us that Æthelwold was the king's chief counsellor. Edgar seems to have been unquestionably devout and he was prepared to heed his monks when they advised him to do things he would rather not. But reform was in his interests too. In 956 his brother Eadwig had granted some sixty landbooks to laymen, roughly the quantity Edgar granted throughout his whole reign. This meant that Edgar started with a badly depleted demesne. He could not possibly hope to resume these estates but the reform of the monasteries gave him an opportunity to divert vast estates into the hands of devoted friends he could entirely trust.

Very early in the reign Edgar demonstrated his intentions. There was a newish archbishop of Canterbury whom Edgar sent packing back to his original diocese and intruded Dunstan in his place. As soon as the sees became vacant Edgar appointed Æthelwold bishop of Winchester and Oswald bishop of Worcester. They expelled those members of their cathedral communities who would not accept their version of monasticism.[22] As they were not permitted to take any property with them they must have looked to their families for support. There is enough information about life in the newly reformed monasteries to show that it was harsh. There is a story told about Abbot Foldbriht of Pershore, who was noted for his austere life. While a simple monk at Abingdon he was preparing a meal for the community when Abbot Æthelwold came into the kitchen and asked him what he was cooking. Foldbriht replied 'dumplings,' and the Abbot ordered him to give him one. Without hesitation Foldbriht plunged his arm into the boiling water and lifted one out. Whilst the *Rule* insisted that a monk should obey the abbots's commands, I do not think Benedict meant the abbot to give commands like that. From then on Foldbriht was a made monk. One shudders to think what life in Pershore must have been like in his day.

Having purged their communities, the reformers turned to their lay tenants. Our main evidence comes from Worcester, where archive keeping was far in advance of anywhere else. The cathedral records contain some seventy 'loans' made by Oswald to his military tenants. Some scholars prefer to call them leases because the term is familiar in the modern vocabulary of land-holding, which is precisely why it is misleading. Æthelwold's Winchester has some, but not much, information about the bishop's activities in this field. But our main information about Æthelwold as abbot and what he did with – perhaps to – his lay tenants comes from his foundation of Ely. There exists a book called the *Liber Eliensis*, the Book of Ely. It is a miscellaneous volume containing material of different kinds gathered together at different times.[23] The most important part rests on a collection of documents and the records of lawsuits originally in the vernacular and made or commissioned by Æthelwold himself. The vernacular version is now lost but what is probably a faithful Latin translation was made of them in the early twelfth century.

Most of Edgar's new abbeys produced very little archive material. Oswald's foundation at Ramsey produced quite a lot of material, printed in the nineteenth century but in no sense edited. This sounds like quite an abundance of documentation but compared with the twenty thousand or so charters of Cluny it is chicken feed.

That Edgar meant to impose a general policy is clear enough. He is said by the first life of Oswald to have given the entire lands of the English Church to the monks. The new monks could not offer their lay tenants uniformity of treatment. What Æthelwold could do at Winchester was rather different from what Oswald could do at Worcester: both differed from what Dunstan could do at Canterbury, which was nothing. Uniformity was impossible to achieve because Edgar's lordship varied in intensity from place to place. Dunstan could do nothing because the king, like his predecessors, had to handle Kent with kid gloves. The lay tenants were very savagely treated at Winchester; they were only more lightly treated at Worcester by comparison.

Oswald granted his tenants – mostly but not all thegns – estates for a term of three lives, which in most cases would fall short of three generations. These loan charters often call themselves landbooks, an example of the dishonesty the new monks were capable of. A landbook gives an estate to a man and his heirs for ever. These loans were of strictly limited duration. The subterfuge suggests that the men had previously held by book and Oswald is restricting their rights drastically, sugaring the pill by clothing the loan in the language of high status. A high proportion of the loans are to members of Oswald's connexion – his kinsmen, and so on – but Oswald was not a local man: he was a man of Viking descent from the other side of England. It is hard to escape the conclusion that they replaced dispossessed men of West Country stock. Oswald was not simply looking after his own. As head of Oswaldslow he had important military responsibilities and, like every other magnate, he had to have men about him whom he could trust. In which case the men one knew were the best bet. At Winchester it is hard to escape the conclusion that Æthelwold was even harsher. Only one loan charter survives. It is a loan for one life granted at the petition of the queen. This suggests the wholesale suppression of bookright. The Church, however, had to provide its quota for the shipsoke. It is possible that when the term of lives ran out the next heir, all things being equal, got a new charter, which would, of course, have to be negotiated. In the end the number of Oswald's connexion who became tenants of Worcester is perhaps the grimmest evidence of what the reformation meant for the lay tenants. What it amounts to is that in every diocese there were ejected clerks and disgruntled lay tenants, sometimes related.

There is another aspect to Oswaldslow. It was not a homogeneous block of territory. Some of it was not even in Worcestershire, but the most important part of it lay in a block of land surrounding the *burh* of Worcester (which was not part of Oswaldslow). The thegns who made up the liberty had to accept Oswald, and his successors, as their *archiductor*, a title probably derived from that conferred on St Bruno, the younger brother of Otto the Great, as head of the great liberty attached to Cologne cathedral: he was called *archidux*. This meant at Worcester that the thegns of Oswaldslow were now the bishop's vassals and no longer the men of Ealdorman Ælfhere, who still held the *burh* with the responsibilities that went with it. At the other end of the country the monks of Æthelwold's Ely got a great liberty called Wicklow. This was not a shipful as far as we know – it amounted to far more than three hundred hides – and it also contained the site of Sutton Hoo, had the monks but known. Had they known, the British Museum would have been deprived of some of its greatest treasures. The local ealdorman, the local half-king, was Æthelwine, a keen supporter of the monks. He was treated very differently from Ælfhere. The monks gave him the liberty to run for them in return for a modest rent.

We do not hear of dispossessed clergy and laymen at Ely but it is evident from the litigation recorded in the *Liber Eliensis* when the death of Edgar made it possible for laymen to sue the monks that many men thought they had been badly treated. It is noteworthy that the monks often settled out of court. The late Professor Whitelock remarked bluntly in her foreword to the *Liber Eliensis*[24] that Æthelwold does not come very well out of a study of that book.

The monastic reformation has left a number of charters not easy to criticise. They are not landbooks because the churches had held landbooks for the estates in question for many years previous to the reformation. They did not, in other words, create title. They do not model themselves on landbooks or exhibit many signs of common form, though they exhibit some. They have been too easily dismissed as forgeries because they look different from landbooks. They look different because they are different. They are to do with the communalisation of the church's property and the right of the new monks to run the endowment of their churches as they saw fit. They also contain provisions concerning specially important monastic business, in particular the proper method of choosing an abbot, or abbot–bishop in some cases. These provisions vary in their phrasing but they do enjoin the same procedure. It is clear the obvious concern was not to elect the right man but to keep the wrong man out. (This is not an insular feature of such charters but is fairly common in western Europe until the eve of the Gregorian reformation, when the last example of such an electoral provision was drafted in the election decree for the papacy itself. This seems to have envisaged an alliance of the reforming party in the Roman *curia* and the emperor to prevent the election of a 'reactionary' Pope. When, a few years later, Henry IV and Gregory VII fell out it was obvious that the day of this kind of election protocol was over.) It is clear the key figure was the king, who held *dominium* in such matters, which made his intervention all right, as against the magnate's mere *prioratus*,[25] which made his intervention all wrong. It is clear that this was not a means of augmenting royal power. Edgar did not choose new abbots or even new bishops. When Æthelwold died it is clear that his successor as bishop of Winchester, Ælfhere, was chosen by Dunstan. If a sensitive see like Winchester was filled on Dunstan's nod it is likely that other appointments were made similarly. It is interesting to note where Dunstan found Ælfhere. It is often said that Ælfhere was abbot of Bath, but Dunstan's biographer tells us that Dunstan was visiting Bath when he was told of Ælfhere, who presided over a small *monasteriolum* near by. He was plainly not of the social class that normally provided bishops and archbishops. This echoes complaints from such men as the contemporary bishop of Lâon, one of the few literate opponents of the reformers, that the reforming monks – he had experience of Abbo of Fleury – encouraged the appointment of men of low birth to the episcopal bench. It is evident that the new abbots came mostly, if not entirely, from the stables presided over by Oswald and Æthelwold.

There is no doubt that Dunstan, Æthelwold and Oswald were sincere and able men. They demanded nothing of their monks they were not prepared to do themselves but they were harsh, hard men, although conventional opinion has glossed over this harshness. Dunstan is portrayed as a patriarch, Oswald as a gentle monastic Fabian;[26] no one seems to be able to do much for Æthelwold.[27] But of recent years something of the dark side of these men has emerged. Dunstan was a man of extraordinary violence[28] and Dr Lapidge has suggested with some force that Æthelwold prepared for his own canonisation.[29] The reformers helped to create some of their own difficulties. The early death of Edgar was bound to make trouble for them. The first biographer of Oswald said he was murdered, though no one else did. His son and successor, Edward the Martyr, certainly was, but the only person to say much about it was Archbishop Wulfstan in his famous sermon, the word of the Wolf to the English, forty years later, and even he does not tell us who did it. It is likely enough that Ealdorman Ælfhere of Mercia was the guilty party. At any rate, he did penance for it. The reforming monks made things more difficult for themselves by their treatment of Edgar's eldest son, Edward. The witness list of the monasticising charter of New Minster makes fascinating reading. Edward was the son of Edgar's first wife, who had her marriage annulled on grounds of consanguinity. His present queen was pointedly referred to as the king's legitimate wife, and her elder son, Edmund, takes precedence over his elder brother, Edward, as his father's legitimate son. Edward, the elder, is merely the king's procreated son. Edward seems to have been proclaimed a bastard. This legitimate son, Edmund, must have died very young, and Edgar's second 'legitimate' son, Æthelred, was too young to succeed when his father died. The reforming party did what is nowadays called a U-turn and decided that Edward was legitimate enough to succeed after all. This example was by no means unique, and reformers everywhere played ducks and drakes with the canon law of consanguinity and legitimacy. The literate clerical conservative Adalbero of Lâon made a shrewd point when he said, with Abbo of Fleury in mind, that the monks made up the law of the Church as they went along.

We know little about Edward the Martyr except that he was unpopular. It was probably because he chose to follow his father's policies. Ealdorman Ælfhere decided it was time he got his own back. The monasteries of Wessex and East Anglia were safe enough, though Ely had to make compromises. The monasteries of Mercia were devastated. Ælfhere dared not attack Worcester cathedral itself but he destroyed Evesham and scattered the community. Abbot Germanus of Winchcombe fled to Fleury. Deerhurst was another victim, as was Pershore. Most of them recovered in the fullness of time, though Pershore never did. This was not due to any lingering anti-monastic prejudice. Even pious kings never forgot economy, and Edward the Confessor used a lot of Pershore's original endowment to fund Westminster Abbey. In medieval England what Westminster Abbey got Westminster Abbey kept.

It is hard to sum up Edgar's reign and do justice to his achievements. The monastic reformation entered its most spectacular phase in his reign. But it could not have happened as it did without the long preparation the three key monks had undergone. It was this generation of experience that taught them the meaning of Benedictine monasticism, that disciplined them to have the will to carry out what they had learnt. But it needed a powerful king willing to put the resources of his kingdom at their disposal, and that Edgar was willing to do. However we look at his reign he was by far the most powerful king of the house of Cerdic. However much Ealdorman Ælfhere hated him, which must have been a great deal, he dared do nothing until Edgar was dead. Edgar's achievements were many of them short-lived, but that was mainly because Edgar himself was so short-lived. He needed time to let what he attempted take root. But he had changed the face of England permanently. The greatest monasteries dissolved by Henry VIII were founded by Edgar, and that is no mean memorial. But he had left a legacy of hatred, bitterness, disaffection, and as it happened the time he did it was the worst possible time.

NOTES

1 Actually it is in the Domesday assessment of Stamford, Domesday Book, i, 336v. I owe this reference to Mr Campbell.
2 Manchester, 1952.
3 S. D. Keynes, *The Diplomas of King Æthelred the Unready*, Cambridge, 1980.
4 'The West Saxon Charters of King Æthelwulf and his Sons', pp. 1109–49.
5 Joseph Fleckenstein, *Die Hofkapelle der deutschen Könige*, 2 vols, Stuttgart, 1966.
6 'The Making of Æthelstan's Empire: an English Charlemagne', in Patrick Wormald (ed.), *Ideal and Reality in Frankish and Anglo-Saxon Society*, Oxford, 1983, pp. 250–64. It is also worth pointing to another Continental importation of Æthelstan's reign and it cannot be done better than by citing Stenton's words in *Anglo-Saxon England*: 'the simple clear and beautiful handwriting known as the Carolingian minuscule had appeared in England before the end of Æthelstan's reign … and it rapidly came to be regarded as the most appropriate for the representation of Latin texts. Long before the close of the tenth century English scribes were employing it with absolute mastery and a sense of the decorative value of the script–pattern which it yielded' (p. 443).
7 Wood, 'The Making of Æthelstan's Empire'.
8 Dom Kassius Hallinger, 'Gorze–Kluny', *Studia Anselmiana*, 22–5, 2 vols, Stuttgart, 1950–1.
9 M. Lapidge and M. Winterbottom, *Wulfstan of Winchester: the Life of St Æthelwold*, Oxford, 1991, p. 11.
10 Eric John, *Orbis Brittaniae*, Leicester, 1966, pp. 221–3.
11 John, *Land Tenure*, pp. 120–1.
12 Eric John, *The Anglo-Saxons*, ed. James Campbell, Oxford, 1982, p. 184. I have attempted to illuminate the economic and financial consequences of monastic conversion in the case of Worcester cathedral in 'The Church of Worcester and St Oswald', forthcoming.
13 I have discussed this case at length; see my forthcoming article 'The Church of Worcester and St Oswald'.
14 Campbell, *Essays*, pp. 155 *et seq.*
15 John, *Land Tenure*, p. 174, n. 1.
16 Stenton, *Anglo-Saxon England*, p. 390, n. 1.
17 Dorothy Whitelock, *English Historical Documents*, i, p. 846.
18 *Orbis Brittaniae*, pp. 155 *et seq.*

19 *Orbis Brittaniae*, p. 157.

20 G. B. Bezzola, *Das Ottonische Kaisertum in französischen Geschichtsschreibung*, Graz and Cologne, *passim*.

21 Carl Erdmann, *Die Entstehung des Kreuzeugsgedankens*, Stuttgart, 1935; trans. M. W. Baldwin and W. Goffart, Princeton, NJ, 1977.

22 John, *Orbis Brittaniae*, pp. 234 *et seq.* P. H. Sawyer, 'The Charters of the Reform Movement: the Worcester Archive', in D. Parsons (ed.), *Tenth-Century Studies*, London and Chichester, 1975, has rejected my claim that Oswald expelled clerks from Worcester, replacing them by monks. I have replied in a forthcoming article, 'The Church of Worcester and St Oswald'.

23 E. O. Blake, *Liber Eliensis*, Royal Historical Society, Camden 3rd Series, xcii, London, 1962.

24 *Ibid.*

25 Dr Pauline Stafford in her *Unification and Conquest*, London, 1989, p. 188, writes: 'At one point the *Regularis* specifies the need to end *secularium prioratus* which has been the ruin of monastic life in earlier times. What the authors meant and the audience understood by this term is not clear. Secular domination could be its meaning, a wholesale attack by the reformers on the noble control of the monasteries. It may be little more than reiteration of the theme of non-involvement in secular affairs. In either case it is given little prominence in the document and it would have been easy to miss the full long-term implications of such a potentially novel idea. Patronage and protection by the king were more than acceptable, he could even intervene in the choice of abbot.' *Secularium prioratus* was a far from novel idea. The secular control of monasteries was condemned by Archbishop Æthelheard at Clovesho in 803. Cf. Simon Keynes, *The Councils of Clovesho*, p. 26. Stenton, *Anglo-Saxon England*, has a number of references to the practice: Dr J. L. Nelson, *Politics and Ritual in Early Medieval Europe*, p. 247, writes, 'at the core of the king's council was a group of bishops ... active in legislation and most notably of all in the promotion of monastic reform – which since it involved the expropriation of laymen and the communalization of monks' property, brought them into sharp conflict with what Æthelwold castigated as *secularium prioratus*. These bishops assigned a a precise and crucial role to the king in the fulfilment of their aims, rightly seeing in royal *dominium* the one effective safeguard against the magnates' local lordship.' I published a study of how extensive the problem of secular domination was on the Continent as well as here, 'Secularium Prioratus and the Rule of St Benedict', *Revue Bénédictine*, 75, 1965, pp. 212–39. I cannot see any ambiguity in the *Concordia* at this point. Dr Stafford seems to think *prioratus* means something like priority but it must surely mean overlordship. She says it is given little prominence in the document, which is not true. It is separated from the main text and included in a 'legal appendix'as a prolegomenon to the abolition of the death duty, the heriot, for monks. Even tenth-century holy men gave prominence to massive tax concessions in their favour. The concession, along with the emphatic statement of the king's duty to intervene in the choice of abbots, is part of the exercise by the king of his *dominium* and are concrete examples of what was forbidden to the mere *prioratus* of a magnate. The royal *dominium* is quasi-sacramental and thus set apart from anything a secular magnate could do. The king's part was not to choose but to enforce the right choice.

26 The 'Fabian' version of Oswald was first aired by the late Dean Armitage Robinson in his 'St Oswald and the Church of Worcester', *British Academy Supplemental Papers*, v, London, 1919.

27 Lapidge and Winterbottom, *The Life of Æthelwold*, do not try very hard and I for one

don't blame them.

28 *St Dunstan: his Life, Times and Cult,* ed. Nigel Ramsay, Margaret Sparks and Tim Tatton-Brown, Woodbridge, 1992, pp. 247–8.

29 *Life of St Æthelwold*, p. ci.

CHAPTER 7

The restoration of learning

I MEAN NO DISPARAGEMENT of the revival of learning undertaken under such difficulties by Ælfred and Æthelstan. Their achievement was small in scale as important movements often are at their inception but large in consequence. By the end of the century there was a literary and ideological renaissance based on the new monasticism, a renaissance that owed everything to the tender but tough sproutings first seen in the time of Ælfred and Aethelstan. From the beginning there was enormous dependence on foreign scholars. From Bishop Asser, himself a foreigner, there was a continuous supply of learned men from Francia, at first mainly from East Francia. By the end of the century, largely owing to the influence of Fleury, the *Quelle* had moved to West Francia. It is important not to see the tenth century and its revival of letters in two halves: there was basically a single movement, but after the reform of the monasteries there were more resources and more native *literati*.

The works of art that changed hands in gift exchanges illustrate this continuity. One of them was the Coburg Gospels, executed at Metz in the 860s.[1] This was given a magnificent ivory cover representing the Ascension. It was enormously influential in English art because the new monks included men who could learn and profit from it. A splendid Ottonian object, the Brunswick casket, was in the East Frankish monastery of Gandersheim by the end of the tenth century. It seems to have been lent to an English house before 970 because its well known representation of the baptism of Jesus is widely regarded as the model for the illustration of the same subject in the Æthelwold Benedictional, one of the most famous artefacts of the early reform movement. It is a little opulent for my taste, a little proto-Victorian, but no one could deny its magnificence. Another object the early English monk artists had to look at was the superb psalter King Æthelstan gave to Old Minster, a ninth-century product of the Liège area. The illustrations were closely – and intelligently – studied and the monks were not afraid to add more illustrations to the book. Cheek, one might think, but they are not unworthy.

But the vital element in the revival was the intellectual side. One reason it was vital was that the conservative clergy could not answer in kind, being mainly illiterate. I have mentioned Adalbero of Lâon before. His satirical verses have no more than a modicum of literary merit and some of his arguments are so obscure as to be unintelligible (it may be due to the copyist) but occasionally his shafts strike home. He pointed out that Abbo of Fleury made up the law of the Church to suit himself. (This is not wholly fair but it is a justifiable debating point.) The trouble the reformers faced was that they were seeking to dress up a radical and innovatory monasticism in what they claimed were the ancient texts of traditional canon law. But that canon law did not support them because it had never encountered their kind of churchmanship before. A little later in time an East Frankish bishop, Burchard of Worms, produced a comprehensive statement of the law of the Church. His 'authorities' are frequently made up by himself.[2] In the middle of the eleventh century Leo IX's adviser, Cardinal Humbert, devised a means of coping in this situation. If, say, Gregory the Great had written something that did not suit him he supposed that the devil had pushed his pen at that point and felt free to correct the text. Abbo, to be fair, produced an honest solution to the problem. He did not pretend that what he thought canon law should be was necessarily to be found in ancient texts. He established a criterion for justifying his choice of what was law by inventing the criterion of the utility of the Church. By following him the reformers could be right without being dishonest (or at least not wholly so). A century later his idea had become universal. As a tailpiece here the most important writer on canon law in Anglo-Saxon England was Archbishop Wulfstan, a second-generation reformed monk. He cited no authorities at all: this was the law, and that was that.

It is obvious that education on the scale needed to support all this could not have come cheap. Had the establishment been united behind the traditionalists the resources available would have been small. Speaking generally, the Church from the papacy downwards would never have been reformed without the emergence of a reforming conscience that made great and powerful men feel guilty about taking money and property from the Church. The things the reformers sought to achieve, the dodges they used to get their way, were not specially English. They were widely found in western Europe but especially in Francia. In the time of Gregory VII a monk of Cluny called Udalric wrote a letter of advice to the abbot of Hirsau, in East Francia, who was seeking to reform his monastery, Cluny-style. He told Abbot Wilhelm that he should see his monastery was always in debt so that the local magnates, if they did not have pious wives who would nag them into paying the abbey's debts, would at least keep their hands off its bankrupt estates.[3] There are traces of the reforming conscience everywhere. Somewhat surprisingly, Ealdorman Ælfhere of Mercia, although he did very badly out of the new monasticism, was a benefactor of Glastonbury. It needs to be remembered that life spans were much shorter than they are now and the prospect that opened up for everyone was not just inevitable death but the certain assignment to Heaven or Hell. The new monks shared these convictions and highlighted them by their lives of self-denial and austerity. When Dunstan was beaten up at Æthelstan's court it was his life style, not his convictions, that enraged his contemporaries. Dunstan was a nobleman with the favour of the king and other highly placed persons and so certain of a great career. It was not simply prejudice that moved his attackers: Dunstan's way of life put the fear of God into those who wanted to carry on in the traditional way. He was telling his contemporaries something they would rather not have heard.

The most important Continental centre of influence on the English monks was Fleury. Around 970 the time came to draw up a set of customs binding on all monks, securing uniformity. Frankish monks were present to advise. Monks from Flanders were present, presumably, as a result of Dunstan's time of exile there but Fleury monks were also present. An early Fleury customal was discovered a few years ago. It has now been published and shows beyond doubt that Fleury was the major influence behind the English reform.[4] Inevitably the ideological issues raised by the Cluny and Fleury reformers touched the English monks too. The most important of the English ideologues of the second generation were Archbishop Wulfstan of York and Abbot Ælfric of Eynsham. In their writings they present a primer of the new theology. Wulfstan was the foremost preacher of his day – though his style was described to me by the late Dr F. E. Harmer as soporific. He certainly sometimes preached to laymen: his most famous sermon, the words of the Wolf to the English, unquestionably was. It dates from the end of Æthelred II's reign, following years of unmitigated defeat at the hands of the Danes. It is a pretty comprehensive indictment of the sins of the English, and the connexion between those sins and the wrath of God is hammered home. Wulfstan had special experience of the troubles of the time. He had written all, or most, of Æthelred's copious legislation – pious, prolix and entirely ineffectual (in the short run, at least). That did not prevent Wulfstan carrying on when Cnut seized the crown:

he wrote both Cnut's codes. He wrote many homilies, mostly directed to religious communities, although they contain observations about secular matters, especially concerning lay intervention in what he thought were spiritual affairs. The germs of the controversy over lay investiture can be found in Wulfstan's homilies. He is credited with some short treatises on status matters for the laity. They have a northern flavour; Wulfstan was archbishop of York. They are brief and laconic and they do contain Wulfstan mannerisms, though that need not necessarily mean he wrote them. Still, he must have known of them and probably authorised them.

A very great number of parishes were created in England at this time, Danes or no Danes. Wulfstan was a pioneer in holding local synods and bringing episcopal power face to face with parish priests. He wrote a remarkable book of canons that I have discussed already and which can have been meant only for such synods.

Ælfric was the most distinguished intellectual monk of his generation. A pupil of Æthelwold, and always proud of it, he wrote a (but not the first) life of Æthelwold.[5] He mostly wrote in the vernacular, and his works can be read where Ælfred's have to be deciphered. These days his Anglo-Saxon has to be learnt as a foreign language, which is misleading. The vocabulary of modern English is much more latinised than Ælfric's was but his grammar and sentence structure are still recognisable. In his classic essay 'On the continuity of English prose' R. W. Chambers claims Ælfric as one of the founders of English prose style. Little interest has been shown in the content of his thought, however. An American scholar, Dr Milton McGatch, has written a study called *Preaching and Theology in Anglo-Saxon England*.[6] He assumes Ælfric's theology was derivative, pastoral and practical. He sees Ælfric not as an intellectual but as a man who wished to make himself an efficient ecclesiastical administrator. There is some truth in this but not much. (As abbot of Eynsham what things ecclesiastical did he have to administer?) Ælfric was not an original thinker. Little of what he says does not or could not come from someone else. But what Dr McGatch does not see is that Ælfric's sources were very much the new theology of the day, as yet neither widely known nor held. Dr McGatch concentrates on the eschatological homilies, which were for Ælfric a burning issue only in the literal sense. Ælfric's important thoughts are to be found elsewhere.

His main works were two volumes of *Catholic Homilies* and two of *Saints' Lives*. The collection had a certain unity for Ælfric. In spite of their title the homilies are lives of popular, mainly non-English, saints. The lives are those of saints of special interest to monks. Both collections had literary patrons, Ealdorman Æthelweard, the apparent author of a Latin translation of the *Chronicle*, and Ealdorman Æthelmaer. The homilies are written in a less literary style than the lives but that does not mean the lives were only for monks. The probability is that Æthelweard knew Latin, in which case he could certainly have read the vernacular. Since it seems that some laymen had been receiving education since Ælfred's day, there is likely to have been a potential lay audience. In his *Rule* c. lx and especially in rule c. lxxiii Benedict had prescribed a very restricted literary diet for monks: the commentaries of Cassian, the lives of the Desert Fathers and the Bible made up most of it. I think Ælfric wanted to bring this list up to date, though the world of the monastic pioneers was not neglected. Ælfric included a life St Benedict would certainly have approved of, that of St Mary of Egypt. This must be the silliest work of hagiography ever written and an example of the limitations celibacy could impose on a very intelligent man. St Mary was a whore who after a lifetime of prodigious fornication underwent a dramatic conversion to chastity and then achieved sanctity by defending what was left of her virtue to the death. The notion that, after the sort of life he describes her as having led, St Mary was hardly likely to have been what is nowadays called a desirable sex object did not occur to Ælfric. (I am not sure I am right about this. In the last few years it has become apparent that rape has little to do with the sexual attractiveness of the victims but stems from a desire for dominance that might be enhanced by a woman like St Mary.) But for the most part these pieces, written for beginners as well as the elite, are full of interesting as well as novel theology.[7]

We need to remember that Æthelwold's school, both at Abingdon and at Winchester, was a nursery of abbots and bishops. By 1000 all English bishops were monks. For all the damage Ealdorman Ælfhere inflicted, the bishoprics with their shipfuls and the jurisdiction that went with them were firmly in Benedictine hands, and behind those hands were monasteries with a lively cultural and literary life. By Cnut's reign the episcopate was open to royal clerks too but they had been subjected to much the same kind of education. Dr Frank Barlow has pointed out[8] that many of the new bishops came from establishment families but there is little evidence that their family connexions had much influence on their behaviour. The revolution had been effected. What they were taught is best seen in Ælfric.

He wrote one of the earliest Latin primers and a useful phrase book with parallel English and Latin phrases – the ancestor of thousands of such books. He tells us that Abbo, who was evidently a great figure in the English monks' world, came from Fleury to Ramsey. Whilst in England Abbo heard the story of Edmund king and martyr from Dunstan and accepted a commission to produce a Latin version, which has already been discussed.[9] Ælfric produced a simplified version of a very sophisticated text – Abbo, in this life, is one of the first, if not the first, writers since classical times to use irony as a literary device. This simplification does not mean that Ælfric disagreed with Abbo. There is little in Abbo here that does not turn up somewhere in Ælfric. He ignores, it is true, Abbo's dislike of bishops – after all, the reform movement in England was an episcopally led movement. There are very few English saints in Ælfric's collections, a demonstration that the new monasticism had a real cosmopolitan ethos.

This goes with an interest in the theology of the Church.[10] Ælfric wrote:

> All churches in the world are reckoned as one Church, and it is called the congregation of God because we are all called together to God's kingdom. Now this congregation is God's bride and continues a maiden like the holy Mary.

(I think Ælfric would have loved the Titian *Assumption* could he have seen it.) Sir Richard Southern, in his *Making of the Middle Ages*,[11] was the first scholar to connect the rise of a sense of the Church with the cult of St Mary. On the same page: 'Also the whole church of God, that is all Christian people, is consecrated to one maiden.'

Abbo has a lot more to say about the relationship of Peter and the Church than Ælfric has. This is not because Ælfric was insular. But Abbo's monastery, Fleury, even Cluny itself, depended for their independence on papal privileges. The English monks were the protégés of the English bishops. The last thing Ælfric would have wanted was a privilege to exclude bishops from the monastic world. Some of the sort of problems the reforming monks were faced with are illustrated by a *cause célèbre* involving the greatest scholar of the day, Gerbert, afterwards Pope Sylvester II.

The new king of the West Franks, Hugh Capet, owed his election largely to Gerbert, who played the main part in denying the Carolingian claimant, Charles of Lotharingia, the crown and elevating the leading West Frankish magnate as king. But for political reasons Hugh would not make Gerbert archbishop of Rheims. The man he chose turned out to be an utter disaster and Hugh threw him out, appointing Gerbert in his stead. By the strict letter of the law Gerbert had been intruded into another's see. His position was strictly parallel to Dunstan's elevation to Canterbury, where Edgar sent the newly elected archbishop back to his original see. The ejected candidate seems to have been a perfectly respectable bishop whereas there is no doubt that Hugh's original choice for Rheims was not. So Dunstan's intrusion was worse than Gerbert's. The papacy was going through the worst period in its history and the Pope of the day was indifferent to the Canterbury succession. Gerbert's Pope, one of the worst in the history of the see of Peter, saw Gerbert as a danger because he had the ear of the imperial court and the imperial court was showing signs of an interest in reforming the papacy. The Pope took a strictly canonical line and ordered the ejection of Gerbert from Rheims. Abbo supported the Pope and ranged himself against Gerbert. He was not in the least sympathetic to the Pope's actions. He said roundly that the Pope's motives were purely venal. But Abbo took the stand he did for the sake of Fleury. If the bishop of Orléans gained entry to the abbey it would be the end of reform, and the only thing that kept him out was the papal privilege withdrawing the abbey from the bishop's jurisdiction. Abbo dared do nothing to devalue papal privileges. The imperial court sympathised with Gerbert but were not prepared to defy a papal decision on canon law, which, however dubious the motives for making it, was undoubtedly legally correct. Gerbert was rewarded with Ravenna. History does not record what the Pope thought of this but it does rather look as though he had been hoist with his own petard. Gerbert in Ravenna was a good deal nearer Rome than he would have been in Rheims. At no point did Gerbert show any animosity to Abbo or Fleury. Abbo had been a pupil of Gerbert and it seems to me was more distinguished than his master. Men like Abbo, Gerbert and Dunstan were clear what they were doing and in broad agreement as to methods. Their aims were common aims and their achievements common achievements that made for a great improvement in European culture. They were forced to fiddle on occasion, and consistency was a virtue they could not entirely afford. Had their opponents been diligent and learned they could not have succeeded but their opponents were neither diligent nor learned and ignorance got what it deserved.

Very strict sexual morality was characteristic of the tenth-century reformers. That they insisted on clerical celibacy goes without saying. They also had a strict code of sexual morality for laymen that had some unintended and unwelcome consequences. Sexual activity was not only confined to marriage but even then was permitted only for the procreation of children. Ælfric is quite clear on this: 'the chastity of the layman is that he hold to his marriage and lawfully, for the increase of people, beget children'. 'They must desist from sexual relations with their wives when they could no longer procreate.' This is not the dictum of a solitary insular monk. A generation earlier the well known reforming bishop of Verona, Rather, had taught the same thing. Rather published his views on the topic in a book intended to publicise the many injustices he had suffered at secular hands, the *Praeloquia*. Rather was a primitive publicist but one of some genius and he got his book very widely circulated. The book was known in West Francia and it is safe to suppose Abbo had read it, and Ælfric was a pupil of Abbo's in a way. Ælfric was then a spokesman for a European tradition. But such a position did make it difficult for a reforming bishop to explain to a prince or magnate whose wife was barren why he could not repudiate her and marry another. What effect this had on the rather cavalier attitude laymen of the period had towards annulment and remarriage can only be conjectured.

Ælfric's most important theological themes concern kingship and here again he speaks as representative of the reforming opinion of the time. The king was not a priest but he was not exactly a layman either. Edgar himself in one of his laws claims only to be a layman. Ælfric says little of this but he had been a pupil of Æthelwold who, in the *Regularis Concordia* which he wrote, had compared Edgar with the Good Shepherd. Another member of Æthelwold's connexion had said, 'A Christian king is Christ's representative among a Christian people.' For these monks the king was a mediator between clergy and laity. The king's lordship or *dominium* was what Æthelwold appealed to, to prevent the tyranny of laymen from appointing abbots. This *dominium* was what Æthelwold underwrote the reform programme with. In other words the royal *dominium* was quasi-sacramental.

A generation ago it was usual to call this kind of theology caesaro-papist, as some scholars still do. The Ottonian empire in East Francia is what these scholars have in mind but there is little difference in principle or detail. The Ottonians normally called themselves, after they had gained papal consecration, emperors. Edgar more usually called himself king, but he used an imperial style on occasion. Ælfric significantly, in his life of St Swithin, called the reign of Edgar a golden age and recalled Edgar's imperial durbar, when he was rowed on the Dee by eight kings in a set piece of imperial symbolism. I said significantly because the durbar is totally irrelevant in its hagiographical context. But before we leave this caesaro-papism we must ask a simple but important question. What did these caesaro-papists think of Christ?

To get to the roots of Ælfric's political thought we need to look at his Christology. Ælfric, like most educated Christians of his day, held a view of the Atonement derived originally from the Cappadocian fathers. The thesis is beautifully summed up by Sir Richard Southern in his *Making of the Middle Ages*:

Man was a helpless spectator in a cosmic struggle which determined his chance of Salvation. The War was one between God and the Devil, and God won because he proved himself as the master-strategist, a majestic awe-inspiring act, justly acclaimed in such a triumphant expression of victory as the *Te Deum*. But there is little or no place for tender compassion for the sufferings of Jesus.

It would seem that in Anglo-Saxon England a subjective, emotional devotion to the intimate sufferings of Jesus, exemplified in the eighth-century prayer books of Cerne and Nunnaminster, not only preceded devotion to the crucifix but exerted considerable influence on the Continent.[12] Sir Richard also drew a connexion between the feeling that the traditional view of the Atonement was inadequate and the cult of devotion to the crucifix but to a crucifix that exemplified the sufferings of Christ nearly naked on the cross (but without a crown of thorns until the mid-thirteenth century). The inadequacy of this traditional theology of the Atonement was the conception of God the master strategist. God went fishing and baited his hook with Jesus. The devil was unable to resist the bait and, in taking it, freed God, who must give even the devil his due, to reclaim mankind, the sin of Adam having been atoned for. On this view man was only a spectator in this cosmic struggle, though a very interested spectator. What was wanted was a view of the Atonement that would involve the individual Christian and give him a part to play. In the end this new, more individualist view was provided by St Anselm. It has not always been realised that the traditional view and Anselm's individualism supplement each other. If the Atonement does not involve a cosmic struggle what room is there for an Atonement at all? It is the brushing aside of the Cappadocian fathers that has led to Anselm's view being dismissed as grocer's shop theology. Anselm added an important dimension to the traditional theology of the Atonement but he did not destroy it.

The new crucifix was much in evidence during the tenth century reformation. Professor O'Carragain allowed me to read a portion of his book on the Vercelli Book in manuscript. The drift of his argument is that representations of the crucifixion were not common before the time of Ælfric, though it is known that King Æthelstan had a devotion to the cross. The Harley Psalter shows a clearly dead, nearly naked Christ upon the cross. It is probably a late tenth-century Winchester production, and the same artist, who was English, executed a charming drawing of the constellation Aquarius at Fleury. It is sometimes said that this is the first representation of Christ dead upon the cross but there seem to be dead Christs on the cross in East Frankish artefacts before the Harley Psalter, notably the

Gero crucifix in Cologne cathedral.[13] In England it is certainly new. In the great drawing in the Bodleian library of Dunstan prostrated before the risen Christ, Christ is not represented as crucified and has more than a touch of triumphalism about him.

Let us now see what Ælfric thought about all this:

> Now some men believe that it must happen for them even as it was determined for them and ordained in the beginning, and they cannot avoid acting amiss. Now we may say truly that if this be so it is a useless commandment that God commanded through David: 'Turn away from evil and do good.'

Ælfric was neither an Anselm nor a Bernard but he saw a century earlier than either some of the limitations of the received theory. He is concerned to emphasise that the individual has a part to play in his redemption.

> He hath given us our own choice. He gave a most steadfast gift, and a most steadfast law together with that gift, to every man until his end, both to poor and rich. This is the gift that a man may do what he will, and this is the law, that God recompenses every man according to his works, both in this world and in that which is to come, whether good or evil, whichsoever he practise.

Since Ælfric also knew and accepted the traditional theory of the Atonement, he can legitimately claim a part in extending that theory.

Ælfric also had thoughts of some interest about Christ and the place of Christ in Christian devotion:

> Verily to his beloved disciple Jesus entrusted his Mother, when suspended on the Cross he redeemed mankind.

> He fled from worldly honour when he was chosen king; but he did not flee from reproach and scorn when the Jews would hang him on a cross. He would not encircle his head with a golden crown, but one of thorns.

> Now if you believe that Christ is the son of God who was hanged on a cross is true God, then I will show you how the Lamb continued undefiled in his kingdom.

For the feast of the Exaltation of the Holy Cross, which as a late seventh-century papal invention had not attracted much attention from homiliarists, he says:

> When that heavenly King, Christ himself, entered in through this same gate

to his own passion, he was not clothed in purple, nor adorned with a royal crown, nor rode he through this stone gate upon a horse but upon the back of an ass.

When he came to write his life of St Martin inevitably he could not resist the deathbed story he found in Martin's first biographer, Sulpicius Severus, but he gives the story a Christological thrust not found in the biography.

Then perceived the saintly man by the Holy Ghost that it was the same Devil, and not his Lord, and said, Our Lord said not that he would come with a crown and clothed in purple, and I believe he will not come to us except in the form in which he suffered.

Ælfric specifically promotes devotion to the crucifix:

My brethren, let us behold the crucified Christ, that we may be healed of venomous sins. Truly as the people of Israel looked on the venomous serpent and so were healed of the serpent's bite, so now they will be healed of their sins who look with belief on the death of Christ and his resurrection.

It is not surprising that representations of the Crucifixion, often surprisingly intimate, were a feature of Ælfric's world. Archbishop Wulfstan, his contemporary, writes:

And at that judgement to which all men must come, our Lord will show us at once his bloody side and his pierced hands and the same cross on which he was hung for our need, and then will quickly demand how we have repaid him for that and how we kept our Christian faith.[14]

The political significance of this should be plain: we should be able to see more clearly what the proponents of 'caesaro-papism' were getting at. Ælfric — and I do not think his views were original to him or even specifically Anglo-Saxon — was inviting kings to identify with the suffering, not the triumphant, Christ. Not that representations of Christ in royal robes were unknown, but they were certainly not common. Dom Kassius Hallinger[15] has an important point to make here. He says that devotion to the crucifix was fairly new in the tenth century, especially the emphasis on Christ's human attributes — he thinks they were of Carolingian origin — and it is through the teaching of Odo of Cluny that this new devotion became widely dispersed. So again it looks very much as though it is the connexion between Odo, Fleury and Abbo that lies behind Ælfric's theology.

But the culmination of the reformed theology of kingship came at a precise time in a specific place, Whit Sunday 973 at Bath, with the conse-cration[16] and coronation of Edgar as king. Almost all we know of the cer-emony comes from Byrhtferth of Ramsey's life of Oswald. Byrhtferth certainly knew and was probably taught by Abbo, and once again we find a Frankish presence at an apparently insular occasion, the coronation of a king of England. All the themes I have been discussing were brought together in a single, spectacular public ceremony, with the symbolism now intelligible to many of those present. The sources suggest that Edgar was twenty-nine, or in his thirtieth year as they prefer to put it, when he was crowned. Significantly the *Chronicle*, as was its wont, gets its years mixed up. Thus the annalist knew that Edgar was in his thirtieth year when he was crowned, independently of his real age. So Edgar's age at the time was a piece of ideology, not chronology. The 'thirtieth year' must be a refer-ence to Luke iii, 23, which says Jesus was in his thirtieth year when he began his public ministry. The ceremony was presided over by Dunstan, who, as archbishop of Canterbury, had the sole right to crown the king. Dr Nicholas Brooks, in his account of the coronation of Æthelstan,[17] argues:

> the so-called 'second' English coronation *ordo*, which is preserved in vari-ous manuscripts of the late tenth century, was first used on this occasion, and that a Wells element can be detected in its liturgical parentage. If so Æthelm himself (he was archbishop of Canterbury and a former bishop of Wells) may have composed it or ordered its compilation – which involved reworking much material from the first royal *ordo* but also introduced many novelties, such as the crown itself, into the English king-making ceremony. This second English order was to be used for royal consecrations, with minor additions and alterations, until the Norman Conquest.

This seems to me quite simply wrong. The *Vita Oswaldi* describes the order used in 973 in such detail as to suggest it was unfamiliar. If Dr Brooks were right this was the fifth time it was used and there could have been little novelty left. It was unprecedented for a coronation to be so long delayed, and I have pointed out the theological implications. The decision to delay the coronation must have been taken early in Edgar's reign and Dunstan must have been party to it. It would be natural to have a new *ordo* prepared for such an occasion, and most scholars have supposed that that is what happened. Byrhtferth had obviously seen the text: the fact that he accurately describes Oswald's part as archbishop of York proves that. He also says that Edgar was decorated with lilies and roses. In the thought world of the reforming monks lilies stood for chastity and roses for martyrdom. Byrhtferth must have been referring to objects among the regalia, since his word 'decorated' implies that Edgar wore them on his person. I cannot identify the roses but the lilies are surely the new lily crown? In the Cambridge manuscript[18] that contains the prose and verse lives of St Cuthbert, the frontispiece shows Æthelstan presenting the book to Cuthbert. Both are in full fig. Cuthbert is wearing a cope and a mitre whilst Æthelstan is wearing the old *Bügelkrone* the lily crown replaced. Dr Brooks mentions that several manuscripts of the second order survive from the late tenth century – exactly what we should expect if it were made for Edgar's consecration. If Æthelm had written it we should expect earlier manuscripts, one of which Dunstan would have used. Finally the Wells symptoms Dr Brooks thinks a clinching argument seem to me entirely inconclusive. Dunstan was born in the diocese and must have been familiar with the Wells liturgy from an early age.

One of the oddest things at first sight is what Byrhtferth says of the coronation banquet. He tells us that Edgar feasted with the bishops and secular magnates whilst the queen feasted separately with the abbots and abbesses. To make things even odder, he calls it a nuptial feast. It has been suggested he was confusing the coronation banquet with Edgar's wedding feast. I remark in passing that it seems odd that the bride and bridegroom should have had separate wedding breakfasts. At that time the word for 'crown' can also mean mitre. This and the delaying of the coronation until Edgar's thirtieth year suggests that his monk advisers saw Edgar as a kind of bishop. A bishop was traditionally married to his diocese, and that is perhaps why Byrhtferth called the banquet a nuptial feast. There is reason to think that what became a familiar *topos* in the high Middle Ages, the marriage of a king to his kingdom, had already made its appearance. The first occurrence known to me is in Flodoard of Rheims, a kind of transitional figure between Hincmar and Abbo in the intellectual history of West Francia, who called the emperor the consort of the empire. Flodoard was a pioneer of the new theology and invented a new kind of church history, the history of an individual church set in the context of the universal Church and illustrated with documents. It is not impossible that Byrhtferth was influenced, directly or indirectly, by Flodoard here. It seems to me that the life of Oswald has some resemblance to Flodoard's 'new' history. At any rate I think it is possible to detect signs of quoted documents in the text but we shall have to wait for Dr Lapidge's new edition of the life for confirmation or denial. In 1025 the young king of the West Franks, Hugh, died and his epitaph says that the kingdom was widowed. The source of the obituary was Fleury. Hugh, like Edgar, was consecrated on Whit Sunday. Abbo must have read Flodoard and, of course, Byrhtferth was his pupil.

The coronation was only the climax of the promotion of the new royal ideology. Every monastery was a centre of sustained royal propaganda. Mass was said daily for the king and he was prayed for several times a day. Most monks came from 'good' families. Abbo was counted of low birth but his family were certainly not peasants. Monks would have contact with their families and some of the pervasive royalism would have rubbed off. The old royal ideology had compared kings with David, most strikingly at the coronation of Pippin in 751. A Davidic kingship was dear to the Carolingians but it had a great drawback from the reformers' point of view. When David behaved disgracefully over Bathsheba a prophet could rebuke him but he was still king. It took a shifty politician like David to get rid of Saul but he could not have done it without Samuel. Even Abbo thought that a *populus* could – indeed, should – choose a king but they could not get rid of him afterwards. But the Christocentric concept of kingship was double-edged if someone chose to draw out its logical implications. If a king were a type of Christ it was blasphemy and sacrilege to oppose him, but if he persecuted the Church he was *ein Unmensch, ein Tyrann*.

The English, like the French, never had to face the nastier consequences of their king being a type of Christ. Gregory VII was the first Pope who drew out the full consequences of the theory. This has led scholars to contrast the caesaro-papism of the pre-Gregorians with the full-blooded harrying of kings by the true Gregorians. But the underlying theses of the Gregorian programme had been available for use if anyone chose to employ them. Until Gregory no one had wanted to. It is obvious that Æthelwold would accept bad kings: he served both Eadwig and Æthelred II, who was very anti-monastic until misfortune made him pious.

There is no odder episode in English history than the tenth-century reformation, but no single generation did more for scholarship and letters. It will now be easy to answer the traditional examination question 'England became part of Europe only after the Norman Conquest. Discuss.' Before 1066, long before 1066, cultural relations with the Continent were far closer than the relations between Normandy and the rest of Europe, even with the kingdom of France. Normandy was the back yard of Europe and taught the English nothing because the Normans had nothing to teach, just a very great deal to learn. Normandy supplied the English with some outstanding bishops after 1066, though the two greatest, Lanfranc and Anselm, were not Normans but two pious Italians mortifying the flesh by working in the backwoods.[19]

NOTES

1 Michael Wood, Æthelstan's empire', p. 260, has a brief, useful discussion of the covers of the Coburg Gospels.
2 P. Fournier and G. le Bras, *Histoire des collections canoniques en occident*, Paris, 1931.
3 The matter is discussed at length by Eric John, 'Secularium Prioratus and the Rule of St Benedict', *Revue Bénédictine*, 75, 1965, pp. 212–39.
4 Ed. Dom Kassius Hallinger, *Corpus Consuetudinem Monasticarum*, vii, 3, Siegburg, 1984. Cf. Veronica Ortenberg, *The English Church and the Continent in the Tenth and Eleventh Centuries*, Oxford, 1992, pp. 244–5. Cf. Professor A. P. Smyth's important remarks on the part played by Fleury in the literary and theological life of Francia and England, *Alfred the Great*, pp. 271 *et seq.*
5 Lapidge and Winterbottom, *Wulfstan*, pp. cxlvi *et seq.*
6 Toronto, 1977.
7 To be fair to Ælfric, the cult of St Mary of Egypt had deep roots in English tradition. It was probably introduced into this country in the days of Theodore of Tarsus by Abbot Adrian: a Neapolitan monk introducing a Neapolitan cult, in other words. The cult was widely popular in his day. Dr Ortenberg, *The English Church*, has a valuable discussion of St Mary and her cult.
8 *The English Church, 1000–1066*, London, 1963.
9 I have been unable to consult Marco Mostert, *The Political Theology of Abbo of Fleury*, Hilversum, 1987.
10 Eric John, 'The World of Abbot Ælfric', in Wormald *et al., Ideal and Reality in Anglo-Saxon Society*, pp. 300–16, for a discussion of Ælfric's theology.
11 London, 1953.
12 T. H. Bestul, 'St Anselm and the Continuity of Anglo-Saxon Devotional Traditions', *Annuale Medievale*, 18, 1977, pp. 20–41. Now see Barbara C. Raw, *Anglo-Saxon Crucifixion Iconography and the Art of the Monastic Revival*, Cambridge, 1992. Ms Raw's book is a valuable compendium of information about Anglo-Saxon iconography but the theology is strictly subordinate to the iconography. Although she does cite St Anselm she does not refer to Sir Richard Southern's work.
13 Raw, *Anglo-Saxon Crucifixion*, p. 201, describes the Gero crucifix as a wooden crucifix showing the dead Christ.
14 *Homilies of Wulfstan*, ed. D. Bethurum-Loomis, Oxford, 1957, No. ii, translation by Barbara Raw.
15 'The spiritual life of Cluny in the early days' in *Cluniac Monasticism in the Central Middle Ages*, ed. Noreen Hunt, London, 1971, pp. 29–55.
16 The late Dr Whitelock drew attention to a passage from Ælfric in this connexion. Ælfric does not use the normal word *gehalgod* for royal consecration but the expressive *smyrad* and states, 'the king after he is consecrated then has dominion over his people'. *Documents*, p. 851.
17 *Early History of the Church of Canterbury*, p. 215.
18 Corpus Christi College, Cambridge, manuscript 183 frontispiece.
19 It was only after writing these words that I remembered Stenton's closing peroration in *Anglo-Saxon England*, p. 687: 'The Normans who entered into the English inheritance were a harsh and violent race. They were the closest of all western peoples to the barbarian strain in the continental order. They had produced little in art or learning, and nothing in literature, that could be set beside the work of Englishmen. But politically they were the masters of their world.'

CHAPTER 8

The ruin of the house of Cerdic

A SAGA CALLED the Jomsviking Saga survives which is set in the late
tenth century. We are fairly sure there was a place called Jomsborg and we
think we know where it was. So far archaeologists have found no trace of
the fort. The Saga,[1] which was written in the thirteenth century, claims
that Jomsborg was founded by an important Danish magnate of the day
called Palnatoki, who, having enjoyed exceptional power and position,
was driven into exile. He established a great fortress in the Baltic, and the
saga describes the fortifications and the harsh discipline enforced therein.
The prospective member of the community had to be of proven prowess,
proved by killing people and not getting killed in return. It was expected
that the postulant would be in his late teens. A special exception was made
for St Olaf, who was enrolled under-age for his proven savagery. In spite
of a lifetime of killing, of numerous wives and a bevy of bastards, there is
a real case for regarding him as a saint. The oldest manuscript of the saga
says that Jomsborg held three ships protected by chains. Other manuscripts
say that it held three hundred ships: the evidence suggests that this figure
is likely to be nearer the truth. Kinship had to be set aside. No member
could take part in a feud in which another member of the 'community'
was involved on the other side. No leave longer than three days was permitted – anticipating the Iron Duke, who in the Peninsular War would
allow his officers only weekend passes on the grounds that two days were
as long as any rational man would want to stay with the same woman.

The saga is important for what it tells of the regimen that obtained in
the fortress. How historical it is is not easy to decide. The chronology can
in no way be made to work but some of the personal names mentioned in
the saga occur in other sources and they seem to refer to men of the same
or similar background. What matters is that archaeologists have uncovered
the remains of four comparable fortresses in Denmark proper. They are
Trelleborg, Fyrkat, Aggersborg and Nonnebakken. It is possible to calcu-
late that they could hold over five thousand men and they are plainly only

secondarily defensive points. Sir David Wilson and Professor Foote[2] have suggested they were the bases from which the attacks on England and other parts of Scandinavia were launched. King Edgar created monasteries that sowed division and dissension, and the Danes created fortresses that could take advantage of those divisions and dissensions. In the light of the archaeological evidence there must be some truth behind the saga. Jomsborg is mentioned elsewhere and it seems to have been neither in Denmark nor under Danish control. This is shown by the career of the most famous Jomsviking, Thorkell the Tall. He was clearly the ally, not the subject, of the king of Denmark. It will appear in what follows that he was a very important ally of the Danes but was never entirely trusted by their kings.

What was the relation between these new Vikings and the old invaders of Britain? The question is too rarely asked. It is likely enough that many of the first lot of Vikings came from Denmark. We tend, perhaps, to think of Scandinavia as three separate kingdoms, which for some purposes is true. But underlying the politics and the societies was a common Scandinavianness which is very relevant to such matters as Viking recruitment. But the leaders of the first Vikings were Norwegian, not Danish, and their essential base was Dublin, not Scandinavia. The manner and style of their campaigns were not Danish but *sui generis*. The aims of the Danish Vikings were different. At some point – when exactly we do not know – the Danish king, Sweyn, formed the intention of conquering England and making himself king of England as well as Denmark. His strategy was always very different from that of the first wave of Vikings. He showed no interest in Dublin or Scotland, but fairly early on he seems to have to come to terms with the leaders of the French Danelaw, Normandy, and secured the best possible base to attack the English. The English defences presupposed attack from the north and west; they did not anticipate cross-Channel attacks on the south and south-east. Wessex was protected by burhs from an attack from Mercia or farther north but not by much from the attacks that actually came. It is an early example of the classic English disease, fighting this war with the tactics of the last.

It is evident that, although the divisions Edgar's reign had created can only have helped Sweyn's designs, a new Danish invasion was inevitable. The Danish king did not have the resources the English king had, not even Æthelred II, but somehow the Danes raised the resources to build what have been described as the greatest fortresses since the Roman empire as well as a fleet of expensive ships. The Danes, moreover had good intelligence of the state of England. The new 'Englishmen' of Viking descent seem to have had little sympathy with the new Vikings or contact with them. There was now a considerable volume of trade between England and Denmark, and Danish 'commercial travellers' could pass on information about English wealth and where it could be found as well as political intelligence. It cannot be coincidence that, from the beginning of these invasions, Sweyn directed his main force against East Anglia and Wessex whilst Mercia was spared for his lifetime. Its treacherous ealdorman, Eadric Streona, was tacitly an ally.

I have already mentioned the new factor in the equation, Normandy. We know little about the terms of the Danish–Norman alliance but one certainly existed. At one point Æthelred actually invaded Normandy and signed a treaty under the auspices of the Pope in 991 which it seems sensible to suppose followed the invasion. It does not seem to have had much effect. In 1002 Æthelred formed an alliance that held by marrying Emma, the daughter of the Norman duke, Richard I, as his second wife. Richard I never seems to have liked or trusted the English and it was not until after his death that there was any real *rapprochement*.

There is great deal of difficulty about the sources. King Sweyn, and presumably many of his subjects, were now Christian, if rather of the muscular variety. But the Danes were still mainly illiterate and the sources about Viking activity were mainly not written down until the thirteenth century. In his magnificent study *The Myth and Religion of the Pagan North* Professor Turville-Petre has shown that much early material is recoverable from the sagas, but even so they were meant as entertainment, not history. Dr Alfred Smyth has made a valiant attempt to extract history out of the saga material.[3] This has caused great controversy, but his critics seem to me to miss the point. Dr Smyth has opened up a new and difficult field but when source material is so scarce we must do everything we can to extract what can be got out of what there is. There is little evidence from the Danish side. An East Frankish bishop, Thietmar of Merseburg, wrote a chronicle that partly survives in his autograph (most of it was destroyed during the war). He was a contemporary of Cnut and well informed about Danish affairs. He also had information about England which, though often inaccurate, is occasionally important. He has been strangely neglected by English historians.

The English evidence is also difficult, though, thanks to the work of Dr Simon Keynes, much less difficult than it was.[4] The main source is a version of the *Chronicle* known as the Abingdon chronicle because in the Confessor's reign it was written at Abingdon. But in Æthelred's reign it was probably kept and written in eastern England. It is the main reason for

Æthelred's disastrous reputation, summed up in his nickname, the Unready. In fact the nickname is a pun on the meaning of his name, Æþelræd Unræd, Good Advice the Ill-advised. We know most famously from Wulfstan's sermon 'the words of the Wolf to the English' and some charter references that the English still retained a sense of what their names meant. It is not until after the Conquest that names become simply names. Dr Keynes has shown that the Abingdon chronicle of Æthelred's reign was not a set of annals, as it appears to be. It is a single narrative written by one man at one time. The time was shortly after the death of Æthelred and very early in the reign of Cnut, 1016 or 1017. In other words it was written in the depths of defeat. There is some evidence that Æthelred was not the criminal incompetent he is sometimes portrayed as. He devised most of the policies that eventually worked – when tried by others. He may not have been a very competent organiser but I think we must believe the Abingdon chronicle when it describes the constant treachery of the English magnates that thwarted him at every turn. When Cnut became king he showed what he thought of them by decimating the old establishment in a bloodbath. The magnates executed had been manifest traitors to Cnut, having sworn fealty to him then going back on it. Probably the main cause of Æthelred's failures was that he either would not or, more likely, could not anticipate Cnut in this matter. At any rate the advent of Cnut was a much bloodier affair than the advent of William the Conqueror a century and a half later.

The English had much poorer intelligence of Danish intentions than the Danes seem to have had of theirs. There is no sign they knew anything of the great fortresses in Denmark. Possibly their confidence that they had solved the Viking problem made them overweening. What the English had solved were the problems of the Norwegian Vikings and the Dublin–York axis. What they were now faced with was a very differently orientated enemy they were totally ill equipped to deal with. By now the men of Viking descent in England, at least at the top level, had been assimilated into English society. In some areas they retained their own law. These areas, known as the Danelaw, consisted of Yorkshire certainly and probably East Anglia too. It has been denied that East Anglia formed part of the Danelaw but the Viking-descended East Anglians had ruled themselves for a generation before they recognised the authority of the English king. There is no evidence that the English kings ever tried to make the East Anglians give up their laws and customs: it must surely have left traces in the sources if they had. These men never allied themselves with Sweyn's lot. At least at first Sweyn and his men were after loot and the Viking-descended East Anglians had as much to lose as their English–descended neighbours.

In autumn 1002, on St Brice's day, Æthelstan ordered a massacre of all the Danes in England, according to the *Chronicle*. In *Anglo-Saxon England* Sir Frank Stenton thought this meant a policy of genocide for decimating the Danelaw and rightly says it would have been impossible. But there was a massacre, for Æthelred himself in a charter for St Frideswide (Oxford) mentions the killing of Danes at Oxford. Oxford was never part of the Viking-occupied territories and can have had few inhabitants of Viking descent. It is more likely that the victims were recent arrivals who regarded themselves as Danes and were so regarded by the English.[5] Most of them must have been traders of some sort and, when one considers the value of the intelligence they could have given the Danes, Æthelred had a point.

Early in the campaign the Danes, with Norman help, seized the Isle of Wight, which provided the perfect base for attacking Wessex. Nothing like a complete reconstruction of the campaigns of Æthelred's reign is possible, because of the problems presented by the composition of the Abingdon chronicle. The first great battle the Danes won was the battle of Maldon in 991 and their final triumph was the battle of Ashingdon in 1016. The consequence was the acceptance of Cnut as king of England in the same year. In other words the Anglo-Danish war lasted a quarter of a century and could not have been the mere procession of defeats the Abingdon chronicle records. The evidence suggests that the English were at first confident they could beat the invaders.

On the beginning of the fighting we have some information from the first life of St Oswald, which survives only in a carelessly written copy made at Worcester. Then there is a very odd source, a poem always known as *The battle of Maldon*, written shortly after the battle.[6] The verse is poor and derivative.[7] The style is very formal. It describes the circumstances in which the battle began and stresses the high morale of the English, led by Ealdorman Byrhtnoth of Essex. The English army is described as the flower of the East Saxon *fyrd*. Maldon is in Essex. The tendency has been to see the engagement as of purely local significance and to deny it any great importance. This is certainly not true. Byrhtnoth was connected with Essex all his life and seems to have been a local ealdorman subordinated to the East Anglian half-king Æthelwine. After the death of Edgar he and Ealdorman Æthelwine were the strong men of the reform party. In the anti-monastic brouhaha of the time the northern half-king, the earl of Northumbria, disappears. There is reason to suppose that Byrhtnoth was promoted in his place. There is important information from two late sources, the *Liber Eliensis* from Ely and the archives of the other great East Anglian monastery, Ramsey. The *Liber Eliensis* is a miscellany of pieces of varying dates. In a late portion of the text it says that Byrhtnoth was *dux* of Northumbria. This late Ely material was drawing on much earlier material because all of what he says can be corroborated except Byrhtnoth's promotion. Even here the poem says that Byrhtnoth had a Northumbrian hostage among his retinue. This was correct practice: hostages were supposed to fight as though they were members of their captor's retinue. But how could Byrhtnoth, as ealdorman of Essex, have acquired a Northumbrian hostage unless he had taken part in a Northumbrian campaign? How could an ealdorman of Essex have done that unless he were earl of Northumbria too? The same late Ely source says that Byrhtnoth was coming to meet the Vikings at Maldon from the north and sought a night's lodging for himself and his men at Ramsey on their way to the battle. The abbot refused him and he turned to Ely, which did not: both Ramsey and Ely are well to the north of Maldon and well to the north of Essex. Although there is no evidence that the sources are related, both tell substantially the same story. As a result, to Ramsey lamentations and to Ely rejoicing. Byrhtnoth left his vast fortune to Ely instead of Ramsey (which got an insulting bequest of one small estate). Although the sources are post-Conquest they are in substantial agreement. In any case the actions of abbots who gained or lost vast legacies tend to be remembered. Byrhtnoth seems to have been the English leader at Maldon and the engagement was not a merely local affair. But Byrhtnoth had only his East Saxon troops, if the poem is telling the full story, and it is not difficult to see why Ealdorman Ælfhere held aloof, as his successor did too for the next quarter of a century.

There is more evidence about the campaign suggesting it was a national matter. The first life of Oswald, which is very little later than the poem, suggests the campaign began a year or so before Maldon. There was a first battle at Maldon which the English won,[8] then the action moved to Devon and the English won again. After defeat at what seems to have been a second battle of Maldon, the ealdorman of Devon took a leading part in the negotiations. In 991 Byrhtnoth seems to have reached Maldon and got his troops ready before the Vikings could land. They put their ships near an island on the river Blackwater on which Maldon stands, within hailing distance of the mainland, where Byrhtnoth and his men awaited them. Byrhtnoth allowed the Vikings to cross to the mainland, for which he has been much criticised by armchair critics. They forget the Viking ships. If Byrhtnoth had refused to let them land they could have taken to their ships and sailed away and ravaged somewhere else. If the Vikings were to be stopped there had to be a pitched battle somewhere and the *fyrd* here were defending their shire and their estates.

The author of *Maldon* was obviously ignorant that one of the Viking leaders was Olaf Tryggvason, one of the most famous warriors of the day. What the poem was concerned to do was to lament the death of Byrht- noth in the battle and to comment on the behaviour of the retainers, pointing out who stayed and who ran away. That Maldon was a national engagement, the climax of a campaign, is shown by the sequel. Peace was negotiated by the archbishop of Canterbury and the ealdorman of Devon. Peace was got by paying for it. From now on tribute was paid in ever increasing quantities and was paid in 994, 1002, 1007 and 1012. Still, five tributes in twenty years is less than one would expect from the lucubra- tions of the Abingdon chronicle, but there is no doubt that Danes obtained enormous sums from the English. In 1018 Cnut raised an enormous trib- ute, presumably to pay off his army, and the last tribute was raised by his son, Harthacnut, for the same purpose. During this period the English, on chronicle evidence alone, paid £250,000 at a time when the largest coin was a silver penny. It is not surprising that Scandinavian museums have such enormous holdings of silver pennies.

By 994 Sweyn had inherited the kingdom of Denmark and had no rival for the leadership of the Danes. At first Sweyn had fought in partnership with Olaf Tryggvason, who was Norwegian. In 994 they had a modest success at London and were paid £16,000. In the negotiations Æthelred showed he was not quite the fool he is sometimes painted. He persuaded Olaf to accept baptism and stood sponsor to him. There was intelligent diplomacy behind all this. Æthelred is likely to have known that the alliance between Olaf and Sweyn was under great strain. Olaf was a descendent of Harold Fairhair and presumably a relative of Eric Bloodaxe. The Danes were already claiming suzerainty over Norway. Olaf promised never to return to England and he never did. He went back to Norway and, presumably on his English funds, set out to defeat Sweyn's ambition to rule Norway. They were henceforth bitter enemies. In 1003 Sweyn killed Olaf and added Norway to his empire. Both Olaf and Sweyn were Christians and many of the Norwegians were still pagan, but Olaf came to be regarded as a Christian champion and a saint. By doing his Christian duty and exercising his diplomatic skill Æthelred had greatly diminished the Danish danger for a decade. He seems to have made very little use of this respite, although he did form a Norman alliance as a kind of insurance policy. But with Olaf dead and Norway apparently subdued the English were in trouble again.

The fact that Olaf was Norwegian and connected with men who fought in the Viking wars of the ninth century suggests a kind of continuity between the earlier and later waves of Viking invasion. This is deceptive. The first Norwegian vikings based themselves on England and Ireland and seem to have had little interest in 'back home'. But Olaf and Sweyn's basic interest was Norway and Denmark. At some point, perhaps after the death of Olaf, Sweyn realised that the English crown was within his grasp. But Denmark was always his base, as it was Cnut's after him.

Sweyn prepared for his renewed onslaught on England by forming an alliance with the king of Sweden and also with the Vikings of Jomsborg. From 1003 the raids got worse. In 1007 a tribute of £36,000 was taken. In 1009 a new dimension was added to Æthelred's troubles. A West Saxon thegn called Wulfnoth raised twenty ships and went into the Viking business on his own account. He must, at some point, have joined Sweyn, because his son, Godwin, was one of Cnut's earliest and most powerful advisers. Æthelred was now married to Emma of Normandy, by whom he had the son known in English history as Edward the Confessor; Godwin's son was Harold II, and another component of the tragedy of 1066 had fallen into place. The ealdorman of western Mercia had two sons. Northman, the elder, was one of the first magnates executed by Cnut for treason, and a younger son, Leofric, became famous as the husband of Lady Godiva. His fate was very different from that of his brother. He was made earl of Mercia and was always loyal to his new masters and was completely trusted by them. We do not know how he earned his promotion but it cannot have been by loyalty to Æthelred II. Leofric and Godwin are not just two individual English renegades. They carried with them retinues of thegns on whom their power rested. The *Chronicle*, in its complaints about English treachery, does not give the half of it.

In 1009 we hear of a great host that ravaged Kent until it was bought off. It was led by Thorkell the Tall, the leading Jomsviking, who had been allied with Sweyn for some time. In 1011 they captured the *burh* of Canterbury through treachery and seized Archbishop Ælfheah. This was the same man who had been picked up in the West Country by Dunstan, made the successor of Æthelwold and then translated to Canterbury. A great tribute was paid and Ælfheah was taken to London, where the Vikings demanded a further ransom. It was now 1012 and Ælfheah, realising that the men of Kent had been bled white, refused to authorise the collection of the ransom. The E text of the *Chronicle*, at that time being kept up at St Augustine's Canterbury, says:

Then on Saturday the host became greatly incensed against the bishop, because he was not willing to offer them any money and forbade any ransom to be given for him. Moreover they were very drunk, for wine had been brought to them from the south. They then took the bishop and led him to their tribunal … and pelted him to death with the bones and heads of cattle, and one of them smote him on the skull with the iron head of an axe, so that he sank down and his holy blood fell on the earth and his holy soul was sent forth to God's kingdom.

There can be no other term but brutal savagery for this: it was also counterproductive. According to Thietmar of Merseburg the murder of Ælfheah shocked some of the Vikings themselves, and Thorkell the Tall and his Jomsvikings changed sides. Thorkell fought hard for Æthelred and was entirely faithful to him but he and his men had to be paid. Æthelred paid them by raising one of the first general land taxes since the Roman empire. This was the famous geld miscalled Danegeld. Its true name was the *heregeld*. It bought nobody off. It paid for an efficient, disciplined body of mercenaries. The English did not like paying land taxes (they never have) and Thorkell was detested by the English. But that should not detract from Æthelred's skill in making a powerful ally of a powerful enemy.

In 1013 Queen Emma returned to Normandy and her brother Duke Richard. Then her two sons, Edward, the later Confessor, and his younger brother Ælfred reached the Norman court. The English magnates began to submit to Sweyn in droves and Æthelred, too, fled to Normandy. Then there occurred an incident of no importance whatsoever except that it is very revealing about the piety of the day. The queen was accompanied to Normandy by Abbot Ælfsige of Peterborough, who made a pilgrimage to Bonneval, where the body of St Florentine was buried. He found the community in desperate poverty because the abbey had been pillaged, so he bought St Florentine from them minus the head for £500 and presented him to Peterborough. (The present-day equivalent is perhaps Royal Holloway College selling its Constable.) On 2 February 1014 Sweyn died and the country was again plunged into chaos. Sweyn had two sons. The probably younger Cnut was to succeed him in England but the elder was to have Denmark. The English magnates were no longer bound by their oaths to Sweyn, so they asked Æthelred to come back if he would govern them better than he had before. Æthelred duly returned to face a young man who had yet to make his mark. In fact it was not Cnut who conquered England but two older men who did it for him. Cnut went north to Lindsey. Æthelred showed that he could be effective and reached the north before Cnut felt he was ready to fight. He fled back to Denmark, leaving his allies to endure Æthelred's very bloody reprisals.

The last months of Æthelred's life are obscure. In 1015 a council was held at Oxford and the ealdorman of Mercia, the treacherous Eadric Streona (he did, however, protect the Mercians from the fate that had befallen the rest of England), procured the murder of two brothers, leading magnates of the northern Danelaw. The reasons for the killing are not known but Æthelred made himself a party to it by confiscating the estates of the two men and ordering the arrest of one of the widows. Æthrelred's eldest son and possibly presumptive heir, Edmund Ironside, defied his father by marrying the widow and seizing the confiscated estates. Edmund was neither hated in the north, like his father was for harrying Lindsey, nor despised like Cnut for running away. He was recognised as lord by the northern Danelaw. Cnut soon reappeared and Eadric Streona recognised him. It is unlikely that Edmund had sufficient forces to defeat Cnut, Eadric Streona's Mercians and the southern thegns loyal to his father. Edmund seems to have reached some kind of accommodation with his father and joined him in London, now likely to be the Danes' next objective. On 23 April 1016 Æthelred died and the English in general accepted Edmund as king. He had been forced to leave the northern Danelaw unprotected and Cnut duly invaded it. In the south of England the West Saxon magnates doubted Edmund's ability to beat Cnut and promised allegiance to Cnut at Southampton; they included bishops and abbots, as well as lay magnates. Edmund did, however, manage to force them back into his allegiance but by now the north had also accepted Cnut. Earl Uhtred of Northumbria was one of the turncoats and was murdered for his pains. Cnut replaced him with the Norwegian who had defeated Olaf Tryggvason in Norway, Eric. Eric was now an elderly man with perhaps the greatest reputation as a warrior in the north. He was joined by Thorkell the Tall. Thorkell had remained faithful to Æthelred until he in effect abdicated, and was largely responsible for Æthelred's safe arrival in Normandy. But he no longer owed allegiance to any English leader and it is clear he was hated by the English in general. The situation was a confusing mess in which no one quite knew where they stood but everyone knew they had a great deal to lose if they did the wrong thing. In Thorkell's case there are stories which may contain some truth that some of his men, including his brother, Hemming, were murdered through English treachery. Thorkell's position was very precarious and it is no surprise that he decided his safest option was to turn to Cnut.

The scene of the action moved to the London area and both sides had some success but Cnut could not take the city. Edmund defeated Cnut at Otford and was immediately rejoined by Eadric Streona. It may be thought he was gullible to accept him but he really had no choice. Ealdorman Eadric commanded a sizeable body of Mercian thegns. As he had protected their lives and their property when the rest of England was ravaged and pillaged it is likely he was popular and trusted by his Mercians, if by nobody else. Cnut withdrew from London and to repay Eadric and weaken his position he ravaged Mercia.

Edmund pursued Cnut but was beaten in what turned out to be the decisive campaign of the war at Ashingdon in Essex. Edmund was still a force to be reckoned with and Cnut came to terms with him. Edmund was to keep Wessex and Cnut took the rest of England. This settlement hardly bears the stamp of longevity but was never tested because Edmund died on 30 November 1016. Cnut was now recognised as the unquestioned king of England. The treacherous English magnates found they could not play ducks and drakes with their allegiance to Cnut as they had with Æthelred and Edmund. He killed several of them, including Eadric Streona, who got what he had been asking for for a very long time.

Sir Frank Stenton, in general an admirer of Cnut,[9] wrote:

> At least four prominent Englishmen – Eadric Streona among them – were slaughtered without any recorded trial in the first months of his reign … two young sons of Edmund Ironside survived but only because a refuge was found for them in Hungary, where Cnut's agents could not reach them.

The 'slaughtered' Englishmen were barefaced traitors who had sworn allegiance to Cnut and then gone over to Edmund Ironside. A century and a half later they would have been tried but I do not think the outcome would have been any different. As for the æthelings I think Sir Frank was not allowing for the nature of the times in the sort of misfortune that had befallen Æthelred's family. It is true post–Conquest sources suppose that the boys fell into Cnut's hands, that he was hesitant about killing them outright and handed them over to the king of Sweden to do it for him, who, however, sent them to Hungary instead. I do not believe the boys would have been allowed to fall into Cnut's hands. In the circumstances the only recourse the young men had was to seek the patronage of powerful kinsmen. Æthelred's young family by Emma was protected by their Norman uncle. The two æthelings' obvious patron would be their kinsman, Duke Conrad, the future Emperor Conrad II. His great-grandmother was Otto the Great's queen, Edith (Eadgifu), who was sister to King Edmund, the boys' great-grandfather. The kinship was remote but probably not too remote to escape the obligations of feuding. Duke Conrad and his Germans took some interest in internal Hungarian politics and at some point in the early eleventh century began to build up a pro-German party at the Hungarian court. It seems likely that this was how the æthelings reached Hungary. Edward married a kinswoman of the future emperor. At any rate Edward showed interest in the English succession only when anti-German feeling made it prudent for him to withdraw from Hungary.

NOTES

1 The relevant portions are printed in Margaret Ashdown's *English and Norse Documents relating to the reign of Aethelred the Unready*, Cambridge, 1930.
2 *The Viking Achievement.*
3 Smyth, *Scandinavian Kings in the British Isles.*
4 Simon Keynes, 'The Declining Reputation of King Aethelred the Unready', *Aethelred the Unready: Papers from the Millenary Conference*, Oxford, 1978.
5 See also J. Blair, *Anglo-Saxon Oxfordshire,*
6 *The Battle of Maldon*, ed. Scragg, p. 32. Attempts have been made to date the poem in the reign of Cnut on the grounds that the title 'earl' given to Byrhtnoth was not in current usage in 991. This has been rejected because the title 'earl' is found in a law of Edgar: but more remains to be said. The law of Edgar designates only his vicegerent in Northumbria 'earl'; his colleagues in Mercia and East Anglia are called 'ealdormen'. It is generally supposed Byrhtnoth was ealdorman of Essex at the time of the battle but no ealdorman of Essex was called anything but ealdorman until Cnut's reign. I have pointed to the strong evidence that Byrhtnoth was earl of Northumbria in 991, in which case the poem was employing the correct usuage for that year. Unless scholars are prepared to accept Byrhtnoth's promotion to Northumbria (it is obvious why Northumbria should be terminologically precocious in this matter of title) the revisionists have a point. In 991 Byrhtnoth was either ealdorman of Essex or earl of Northumbria with or without Essex as well.
7 The late Dr Harmer, who taught me Anglo-Saxon, once said to me, 'You could write a poem as good as that if only you knew enough Anglo-Saxon.' When I was first appointed to Manchester I wanted to start the Medieval English History course at 1066 but wasn't let. I therefore went to Dr Harmer and asked if I could sit in on her Anglo-Saxon course for English honours students. She said she was so surprised that an historian should want to learn the language of the sources that she would teach me herself. I was joined by the late Eric Stone, most closely associated with Keble College, Oxford, but then at Manchester. Dr Harmer always began by making us read aloud the passage she had set us for preparation. When it was the turn of the *Battle of Maldon* we read a long section each and it was obvious that Dr Harmer, who was not a frivolous lady, was preventing herself from laughing only with an effort. It turned out that Eric Stone and myself quite unconsciously surrendered to the rhythm of the poem and were waving our shields and brandishing our swords. So perhaps one should allow the poem more merit than I have done.
8 Eric John, 'War and Society in the Tenth Century: the Maldon Campaign', *Transactions of the Royal Historical Society*, 5th series, 27, pp. 173–95.
9 *Anglo-Saxon England*, p. 397.

CHAPTER 9

The northern empire

THE SOURCES FOR THE REIGN of Cnut and its immediate aftermath are, as usual, tantalising and scrappy, but they begin to take on some new and interesting characteristics. One of the most important sources for the period is also one of the oddest in English history, the *Encomium Emmae Reginae*, the praise of Queen Emma.

The lady in question was Æthelred's widow, Queen Emma, who quickly married Cnut. She is unlikely to have had much choice in the matter, since she was wholly dependent on her brother, Duke Richard II. Cnut wanted a Norman alliance. As Stenton pointed out years ago¹ Cnut wanted as much continuity as possible in his rule. He also knew that his attraction for the English was his ability to prevent attacks from Scandinavia, and a Norman alliance was a useful part of that policy. Duke Richard was willing and the marriage sealed the alliance. So long as Duke Richard lived the alliance endured. In the early twelfth century the widowed empress Matilda was forced to marry the count of Anjou. She very much resented her demotion from empress to countess. At least Emma was a queen again, and she does not seem to have resented her husband. What she did resent was that Cnut, in Scandinavian style, had an English wife too, by whom he fathered a son, the future Harold I.

The *Encomium* was written at Emma's request by a Flemish cleric. It is a very strange and very much misunderstood work. Its best editor is its latest: the late Alasdair Campbell. But Dr Campbell misunderstood both Emma's motive in commissioning the *Encomium* and its author's intentions in writing it. He thought it belonged to the genre of hagiography. He cited what he thought were two fairly recent precedents, two lives of East Frankish royal ladies, the life of Henry the Fowler's widow, Queen Matilda, and an obituary of Otto the Great's empress, Adelheid. The life of Matilda at least has an obvious political *Tendenz*. Dr Campbell calls these two books 'eulogistic accounts of royal ladies which recall the Encomium in matter, tone and style'. Most commentators agree with Dr Campbell, and the book has been relegated to the ranks of hagiography and interpreted accordingly. In my opiniion we are faced with a new and quite different kind of writing. Let me first point out why I do not think we are in the world of hagiography. That world has general and well nigh universal characteristics. The subject is endowed with a plethora of virtues and a great deal of Christian piety from which flow a concatenation of wonders, signs and portents. The *Encomium* is quite different. Its author credits Emma with only two virtues. She was good to the poor and when in exile in Flanders she cost nobody anything. Nothing wonderful follows from these rather untheological virtues. There are no wonders but there is an implied threat to the English if they do not heed the queen. Piety, Emma's nor anyone else's, plays no part in the *Encomium*. If this be hagiography it is without religion, miracles or conspicuous virtue. Further it is a work commissioned by Emma: the fact that it has survived shows that it met her needs. It was what she wanted. The book is a very important sign of the growing literary sophistication of the period. It is about politics directly – politics quite separate from religious considerations.

We are immediately up against a difficult problem. The *Encomium* does not suppress all reference to Emma's first husband – it never mentions him by name but refers to him respectfully as *princeps* – but it never says Emma had been married to him and it could be taken to mean that Edward and Ælfred were the sons of Cnut. If we suppose that the *Encomium* was a work of hagiography that could mean only that the encomiast was a liar on a large scale. Works of hagiography were not written for the here-and-now or for those in the know but for a possibly quite remote posterity. I want to suggest that the *Encomium* is not a work of hagiography, and that must make a difference to how we interpret its author's 'suppressions'. We need to look closer at what exactly the encomiast would be at.

A drawing that prefaces the oldest manuscript provides a clue. It shows the author presenting the work to the queen. She is enthroned and crowned, flanked by her two sons, Edward and Harthacnut.[2] After the death of Cnut Emma's family situation was complicated, not to say bizarre. With the advent of Harold I it must have been apparent to Emma and her two families that whatever divided them was trivial compared with the brutal fact that so long as Harold I was around they none of them had any great part to play in English politics. The *Encomium* was addressed very precisely to three people and their immediate entourages, and had a precise date, 1042. The book has nothing at all in common with the two books Dr Campbell cited: if one had to name a genre to which it belongs I cannot think of anything closer than Andrew Morton's biography of the

Princess of Wales. Not surprisingly the encomiast finds it unnecessary to deal out names and labels all perfectly familiar to each of the protagonists. There is no dimension for posterity: once Edward had succeeded Harthacnut and quarrelled with his mother the role of the *Encomium* was finished. It is not surprising that it is almost unknown in subsequent English historiography.

The encomiast has a related theme summed up in the quotation from the Vulgate: 'A house divided against itself cannot stand.'[3] He knew that his readers, even if they numbered only a few, must remember the miseries of Æthelred's reign. So Emma is not only the bearer of legitimacy but the focus of unity too. Once married to Cnut she has little part to play in the narrative until the advent of Harold I, which meant she was needed to restore legitimacy once again.

The writer was not a liar on a grand scale, writing to deceive posterity into believing that Emma was a saint of prodigious virtues, nor is that what Emma paid him for. He was doing the best he could for her by writing an intelligent version of current history – too intelligent for readers of the time – tying Emma to the best way of avoiding the perils of disunity and illegitimacy. In fact Emma was too politically compromised to serve this function. Her obvious lack of any base in English politics, her association with the most disastrous reign in English history, and the fact that on the death of her brother the Norman court turned against her and repudiated the English alliance, made the whole enterprise chimerical. But the encomiast did his best. He is never warm towards his subject, and it is difficult to think he believed all she told him. But he allows us to read between the lines.

Now the *Encomium* is an important and neglected source. It has its limitations. The author never seems to have set foot in England, and he had no set of annals, so his chronology and topography are of little, if any, use. But his account of Cnut's succession is the best we have. He tells us that after Sweyn's death Cnut returned to Denmark, which we already knew. He went presumably to get help from his elder brother, Harold. Sweyn must have known that Cnut could not hope simply to carry on where he had left off: he would have to fight to succeed. Denmark was the safe part of the inheritance and presumably went to the elder son.

We know that Thorkell the Tall was made earl of East Anglia in 1017.[4] The encomiast is the only one to say anything about what went on between Thorkell and Cnut in these early years. (Emma must have known Thorkell personally and her two husbands could inform her of his activities.) He says that Thorkell joined Cnut before Cnut left for Denmark;

Thorkell remained in England on Cnut's orders. This is very improbable and has been held against the encomiast's veracity by those who have not read carefully what he says. He claims only that some say this is what happened, which, with this writer, means, I think, that he did not believe it. Cnut returned to Denmark with only forty ships and accused Thorkell of keeping most of the Danish forces under his command. Cnut told his brother he thought Thorkell would be against them. It looks as though Thorkell had recognised Cnut before Cnut left for Denmark. Cnut ordered Thorkell to accompany him and Thorkell would not: that is why Cnut told his brother he thought Thorkell would be against them. Thorkell was in a difficult position. Trusted neither by the English nor by the Danes, he yet needed allies. In the end Cnut was Thorkell's only possible ally, but he never fully trusted Cnut, and vice versa. Thorkell then suddenly appeared in Denmark, where he patched up an alliance with Cnut, who needed Thorkell's prestige and abilities. When the invasion force returned to England he and Earl Eric were the real commanders of the Danish forces, and the encomiast thought they had made Cnut king of England. After his succession Cnut certainly behaved like a politician with debts to pay. He made Eric earl of Northumbria and Thorkell earl of East Anglia, although in the witness lists of Cnut's charters Thorkell always takes precedence. In 1019 Cnut had to return to Denmark. At some point Cnut's brother Harold died and Cnut succeeded him as king of Denmark. I think that is why Cnut returned to Denmark at this point. During his absence he left Thorkell as regent but in 1021 suddenly exiled him. The quarrel, whatever it was about, was soon settled but Thorkell never set foot in England again. He was given great power in the north, and he and Cnut exchanged their sons as hostages. If Cnut's son was Harthacnut – and he is the only child we know Cnut and Emma had – he was far more Danish than English when he succeeded, and a virtual stranger to the English magnates. The English sources give the impression that he was a tiresome foreigner.

Cnut's first political act was to marry Emma. The encomiast says she made it a condition that her firstborn should rule England. This cannot have pleased Edward. Cnut made an important visit to Rome. This is a vexed question. I agree with Dr Campbell that the evidence forces us to suppose that Cnut paid two visits to Rome, in 1027 and 1031. Two versions of the *Chronicle* put the visit in 1031. They are joined by the Latin chronicler usually known as Florence of Worcester,[5] who is the main source for Cnut's reign. This book was last edited in 1848 – the new edition was promised when I was a young university lecturer and is still eagerly awaited – and the editor made no attempt to identify the book's sources. He could hardly have been expected to in 1848. The edition of the pre-1066 portion has now (1995) appeared. Although the identity of the *Chronicle* texts Florence used is kept open for a later volume Dr McGurk has identified the other sources. Florence had a text of the *Chronicle* related to the D text, which in my view is a Worcester text. He also had Asser and the first life of Oswald. (Dr McGurk points to other saints' lives he quoted from.) The author, or more probably authors, were Worcester men and often give Worcester information no one else has. During the last years of the Anglo-Saxon state for which Florence is a prime source, some of the bishops of Worcester were national figures, and this is reflected in his pages. This is true of Bishop Lyfing in Cnut's reign and even more true of Bishop, then Archbishop, Ealdred in the Confessor's. Ealdred held both Worcester and York for a time. As a result Florence is full of northern information and reads in places like Ealdred's memoirs as told to a Worcester correspondent. It is probable that it was from his version of the *Chronicle* that Florence took his date for Cnut's Roman visit, 1031.

Florence also knew of a letter Cnut sent to England by the hand of Lyfing, abbot of Tavistock and later bishop of Worcester. It is likely though not certain that Cnut wrote in the vernacular. Florence always writes in Latin and he may have translated the letter for his book. No one doubts its authenticity. Cnut says he has spent Easter in Rome and that a number of princes were present, notably the emperor Conrad and Rudolf of Burgundy. He says that these two princes have promised that English pilgrims to Rome shall have free and unimpeded transit through their lands. We know what Cnut was doing in Rome from Continental sources, notably the *Vita Cuonradi*. He was attending the coronation of the emperor, which took place at Easter 1027. Cnut returned from Rome to Denmark and wrote to the English from there. Lyfing was shortly afterwards made bishop of Worcester and it is probably from him that Florence got the text of the letter, but he did not know the date of the imperial coronation (although Lyfing must have known), so he got from the annals the wrong date, that of a later visit to Rome.

Professor Whitelock in her translation of the *Chronicle* had an alternative explanation for the confusion. She accepted that Cnut visited Rome in 1027 but she assumed that the chronicler knew that the visit followed a great battle in Scandinavia. She thought he had confused the battle of Stiklestad in 1030 with Holy River, in 1026. Florence shows little interest in Scandinavian politics, an indifference he shares with other English sources, but his annalist may have done. This is plausible but unprovable. An important Continental source for Danish history is Adam of Bremen. He says Cnut visited Rome in the pontificate of Archbishop Libentius of Bremen, 1029–32, and he says that Cnut was accompanied by the emperor Conrad. Adam cannot have supposed he was referring to Conrad's coronation and he knew that the two monarchs had a marriage alliance in mind. The saga material says that Cnut visited Rome towards the end of his life, as does Goscelinus, a Flemish author who mass-produced Anglo-Saxon saints' lives. What seems to clinch the fact that Cnut did make two journeys to Rome is the encomiast's eye-witness account of his passing through Saint-Omer. In 1027 Cnut went to Rome from Denmark and returned there. To pass through Saint-Omer *en route* from Denmark to Rome would take some explaining.

Why does all this matter? Many scholars have argued that before 1066, when the Norman Conquest took England into Europe, England was part of the Scandinavian world. I have consistently argued that English connexions with the Continent, especially the Frankish part of it, have been played down. All this helps towards a truer picture of the real position. The English sources are indifferent to Scandinavia as long as they can be. But in Cnut's reign the English were bringing Scandinavia into the European mainstream. I do not think Cnut would have been invited to the imperial coronation in Rome unless he had been king of England. There were few Continental contacts as visible or as status-creating as a visit to Rome, especially for such an occasion. Cnut had become very much more than a Viking, and for the first time a Scandinavian ruler was invited to take a central role on the European scene, but only because he was king of England.

In spite of the encomiast Cnut married Emma to secure not legitimacy but a Norman alliance. Cnut ruled Norway and Denmark too. Given such a political structure, the centre point of Cnut's polity cannot have been Wessex but must have lain farther north. In the letter he wrote to Thorkell when the latter was acting as regent in England, he made it clear he knew what his attraction for the English was. He says more or less literally, 'You have had much trouble from the north. Hold fast to me and I will see you do not have any more.' This would be so only as long as he controlled the north, and that meant he had to appear there from time to time and sometimes fight campaigns, especially in Norway. With a Norman alliance he could assume that Wessex was safe and devote his time and attention to the north. In 1027 the queen's younger nephew, Robert the Magnificent – or the Devil; it is a matter of taste – inherited the duchy. He took the part of his exiled cousins. In an attempt to preserve the alliance Cnut married his daughter to the young duke but he soon repudiated her. There-after Cnut had to rule without a Norman alliance but circumstances, notably the early death of Duke Robert, leaving a child – and a bastard, at that – as heir, meant he had no great problems from that quarter.

Cnut governed England much as his English predecessors had done, through super-earls, assisted by subordinates also with the title of earl. But he had to make special arrangements for Wessex. His predecessors had directly ruled Wessex for themselves but the extent of his empire, the vast distances it involved in travel, made that impossible for Cnut, yet the greater part of his revenues came from Wessex. His solution was to appoint a super-earl of Wessex, and he chose Godwin, the son of the West Saxon thegn Wulfnoth, who had set up in the Viking business on his own account. When Earl Eric of Northumbria died he was replaced by Siward, a Dane of whose early career we know little. Godwin, Leofric of Mercia and Siward were Cnut's principal counsellors for the rest of the reign, and between them they dominated English politics for a generation – until only a few years before the Conquest, in fact.

It has been suggested that the weak point in Cnut's empire was Norway. He fought several campaigns there but by 1028 seemed to have gained complete and permanent control. He held a great court at Nidaros (now Trondhjem). He made his heir Harthacnut sub-king of Denmark. He received the submission of the Norwegian magnates and made Earl Haakon, the son of a former earl of Northumbria, viceroy. Haakon seems to have been competent and to have understood the Norwegians. He was soon drowned. Cnut then made a disastrous mistake. He sent his English 'wife' Ælfgifu – he had taken up with her before he married Emma but there was never any Christian ceremony – as vicegerent. It is possible that the Cnut who hobnobbed with emperors and attended coronations in Rome was becoming a little embarrassed by her. She was, however, a very well connected lady of a great landholding family, her father had been earl of Northumbria and she may have been connected by birth with her pre-decessor, Earl Haakon. Repudiation was not on the cards, and perhaps Cnut sent her to Norway to relieve embarrassments in England. At any rate she, assisted by her son by Cnut, Sweyn, was catastrophically incom-petent. We do not know much about her mistakes but we do know that she was held in hatred by the Norwegians for a very long time. First she had to meet the attempt by the local native resistance leader, the Norwe-gian saint, Olaf Haroldson. She won the battle, killed the saint and ruined herself all at the same time. In 1033 she lost Nidaros and by 1035 was back in England.

Olaf Haroldson dead was much more damaging to the Danes than he had been in life. His cult rapidly developed, cult centres, churches dedicated to him, proliferated throughout the Baltic, and always they served as centres of resistance to Danish imperialism. This is a good place to look at hagiography and its political importance, a comparatively recent historiographical development. A less well known cult is that of St Mildrith.[6] She was of little importance as a personality but she was an early Kentish princess. We now realise that the Kentish royal family inherited and transmitted great prestige as the first English Christian dynasty. Quite a number of Kentish rulers sought to make political capital out of Kentish sanctity. The saints concerned were all descendants of Æthelberht, the first Christian king. His great-granddaughter, Domne Earfe, was married to the king of the Magonsaetan, who inhabited what we now call Shropshire more or less. She had three daughters, all regarded as saints, two of whom, Mildrith and Mildburg, were abbesses of Minster in Thanet and Much Wenlock respectively. Their mother left her husband for the religious life and by a tradition that may well be true had founded Minster before 700. According to the legend she got the land on which the Minster was built as a sort of a wergeld for the murder of her two brothers, Æthelred and Æthelberht, by their cousin King Ecgbert of Kent. The details of the way the boundaries were calculated have Frankish parallels that lend plausibility, though not proof, to the story. The two boys had no Kentish cult: that could only have been a permanent embarrassment to the Kentish royal family. Their bodies and their cults were taken to East Anglia, first to Wakering in Essex and then to Ramsey. Since the East Anglian royal family was related to the Kentish royal family but none of their members was in any way involved in their killing, their cults were copiously recorded. From these records we learn important and rather surprising facts. It seems that in Kent what mattered were the minsters associated with royal ladies. Minster in Thanet was a more important house than St Augustine's, even though the monks there had the body of St Augustine and the abbey was the burial place of the kings of Kent. In the end St Augustine's got St Mildrith and most of her lands. Curiously, it was the incursions of the Vikings that brought this about.

The two young martyrs crop up persistently in later English politics. Byrhtferth of Ramsey, in addition to his life of Oswald, wrote an important version of their legend. The resemblance between the manner of their death and that of Edward the Martyr must have been part of the reason for writing it. Dr Rollason thinks that, writing in Æthelred II's reign, Byrhtferth intended a pointed allusion to the circumstances of his accession. He may well have been reminding Æthelred that martyred brothers can go in pairs. Thus a Kentish martyrdom the kings of Kent would have no truck with had been turned into an important ideological weapon by the new monks. Then it looks as though Cnut thought the boys might help him and he sought actively to promote their cult. It looks as though the Kentish royal family conferred a collective charisma unequalled by any other Anglo-Saxon family. It made sense for Cnut, who was weak on legitimacy, to join that particular bandwagon.

It is not easy to turn this sort of thing into hard political currency but it must have had some. The success of the cult of St Olaf and its disastrous results for the Danes are readily intelligible. But the survival of the cult of two early Kentish princes and the fact that the later members of the house of Cerdic and the Anglo-Danish Cnut in his turn thought the promotion of their cults could add prestige to their governance are something we must note, accept that it was important and remain uncomprehending.

The days of Cnut's prestige were over. He had given away or lost some of his most important provinces, and his power to make his earls do as he bade them was based on habit as much as anything. He no longer controlled the north and he could give the English no guarantee against a recurrence of the Viking raids. If he had lived a little longer his reputation might have been much lower than in fact it is. In 1035 he died, leaving England on the verge of chaos. His lawful heir was Harthacnut, who was, however, tied up in Denmark coping with the collapse of the Danish empire in the Baltic, and not likely to be available in the immediate future. Whilst the English knew the raids could come again their great men could not agree on what to do.

NOTES

1   Stenton, *Anglo-Saxon England*, p. 397.
2   *Encomium Emmae Reginae*, ed. A. Campbell, Camden Society, 3rd series, London, 1949.
3   Eric John, 'The Encomium Emmae Reginae: a Riddle and a Solution', *Bulletin of the John Rylands Library*, 63, 1980–81, pp. 58–94.
4   *Anglo-Saxon Chronicle*, C, *sub anno* 1017.
5   Too recently for me to take full cognisance of it, Florence has recently achieved a new edition, *The Chronicle of John of Worcester*, ed. R. R. Darlington and P. McGurk, Oxford, 1995. Only vol. ii has so far appeared, which contains the text of the pre-1066 section of the chronicle only. We must wait for the vital vol. i, which is to discuss the relations between the chronicle and the *Anglo-Saxon Chronicle*, until after vol. iii has appeared. Dr McGurk offers reasons for supposing that the author of the chronicle was a certain John of Worcester. The attribution of the authorship to Florence depends on the annal for 1118 which records his death and attributes to him the authorship or

chief authorship of the chronicle to that date. The chronicle continues for another generation; there is no break in style after 1118; it incorporates annals from the year 1102 derived from Eadmer's *Historia Novorum* which could not have been inserted before 1122; Orderic Vitalis, himself a notable chronicler, ascribes a Worcester chronicle, recognisably this one, as being written by one John. Obviously Florence could not have added the quotations from Eadmer and clearly the chronicle was continued by John (of Worcester). But the *obit.* of Florence cannot be ignored, especially on the arguments presented here which suggest that John wrote it. Dr McGurk says, 'the part played by Florence remains elusive'. p. xviii. Well, yes, but he did play a part, and it seems that John assigned him a high part. If we prefer to call the pre-1118 portion of the chronicle by its traditional name, Florence of Worcester, we have John of Worcester's sanction. Dr C. R. Hart, 'The early section of the *Worcester Chronicle*', *Journal of Medieval History*, ix, 1983, pp. 251–315, argued that the Worcester Chronicle (if it must have a new name this is as accurate as any) up to 1017 was a Ramsey compilation. His arguments in so far as they are purely stylistic are summarily dismissed by Dr McGurk, p. lxxix, but his stylistic arguments are much stronger than Dr McGurk represents them. Dr Hart brings the *Annals of St Neots* into the discussion. He supposes them to have been written *c.* 1000, also at Ramsey. Dr McGurk, relying on David Dumville's edition of the annals, claims they were composed in the first half of the twelfth century, thus ruining Dr Hart's argument. But agreement is growing that Dr Hart's date is correct. Dr Alfred Smyth in his new book on Ælfred the Great supports him, and I have myself argued for a similar date from quite a different direction in an as yet unpublished paper on the *Annals of St Neots* and the defeat of the Vikings.

6   D. W. Rollason, *The Mildrith Legend*, Leicester, 1982.

CHAPTER 10

The avoidance of chaos

AN INFORMED AND INTERESTED observer in 1035, when Cnut died with his Baltic empire collapsing about his ears, must have anticipated the worst. Long and bloody battles over the succession to the crown, renewed Viking raids and a totally unpredictable outcome. Except for the last he would have been wrong. There were squabbles over the succession, followed by a quarter of a century's peace when the English had neither to die in, nor pay for, expeditions to Norway. This was no chance concatenation of events. The worst did not happen because the English political class were determined it was not going to, and although there were profound disagreements among them about key issues they were kept under control. The years immediately following Cnut's death are not glorious in English history, they are sordid and shabby in many ways. None of the protagonists covers himself – or, in the case of the queen, herself – with glory. Earl Godwin's part was especially vile. But they were not competing for personal advantage alone, merely determined that chaos should not come again. Had they failed, a lot of Englishmen must have died and a lot of misery would have been caused.

The English had learnt some lessons. They had acquired a remarkable capacity for organisation, most obviously exemplified in the new monasticism. Unpopular the new monks may have been with some but they were now organised into centrally directed communities. They could be looted still but if the organisation held, as it usually did, the damage could be repaired with comparative ease. In spite of all that had happened they emerged from the reign of Æthelred II relatively well-off and by the death of Cnut were an unquestioned part of English society. Until Cnut's accession they supplied the English with a set of bishops of outstanding quality.

Another factor that may well have been decisive was that the English had learnt, from what we might call the 'Æthelred' experience that disunity meant ruin. From 1035 to 1065 the English magnates – and lesser members of the warrior class must be included with them – made a remarkable attempt to secure consensus. They were aware of the nose for trouble the Vikings had, and although, as 1066 approached, division within the ruling class became more acute, it was not until one family, the house of Godwin, discarded consensus and made a bid for supremacy that England could be invaded again.

Cnut had to face what the sociologists would call a serious structural problem created by the nature of his empire. This was a world divided into face-to-face societies. A man knew his neighbours well, and also knew his superiors. If he saw them less often he saw them sometimes and helped them conduct business. Royal government was peripatetic, moving round the country and living off the royal demesne by eating the food rents. So many people must have seen the king of the day, especially if they lived in Wessex, where most of the royal demesne lay. Beneath the kings were the earls, who must also have been largely peripatetic. But the system ran into difficulties if the king, and sometimes his principal magnates, was away for long stretches in Scandinavia. The system could work only by an extension of the traditional English usage, the delegation of power. Cnut was an exceptionally able delegator, only his wife Ælfgifu was a total disaster. As a chain shows its strength by its weakest link, the collapse that followed after her expulsion from Norway shows that Cnut's empire, though successful for quite a long time, was in the end precarious. (The next 'empire' of which England formed a part, the Angevin, also fell to pieces for much the same reasons.)

We need to look next at what happened when Cnut died. He left at least two sons, Harthacnut by Emma of Normandy, whom he had designated heir, and Harold by Ælfgifu, his English 'wife' It seems that then, or perhaps before, Emma circulated a rumour that Cnut was not the father of Harold. The Abingdon chronicle accepts this preposterous story at its face value; the E text is only slightly less credulous. The encomiast has the story which suggests that Emma herself was the author but he does not seem to have believed her, since he says that Cnut had two sons by another woman. This could only have been Harold and his brother Sweyn, who died in 1035. Harthacnut, Emma's son by Cnut, was unquestionably the legal heir. Primogeniture more or less obtained in England but the succession to the crown was determined by the will of the old king. Thus when William I lay dying he nominated his second son Rufus as heir to England but he could not similarly disinherit his eldest son Robert in Normandy, where strict primogeniture prevailed. He clearly judged that Rufus was an abler man than Robert: subsequent events were to show he was right. But the important point is that he could disinherit Robert in England: nominating a successor was an indubitable part of royal prerogative. Harthacnut was nominated heir by his father. He was obviously little known to the English, who did not like him much when they did know him, but he was backed by his mother and Earl Godwin. Emma held the royal treasury at Winchester. Had he been on the spot when his father died or had he been able to leave Denmark immediately he could not have been denied.

The other great earls, Leofric and Siward, wanted Harold, who was in England. It needs to be recalled that Cnut's power base was precisely their earldoms. Wessex was not in any danger. Normandy, the obvious source of any threat to Wessex, was rendered helpless when Duke Robert died on a pilgrimage to Jerusalem, leaving as his heir a child, his young bastard William. So in 1035 Godwin was not threatened in any way and could do as he would over the succession. He opted to join the queen and support Harthacnut. The general fear of the likely consequences of a long inter-regnum and the fact that no single earl would have been acceptable to the others as regent caused Emma and Godwin to change their candidate. Emma's detestation of Harold I was, no doubt, partly due to perfectly natural jealousy but she must have known that she could expect little respect or favour from him. As she had broken with the Norman court – or, more correctly, it had broken with her – she had no natural refuge. In the circumstances she turned to her first family and invited her elder son, Edward, to claim his inheritance. Edward, who was far from being the 'holy simpleton' Maitland called him, pointed out that he had no assurances from the English magnates and refused. In other words he was telling her he knew she was acting on her own and she did not have the powers of a kingmaker. Emma then turned to his younger brother Ælfred, with tragic results.

The various recensions of the *Chronicle* are interesting here. The E text, from now till 1066 a Godwinist propaganda sheet, never mentions the affair. Not even it could disguise the treacherous part Earl Godwin played in it. The *Abingdon Chronicle* says that in 1036 Ælfred came to visit his mother at Winchester. But Godwin would not allow it 'because the popular cry was greatly in favour of Harold'. The chronicler deplored this and went on: Godwin stopped him and put him and his men in captivity; some were sold for money, some were cruelly killed, some were put in fetters, some were mutilated, some were scalped. Ælfred was blinded and sent to Ely, where he ended his short life and was buried by the monks.

The encomiast agrees broadly with this version of events but is more detailed and highlights Godwin's treachery. He must have been told Emma's version of events and she meant him to write it up. It is this section, in my opinion, that is the *raison d'être* of the whole *Encomium*. Although the encomiast does not accuse her, naturally, she does not come well out of the affair. Ælfred came to England after receiving a letter in her name. The encomiast claims the letter was a forgery written by Harold or his henchmen so he could lure the princes into his power and murder them. I should have thought that the house of Cerdic would by now have been a fast fading memory, and the last person Harold would have wanted in the game was another potential political rival. Since the book is largely a political justification of her conduct directed to Edward, Edward must have known the letter was genuine – she had certainly sent a similar invitation to him – and so, I think, did the encomiast. He is more explicit than the annals and says that Ælfred came to claim the crown. Unless the visit was politically motivated why should he have chosen a moment of crisis to visit the mother he had never seen since he was a baby? Once Ælfred had arrived, Emma faded out of the picture and Godwin took the centre of the stage. The encomiast never makes the slightest direct criticism of Godwin's conduct, which has led some scholars to think he exculpates him. This is impossible. When he was writing Godwin was the most powerful man in England, where Emma had to live, and discretion was called for. The author was a subject of the count of Flanders, who until 1066, even though he married his daughter to Duke William of Normandy, was in English politics a firm ally of the Godwin family. We also know from Florence that when Harthacnut became king he tried Godwin for Ælfred's murder. Godwin did not protest his innocence. He paid what looks like a large wergeld – and made the classic excuse: Harold was his lord, and he was only obeying orders.

With this in mind we can see better what the encomiast would be at, which is to show that Godwin's defence was false. Godwin met Ælfred near London and guided him to Guildford. It is plain Ælfred thought that Godwin was an ally: his mother could not have invited him without Godwin's knowledge and consent. When they met, Godwin took Ælfred under his protection and became his knight by the swearing of an oath. In Flanders people were familiar with terminology such as this, and he is telling us that Godwin became Ælfred's vassal by an oath of fealty. Godwin is also made to say that he withdrew to his lodgings so that he might serve his lord with due magnificence. By these apparently innocuous and pointless details the encomiast sets out to destroy Godwin's defence. Ælfred was his lord, not Harold, and it was his lord he betrayed, not his lord he obeyed. Godwin is implicated in what at first sight seems a trivial detail. He arranged the billeting of Ælfred's men in small dispersed groups. Ælfred must have had complete trust in Godwin to let that happen. Ælfred's men were entertained – and doubtless well plied with drink. Thus when Harold's men suddenly appeared they had no chance to regroup and were soon overpowered. The encomiast never accused Godwin directly, but only weeks before the *Encomium* was written Godwin had been tried for Ælfred's betrayal. In such circumstances not to excuse is to accuse. Besides, the encomiast gave the lie directly to Godwin's only defence. Godwin, of course, was acquitted because the other earls, who had also been for Harold, stood surety for him. In other words Harthacnut was warned of the limits of what he could do to Godwin.

No one could pretend that Godwin's role was anything but vile. He cannot be blamed for giving up Harthacnut. It is clear that Harold was the more popular of the two candidates. Even Emma realised that Harthacnut was a non-starter but she could not opt for Harold. Godwin could and he did. One would have thought he could have told her so. He could surely have prevented Ælfred's arrival had he so wished. He was, one must remember, earl of Wessex, and there may have been more residual support for the former royal house than the sources report. But it looks as though Godwin was paying his late entry fee for joining Harold's party. Even the archbishop of Canterbury reluctantly accepted Harold. Petitioned by Harold for coronation he shilly-shallyed for a whole year. During that time Harold ruled as regent for Harthacnut without the latter's consent. We have a piece of hagiography from Ely, where Ælfred was naturally of interest, which says that Harold ruled a full year before becoming full king. Presumably the archbishop gave way in the end.

Harthacnut was at last free to leave Denmark, and, taking a fleet with him, he sailed to Bruges in Flanders, where his mother had taken refuge. Harold had seized the treasury from her as he was entitled to when he was recognised as king, but from what the encomiast says she was not short of funds. But she could not have commanded money on the scale Harthacnut needed, and according to the encomiast he was on the verge of giving up when he was warned in a dream that Harold would not live long. Whether he really had a dream or whether he received more mundane intelligence, he neither attacked nor made any move to return to Denmark. On 17 March 1040 Harold duly died, so far as we know without issue. On 17 June 1040 Harthacnut appeared off Sandwich. There had been plenty of time for negotiation and the English accepted him.

The *Chronicle* is markedly hostile to him. The English had to pay off his fleet, and Harthacnut insisted on a sum of £32,147. The *Abingdon Chronicle* says: 'He never did anything worthy of a king while he reigned.' In

1041 two of his men collecting the geld in Worcester were murdered and he had the whole county harassed by way of punishment. Among his first acts was what seems a very odd thing to do. He recalled his half-brother Edward from Normandy and seems to have made him some kind of joint king. No source says why he did so but it does make sense of a sort. As king of Denmark without control of the rest of the north it was useful to have a kinsman to act as regent when necessary. It is unlikely he trusted any of his earls; he was very foolish if he did. But the act also falls into place in what was now becoming a tradition, a bid for an alliance with Normandy. Normandy might be not important at the moment but it was not going to stay that way. His co-ruler, Edward was later to make the most spectacular attempt at such an alliance.

Harthacnut was as yet unmarried and younger than Edward, who had almost certainly taken a vow of celibacy.[1] Edward was now about forty years of age, without resources but with a magnificent pedigree. Pedigree like Edward's was very marketable and he could have made a magnificent marriage. His half-nephew, Edward the ætheling, did just that and married a princess probably a relative of the emperor, Henry III. (He was correctly the emperor Henry II or King Henry III – Henry I of East Francia was never crowned emperor – but usage usually dubs him Henry III.) It would seem that Edward presented no threat to any children Harthacnut might have. It may be that Harthacnut knew that his health was poor. As for the English, they knew that with Edward there would be no fleet to pay off as there had been with Harthacnut.

In June 1042 Harthacnut died 'as he stood at his drink'. The Swedish historian, Dr Sten Körner, in a flight of Scandinavian imagination, maintains that Edward killed him.[2] The *Abingdon Chronicle* says he was seized with a horrible convulsion that sounds like a stroke. If so, at Harthacnut's age it was likely to be a severe one. Harthacnut had already had Harold's body dug up and thrown in a fen. He himself was buried beside his father. What the English felt about yet another interregnum was shown when they elected Edward king before his brother's burial. He was consecrated with great ceremony the following Easter. The encomiast wrote just before Harthacnut died and he thought, or said he thought, the reunion of Emma and her two sons was the ideal solution to the problems of contemporary government. It was, in fact, no solution at all. Edward plainly detested his mother, which makes me think Emma's alleged letter to Ælfred was genuine The first thing he did was to deprive her of her status and all her property. She might as well have plumped for Harold I in the first place.

Edward inherited a difficult situation. He clearly felt the death of his brother strongly and raised it whenever he had the chance. Whether this was from personal affection or because a man in his world was supposed to avenge the murder of kinsmen, we cannot know. He knew Earl Godwin had brought about his brother's murder but Godwin was now the richest man in England. Further, he was the earl of Wessex, where most of the royal demesne lay and where Edward had to live most of the time. In 1045 Edward did what in most circumstances would have been the natural thing to do, he married Godwin's daughter Edith. It is obvious the move was very distasteful to him. It is unlikely he wanted a father-in-law at all, let alone his brother's murderer. He was already middle-aged and, although it was the obvious thing to do, he put it off for three years. When he was briefly free of his father-in-law he sent her off to a nunnery presided over by his and Ælfred's sister. It is clear there was never any sexual side to the marriage.

The main source for Edward's reign is the *Vita Eadwardi*, the life of Edward, probably written by the prolific Fleming, Goscelinus. It is really an encomium to Queen Edith and bears some resemblance to the *Encomium Emmae* but its author was less intelligent than the encomiast and less disinterested. The life of Edward, unlike the *Encomium*, was written at the nadir of Edith's fortunes. She had lost virtually her entire family, and even before Hastings it is clear she detested her brother Harold. In the event things worked out better for her than they did for Queen Emma, and the Conqueror treated her with more consideration than her husband had her mother-in-law.

The reign of the Confessor is an enigma and I do not pretend my interpretation is the only possible one.[3] I interpret it the way I do because I know that this was a world where feuds, kindred groups and vows of celibacy were part of the social furniture and need to be taken seriously. I also set great store by the Norman evidence, which seems to me less partisan and tendentious than the English. In the eyes of Edward Augustus Freeman, the author of the weightiest tome, *recte* tomes, ever written about the Norman Conquest, Edward was a French quisling and Harold Godwinson a national hero. Maitland, a much more intelligent but not more learned historian than Freeman and the greatest legal historian we have ever had, wrote Edward off as a 'holy simpleton'. Maitland produced a prodigious body of work for a historian who began at thirty and died in his mid-fifties but there is hardly a human being in any of his books. When he wants to illustrate a point of law he invents imaginary litigants. His famous essay on the proposed treatment of criminous clerks in the constitutions of Clarendon, which Thomas Becket so bitterly denounced, is all sweetness and light. He unravels the procedures Henry II proposed to follow and shows how moderate and sensible they were. He is writing pure theory. I am sure that Henry hoped the Pope would take it exactly as Maitland interpreted it. That procedure, in the hands of a brutal authoritarian like Henry II, would have had rather more in common with the KGB than what we think of as a court of law. It was Maitland who was the political simpleton, not Edward.

The first serious attempt to see what Edward's reign was really about was made by Sir Frank Stenton in his *Anglo-Saxon England*. That is where any serious study of the reign must begin. In 1953 Professor D. C. Douglas wrote an article in the *English Historical Review*[4] that, by taking the French sources seriously for the first time, put the reign in a new light. In 1957, also in the *English Historical Review*, Professor T. J. Oleson suggested some corrections to Dr Douglas's arguments that in my opinion are valid.[5] In 1979 I published what is still my general view of the events of the reign, again in the *English Historical Review*.[6]

The trouble is that national bias has played a great part in the discussion. Until Dr Douglas made it impossible to ignore the French sources most historians took the French or English side. (The French monument on the site of the battle of Hastings is a *casus classicus* of nationalist fatuity.) In 1966 the nine-hundredth anniversary of the battle was celebrated, mostly orchestrated by General de Gaulle, as a great French victory over the English. In 1066 France did not exist – even in 1900 only about a third of the French spoke French. Duke William was the vassal of the French king, though that does not seem to have inhibited him much. King Harold was scarcely the prototype public school prefect Freeman imagined him to be. Grandson of a genuine quisling, his family had made their fortune by pillaging their neighbours. The only thing more absurd than Harold taking afternoon tea with the Queen at Balmoral would be William dining with President Mitterand at the Elysée Palace. If one sought a place where both would have been at home I cannot think of anywhere more congenial than former Yugoslavia or Afghanistan. It is pointless identifying with either side.

Having said that it is obvious that the reign of the Confessor was a very dangerous time for England. The king had no independent power base. His resources were only the royal demesne, and that was under the eye of Earl Godwin. He had considerable powers over the coinage, very lucrative powers, and these seem unlikely to have been taken over by Godwin. He was not going to have an heir, and it would have solved no problems if he had. When Edward married Edith it was clear that William would soon be the unquestioned master of Normandy. Edward thought highly of William, whom he had known all his life, and it only took the decisive victory of Val-ès-Dunes to make him determined to make William his heir. That could never be acceptable to the Godwins, who knew that William could only be a deadly enemy. There was no reason for Earls Leofric and Siward to fear a Norman succession, and the disparity between the fortunes of the Godwin family and the other two earls was becoming obvious and obviously growing. But the perceived dangers of an internal quarrel still held tensions in check, and some of the restraint was due to the king. I have said that the Confessor's reign was an enigmatic one. It will appear less so if we remember that the three greatest men in England had all taken part in the campaigns of Thorkell the Tall and Cnut. Many men had lost family and property in those campaigns and many still living could remember what a Viking campaign was like. In 1066 a man of sixty could have seen King Sweyn in person. Many knew how long those raids had being going on: the various recensions of the *Chronicle* would see to that. No one could be sure those days would not come back. Enigmatic or not, tremendous issues were decided by Edward's reign. If the king had had more of his way the decisions would have been much less painful except for the Godwin family and they were a cancer on the body politic that had to be cut out.

NOTES

1 Eric John, *Analecta Bollandiana*, 1981.
2 Sten Körner, *The Battle of Hastings: England and Europe*, Lund, 1964, p. 73: 'The possibility cannot be excluded that Hardacnut's sudden death at so early an age was a factor in a decided political plan.' I do not see that this can mean anything other than that Edward had Harthacnut poisoned.
3 I have argued my interpretation in some detail in 'Edward the Confessor and the Norman Succession', *English Historical Review*, 94, 1979, pp. 241–67. Pauline Stafford, *Unification and Conquest*, p. 93, offers a very different interpretation that seems to suffer from an excess of political naïveté. '1049–52', she writes, 'did not cause the dominance of Godwin's children. [What did? Sheer damned merit? – E.J.] Edward allowed Harold to succeed to his father's earldom in 1053 and advanced all his brothers during the 1050's and 60's.' Surely the wholly improbable assumption that these appointments were Edward's to give or withhold requires at least an attempt at proof? She has overlooked Stenton's remark (*Anglo-Saxon England*, p. 547), 'There was a natural tendency for a son to succeed a father in his earldom, and by the end of the Confessor's reign the houses which Godwine, Leofric, and Siward had raised to greatness were settled in power beyond the risk of any action that the king might take.' 'Edward did not have, perhaps did not seek, the freedom of manoeuvre Æthelred had exercised in the

990's' again requires something vulgarly known as evidence. What does Dr Stafford think Edward was doing in 1049–52?

4   'Edward the Confessor, Duke William of Normandy and the English Succession', *English Historical Review*, 68, 1953, pp. 526–43.

5   'Edward the Confessor's Promise of the Throne to Duke William of Normandy', *English Historical Review*, 72, 1957, pp. 221–8.

6   'Edward the Confessor and the Norman Succession', *English Historical Review*, 94, 1979, pp. 241–67.

CHAPTER II

Götterdämmerung

FOR THE FIRST TIME in Anglo-Saxon history we have a period with a variety of sources presenting different, sometimes conflicting, points of view. We can, in other words, construct a political narrative and make judgements in a modern sense that no previous reign would permit. I have already suggested that an interpretation of Edward's reign depends on a comparative evaluation of sources, partly comparing the English sources with the French sources but also comparing the English sources with each other. I mean taking account of the often radical differences in what they say and evaluating the significance of their often long periods of silence. The articles by Douglas and Oleson already mentioned have done much to clarify the reign by taking the French sources seriously. The latest full-length study of the reign, by Professor Frank Barlow, tends to revive the once traditional denigration of the French sources. By denying, sometimes but not always, Edward's vow of chastity he contrives to make the reign a concatenation of pointless quarrels by magnates full of pique.

Among the sources it is essential to begin with the *Vita Eadwardi*, superbly edited by Dr Barlow. I have already pointed out its resemblance to the *Encomium Emmae*. Its interpretation is further confused by the late split in the Godwin family between Harold and his brother Tostig. We know from Florence of Worcester that Queen Edith had a Northumbrian thegn opposed to Tostig murdered. One would not gather she was that kind of lady from her husband's biography, in which she plays a central role. At the end of the reign Harold came to terms with the Northumbrian rebels and threw his brother Tostig to the wolves. It is not surprising that the *Vita* is venom itself when dealing with Harold's behaviour at Edward's deathbed, which is not to say it was not telling the truth. It is also noticeable that Dr Barlow has shown that the book was begun soon after the fall of Tostig. It sounds as though Edith realised she needed what would now be called public relations, which Goscelinus was set to provide.

The most famous and most difficult source is what is conveniently, but misleadingly, called the *Chronicle*. For Edward's reign we depend on three recensions, C, D and E. Recension C is what is called elsewhere in this book the *Abingdon Chronicle*, with capitals when it is an Abingdon chronicle, without when it is an unplaced source from eastern England. It is vigorously opposed to the Godwins and lapses into silence at the time of their greatest ascendancy. The reasons for its attitude are a mystery. Earl Godwin was no enemy of Abingdon and tried to make its abbot, Spearhafoc, bishop of London. It looks like an expression of personal opinion. But annals are not normally personal or private things. The author is using the abbey's time and materials to write his book, and his fellow monks would normally read it or at least know what was in it. Unless the mood of the house was also to some degree anti-Godwinist it is difficult to see how the author got away with his opposition. The E text, by contrast, is pure Godwinist propaganda. The final version was written at Peterborough and is sometimes called the Peterborough Chronicle. Freeman, who approved of the Godwins, called its author 'the democrat of Peterborough'. It earned Freeman's approval because he saw Harold as a prototype Whig.[1] At the time it was being written at St Augustine's Canterbury. (The democrat of St Augustine's sounds even odder than the democrat of Peterborough.) For this reign the E text is a Canterbury text, and it sounds as if the community at St Augustine's, like the community at the cathedral, was pro-Godwinist. (The seat of the Godwin families' power lay in what is now East Sussex, but was historically part of the kingdom of Kent.) The D text is the shiftiest of the three. Its provenance is disputed and seems likely to have been either Worcester or York,[2] ruled for most of the reign by the same prelate, Ealdred. Worcester was far more of a literary centre than York. It certainly has information of a northern origin but Ealdred must have moved freely and fairly frequently between Worcester and York and some of his *familia* must have moved with him, so information could easily flow from north to south or vice versa. Archbishop Ealdred seems to have been a West Saxon. First abbot of Tavistock, then bishop of Worcester and archbishop of York in tandem, he survived the Conquest and continued to matter in the Conqueror's reign. He was never deposed, knew a great deal and concealed less than one would have imagined.

The best source is the post-Conquest chronicle usually known as Florence of Worcester. (The editors of the projected Cambridge edition of the *Chronicle* prefer to call him John of Worcester. Since they refused, on the grounds of customary usage, to change the title of the *Annals of St Neots*, although the annals in question have no connexion with that abbey, the attempt to drop the customary title Florence of Worcester for annals much more frequently cited than the *Annals of St Neots* savours of inconsistency.) Florence tells us most of what we know of the nastier side of Godwin rule in the north of England, and it must have come from Ealdred at first or second hand. Florence is much fuller and less discreet than the D text but he is writing after 1066 when the need for discretion had passed.

The E text is pure propaganda but propaganda on the hoof, as it were. There are few signs of hindsight. The French sources can only be called triumphalist. The main one is the *Gesta* of William of Poitiers. It is generally thought to be based on the inferior but still indispensable book by William of Jumièges (though no one has yet proved as much).[3] Triumphant parties do produce their own propaganda but William of Poitiers had neither anything to hide nor the need to lie. He does present Duke William winning the battle of Hastings like a Russian grand master winning a game of chess but a visit to the site of the battle suggests his version is certainly plausible and probably true. The best known feature of his account is how he got Harold to abandon the almost impregnable high ground where he had drawn up his troops, which William's cavalry could not take, by a feigned retreat. It seems to me that only by some such stratagem could the English have been delivered to the Norman archers, who did most of the harm. If ever there was a battle won by consummate generalship and lost by overweening self-confidence it was Hastings.

Another source is the Bayeux tapestry, a striking visual representation of the events that led up to the Conquest and the battle of Hastings. It was woven by order of William's half-brother, Odo, bishop of Bayeux. It used to be thought he intended it to be hung in his cathedral but it does contain matter nowadays known as adult viewing and it has been suggested it was meant for his banqueting hall. It is only two feet wide and I imagine it was more visible and more striking in the banqueting hall. Like all visual sources it presents problems. The danger is to treat it like a television newsreel. The designer had to make it clear at a glance which were Norman and which were English warriors. They are shown as wearing surprisingly similar armour but they have differently shaped shields and the English do not wear spurs. Whether this is historical truth or an artistic device is anyone's guess.

Having looked at the main sources, let us return to the politics of the reign. If, as seems certain, Edward was celibate on his accession (the main source is the *Vita Eadwardi*, whose source was the queen, so it seems good evidence), the succession problem was raised on the first day of his reign.

The *Vita* gives clear evidence that men were worried about the succession very early in his reign. Bishop Brihtwald of Wiltshire, whilst a guest at Glastonbury, of which house he had once been abbot, had a prophetic dream. He saw St Peter consecrate a decent man and a dedicated celibate as king. This is obviously the Confessor, who was consecrated at Old Minster, then dedicated to St Peter. The bishop died in 1045, a few weeks after Edward's marriage to Edith. The point of the vision is that the bishop asked St Peter who would reign over the English after the decent man's death. St Peter replied, not to worry: God had just the man in mind. There is no hint of who he might be. It defies belief that the author of the *Vita*, writing for an audience of courtiers, would have told a story like this if Edward were not celibate and known to be so. The author of the life wrote most of the book before Hastings. He is hedging his bets. He must have known there were only three possible candidates, Harold, William and the king of Norway (another Harold), whose chances seemed quite bright before he was killed at Stamford Bridge. His treatment of Harold at Edward's deathbed suggests his money was not on Harold.

Edward's attitude to Edith must be judged not on the idyllic picture of domestic bliss painted by the *Vita* but on how Edward treated her when he had a free hand. When he forced Godwin into exile he immediately had the marriage annulled and sent her to a convent presided over by his sister and that of the murdered Ælfred. The feud over Ælfred was never healed. When Edward thought he had ruined Godwin he brought up the matter of the murder again and his *Life* says he would have killed Godwin if he could have got hold of him.

Obviously there was no love lost between Edward and his father-in-law from the beginning but crises were avoided. One of Edward's first acts as king was to deprive his mother, now dowager queen twice over, of her money and her dignity. There is no evidence that Godwin was involved in this, although it is not likely they were at all friendly. Edward reckoned her chief and evil counsellor was Stigand, the recently created bishop of Elmham. Stigand first appears in history as head of the community Cnut founded to celebrate his victory at Ashingdon: there can be little doubt where his sentiments lay. By 1047 Stigand had become the successor of Æthelwold and Ælfheah at Winchester, now one of the richest sees in Christendom. As Stigand had a fair claim to be the worst bishop in Christendom, only Godwin could have forced his election. If Edward thought him bad enough to be ejected from Elmham he would never have appointed him to Winchester if he could have helped it.

The *Abingdon Chronicle* tells us that Abbot Siward of Abingdon was made coadjutor to Archbishop Eadsige of Canterbury on the advice of Earl Godwin. Such an appointment would have normally meant that Eadsige was unable to function for some reason, usually poor health. But in 1048 Siward was forced to resign because he was ill and Eadsige resumed his office as sole archbishop of Canterbury. The chronicler is clear there was a clandestine aspect to the affair but he does not say what it was. Siward was never reckoned among the successors of St Augustine. In spite of all this evidence of power, Godwin was never mayor of the palace: that was reserved for his son Harold. Godwin's eldest son, Sweyn, was a complete maverick and he seems to have been regarded as such even in his own family, since his younger brother Harold was preferred to him as earl of East Anglia, still probably a super-earldom.[4] It is unlikely that this display of power was welcome to Edward, nor were Leofric and Siward likely to have viewed the rise of the Godwins with equanimity. Sweyn killed a kinsman for reasons not at all clear and abducted an abbess. Harold acting as Jacob to Sweyn's Esau, headed the opposition to his brother, who was not surprisingly protected by the king. Edward's motives are obvious but he achieved little, since Sweyn, showing more sense than Tostig did at the end of the reign, remembered the adage the family that slays together stays together and, although his family had let him down, he stood by them in 1051.

It is probable that the accretion of power and wealth by the Godwins was unwelcome to Leofric and Siward and their families. From Domesday Book, which does not give the date of the acquisition of the estates it records but does give a picture of English land-holding 'on the day King Edward was living and dead', it is obvious that the Godwins were into property development on some scale. Harold held land in several Midland shires, though not in the Mercian heartland. What is astonishing is the amount of land he held in Yorkshire.

All this time the issue of the succession hung in the air. Edward was in theory only the head of a junior branch of the house of Cerdic. In theory again the head of the house on Æthelred's death was Edmund Ironside, and his role had now passed to his son Edward the ætheling. He had married into the imperial family and lived in Hungary as a leader of the pro-German faction at the Hungarian court. It is possible he could no longer speak English and it is doubtful whether he thought of himself as a candidate for the English crown. By 1047 Duke William had to be taken seriously as a possible successor to Edward. Few of the political class could fail to see the need for a new Norman alliance now that William was the master of his duchy. Such an alliance had been a centre point of English policy for the last half-century. Although no one stood to gain from such an alliance more than the West Saxons, the Godwins could not be expected to accept William as a possible future king. This was a weakness they never overcame. They could see as well as anybody the importance of a Norman alliance but they could never make an alliance with its duke. So the Godwins moved into Europe to thwart Norman power.

English historians are more familiar with the French political scene after 1066 and do not always realise how the events of that year transformed the French situation.[5] There are no natural features separating Normandy and the Ile de France and therefore no natural boundaries.[6] The French king and Norman duke were faced with a choice between alliance and total enmity. Before 1066 they did the sensible thing and were almost always allies. Early in the century one of the leading magnates of the duchy of Burgundy, Otto-William, was the son-in-law of the duke of the day. When the old duke died Otto-William tried to succeed him. But in the circumstances it was the right of the French king, Robert the Pious, to choose, and he was not going to choose a man who already held most of the Burgundian counties. Had Robert accepted his claims the French crown would have been reduced to a cypher. Robert did not give way but forced his own son on Burgundy. He succeeded only after years of a war won with the help of the Norman duke. Even then he was unable to destroy Otto-William, who, widowed, married into the Norman ducal family, who pressed Robert into making peace with him. The kings of France before 1066 looked to Blois–Champagne–Burgundy as their sphere of influence. Brittany, Flanders and Anjou were the sphere of activity of the dukes of Normandy, who were usually at enmity with all three. It was obvious in Duke William's early lifetime that if he did succeed Edward as king of England the delicate balance of French politics would be overturned. We know with the advantage of hindsight that, with the passage of time, the lifetime of William and his two younger sons, the Conquest benefited first the Angevins and then the Capetians, but no one could have foreseen that at the time.

Godwin saw that his natural ally was the count of Flanders, Baldwin. Baldwin married his daughter to Duke William, it is true, but that seems to have been something to fall back on, just in case. In either 1050 or 1051 he married his half-sister Judith to Godwin's son Tostig. Baldwin obviously wanted to keep the *status quo* and he worked for this by helping the Godwins, who without him must have been ruined in 1051. Baldwin sheltered Godwin during his period of exile and helped him make his comeback. In 1065 he received the recently exiled Tostig and made his joint venture with the Scandinavians possible. Not long before 1066, in a new departure, the French king formed an alliance with the count of Anjou that was clearly intended by both parties as a weapon against Duke William. The French sources praise Harold's skilful diplomacy; he presumably had a finger in all these pies. But diplomacy is not proof against the unexpected, as we shall see.

In 1050 Archbishop Eadsige died and Edward decided to make it clear he, not Godwin, was the ruler of England. Dr Douglas has shown that Edward had decided to make William his heir before Eadsige's death. The vacancy precipitated a crisis. The monks of Christ Church wished to elect as archbishop one of their number, who just happened to be related to Godwin. Godwin, of course, supported the monks. Edward overrode him and translated the bishop of London, Robert, to Canterbury. Robert was a Norman who had been abbot of Jumièges and was obviously the king's man, not Earl Godwin's, who proved it by ravaging the estates of Christ Church. This seems rather foolish. The monks were his allies. He may, however, have ravaged the estates of the archbishop, not those of the community. Edward was prepared to placate Godwin, or appear to, by appointing a Godwin ally, Abbot Spearhafoc of Abingdon, to succeed Robert at London. Godwin could not displace Robert, who left immediately for Rome to get his pallium – the ceremonial scarf that symbolised his metropolitical power and which it was now customary for archbishops of Canterbury to get from the Pope in person. He had to pass through Normandy, and Dr Douglas showed for the first time that Robert took the offer of the English succession to William. He returned with his pallium and the duke's acceptance of the English succession. He also informed Edward that he could not consecrate Spearhafoc as bishop of London because the Pope had rejected him as simoniac. I suspect, though I cannot prove, that this was what Edward wanted and expected to happen. Spearhafoc was not reinstated at Abingdon. The new abbot was a kinsman of the king and the new bishop of London another Norman monk. None of this, especially the offer of the succession, could have been done without the assent of Leofric and Siward. Edward had told his mother he would not be a candidate for the crown without the assent of the magnates. Unless Leofric and Siward had given their assent the offer was worthless, and William knew it.

The next move was the arrival in England of the king's brother-in-law, Count Eustace of Boulogne. We do not why he came but his visit was certainly significant. The late Professor R. Allen Brown suggested very plausibly that, just as late in the reign Harold promised to hand over Dover castle to William, a similar arrangement for Eustace to hold it on his behalf was made in 1051.[7] (I think this very likely, but Professor Brown had no right to say so, since he always maintained there were no castles in England before 1066.) The *burh* of Dover was on the site of the post-war castle, whose chapel was certainly pre-Conquest. By the time of Henry II Dover castle covered the whole site of the *burh*. The number of manuscripts of the Burghal Hidage which have survived shows that burhs were not simply replaced by castles after 1066. (Castles and burhs were not normally the same thing except in the case of Dover, where continuity between castle and *burh* seems abundantly clear.) If so, Godwin's situation was nearly desperate. If Count Eustace held the *burh* of Dover while one friendly bishop held London and another Canterbury (the most ancient and principal parts of the Canterbury estates were a solid block of land in eastern Kent), then the king's communications with Mercia and Northumbria were safe whilst Godwin's communications with his ally Count Baldwin were severed. The king was obviously bent on provoking a crisis and meant to get rid of the Godwins for good and all. The fact that he very nearly succeeded shows he had a good basis for his plans. I do not think that Edward expected the Godwins to submit tamely. His biographer suggests he intended to kill Earl Godwin. The king must have been ready to fight and he must have known he had allies. According to the D text Eustace's men got into a brawl with the men of Dover over billeting. The E text and Florence suggest something more significant was at issue.

After an encounter with the townsfolk, Eustace's men moved towards the *burh* of Dover. Serious fighting broke out between Eustace's men and the burhmen. Historians have been too ready to suppose that burhs and burhmen became boroughs and citizens before they did. In this case there is no ambiguity. We are in the world of fortresses and garrisons, not of local government units. The burhmen are identical with the *burgweard*, the men who manned the garrison. Eustace's men go up to the *burh*. Dover castle is on a cliff. Florence says Eustace's men actually got hold of the *burh* and some of them were Norman. It looks very much as though Professor Brown's conjecture is right. Godwin's situation was now desperate.

The king ordered Godwin as earl of Wessex to punish the men of Dover. This may be thought of as rubbing it in a bit. I doubt whether Edward expected Godwin to obey, and he did not. On 1 October Godwin and his elder sons, Sweyn and Harold, assembled an army at Tetbury, near Gloucester. Godwin probably sheered away from an open act of defiance but Edward, who must have been aware he had a strong hand, demanded the surrender of Count Eustace. He summoned Leofric and Siward to his aid. They joined him at Gloucester with their thegns. The D text has a most significant remark:

> Then some of them considered it to be a great folly if they joined battle because well-nigh all the noblest in England were present, and they were convinced they were leaving the country open to invasion, and be bringing utter ruin amongst ourselves.

Godwin's army faded away as he was preparing his counter-plea to the king at Southwark. Godwin then fled to Flanders to save his life; had Baldwin refused to receive him he must have been ruined. The next day the king held a *witenagemot*, a council, and all the *here* (a century earlier this would have meant a force of invading Vikings, with overtones of banditry – one of the earliest examples of a term of abuse, like 'fascist beast'; now it is a synonym for *fyrd*) declared Godwin an outlaw. Then followed the division of spoils which spells out that Edward had discussions with the other earls beforehand. The promise of William's succession was confirmed. Ælfgar, Leofric's son, was made earl of East Anglia in place of Harold, who had fled to Ireland. Edward's victory had a price. The re-creation of Greater Mercia, which the tenth-century kings had avoided, was now a serious possibility. At least for the time being Edward had solved the under-mighty king problem; he had not solved the over-mighty subject problem.

At this point the D text has an entry that has caused some quite unnecessary puzzlement. It says that William came over the Channel with a large company of Frenchmen and 'se cyning hine underfeng' and as many of his companions as suited him. Before Dr Douglas wrote, it could be argued that William came to be offered the succession. But there is no doubt that the succession had been offered and accepted some months earlier than William's visit. The succession was a cause of the crisis, not a consequence. How then to explain the duke's visit? Dr Douglas put it down to the annalist's imagination, as he thought William could not have left Normandy at that time. In his book on the battle of Hastings Dr Körner seems to have rebutted this argument. Dr Barlow seems to deny both the visit and the offer.[8] It is a weakness of his book that he never faces the question of the succession and on occasion leaves one unsure of what he thinks (but never of what he feels: little-English and anti-French). He seems inconsistent about Edward's celibacy and he is in two minds about the visit. He writes: 'If William came he probably came as a petitioner. He, like Eustace, wanted to know where he stood.' William's visit and the annal require more explanation than that, if it can be called an explanation.

It is usual to translate *underfeng* as 'received'. The King is supposed to have received William and some of his men like a lot of debutantes at a royal ball. The annalist obviously thought the visit was important and he stressed that Edward 'received' some of William's men but not others. *Underfon* and its cognate *onfon* have a revealing use in legal and political contexts and the annal seems to fall under both headings. Ælfred 37.2 deals with the case of a man who wishes to leave one district for another and to take a new lord. The law assumes the petitioner is up to no good and if he committed an offence before he left his old district his new lord will have to pay a fine and compensation. The new lord is defined as the man who has received (*onfo*) the man as his vassal. In a law of Edward the Elder no man may receive (*underfeh*) another man's vassal without leave. In one of Ælfric's best lives, that of Oswald of Northumbria, he says Oswald's kingdom had become so large that four peoples received him as lord: *se thæt feower theoda hine underfengen to hlaford*. What the D text is saying in clear enough Anglo-Saxon is that Edward received William and some of his men as his vassals. There is corroboration in the French sources. William of Poitiers makes William call Edward 'my lord and kinsman' in his statement of William's claim to the English crown. No emphasis is put on the vassalic relationship, which did not affect the claim either way. Neither a Norman duke nor a Norman archdeacon would have referred to Edward as William's lord unless William had done him homage and fealty. This was not mere ceremony. Edward did not propose to give away the English succession for nothing. William now owed Edward service and loyalty to be rendered when the King saw fit. At the very least no Viking fleet would be received in Normandy (and the king of Norway had some sort of claim to succeed Edward which he came very near to translating into fact). He could hope for help against the count of Flanders should he turn difficult and he probably had in mind military aid if Godwin tried to make a come-back.

In the event Godwin reappeared in England in 1052. He got sufficient support from the West Saxon thegns to make civil war possible. Leofric and Siward cannot have wanted Godwin's restoration. It meant certain humiliation for Leofric's son Ælfgar, who would be expelled from East Anglia with his tail between his legs. (He was.) But Godwin was desperate, since he faced certain ruin, was prepared for civil war if necessary and had the means. The other earls were no more prepared for civil war than they had been the year before and gave way. Dr Oleson pointed to a significant statement in William of Poitiers that Leofric and Siward recognised the Norman succession. It would be natural to refer this to 1051 –

life would be much easier for historians of the Norman Conquest if William of Poitiers gave dates. He also claimed that Godwin and Archbishop Stigand recognised the succession too. But Stigand was intruded into Canterbury only after Godwin's restoration. If we believe William, and I see no reason why we should not, Godwin's restoration was conditional. Godwin, at least at first, accepted the Norman succession – the king's face needed saving – but I doubt if anyone expected Godwin would abide by it. His expulsion of Archbishop Robert and his replacement by a corrupt pluralist was an act of pure folly. It made an implacable enemy of the reforming papacy, and that was to be a factor in 1066. The strength of the case for believing William is that his man won and when he wrote the attitude of Edward's long-dead earls did not matter. Duke William won England by right of conquest but his victory was legitimated by Edward's bequest, by the Pope himself and by consecration at the hand of shifty Archbishop Ealdred.[9]

Dr Oleson, then, is I think right in arguing that the Godwins accepted the Norman succession in order to secure an easier restoration. William of Poitiers has a further claim on our belief. He says Godwin handed over his young son, Wulfnoth, and his great-nephew as hostages. Wulfnoth was still in William's hands in 1087, and as he is the only member of his family not provided for in Domesday Book he must have been very young when he fell into William's power. All this shows that Edward did have the timorous support of the other earls: the conditions could not have been imposed without it. I think their support was timorous not because it was half-hearted but from fear of Godwin.

There is also the Continental dimension to be considered. If Count Baldwin had not supported Godwin, Godwin would have been ruined. If William had intervened in 1052 he would have risked having all northern France against him.

Earl Harold was duly reinstated as earl of East Anglia but in 1053 Godwin died and Harold became earl of Wessex. Ælfgar was reinstated in East Anglia. Harold was not yet all-powerful but another Godwin was made a subordinate earl there. As the second generation of the great Anglo-Danish families came to power the opposition between them grew stronger. In 1055, wasting no time, Harold got Ælfgar deprived of his earldom and sent him into exile. The E text says he was guilty as charged, the C text says he was innocent and the D text that he was exiled almost without having done anything.

Just before Ælfgar's exile Earl Siward died. He has earned immortality by his brief appearance in Shakespeare's *Macbeth*. Although of Danish origin and appointed by Cnut, Siward had been an appeasing earl of Northumbria. The Anglo-Danish element in Northumbria and Siward's power base lay in what had once been Deira. The northern Northumbrians were mainly of English descent and lived in what was once Bernicia. Siward courted them. He married into the house of Bamburgh and his youngest son and eventual heir was given the very English name of Waltheof. One important task of the earls of Northumbria was to keep the Scots out. This was particularly important to the English Northumbrians, as they stood between the Scots and the Danish south. Siward, of course, was a contemporary of Macbeth, whose character and situation were not quite as Shakespeare represented them. The civil war in Scotland made Siward's task very much easier, since the Scots were too busy killing each other to have time for raiding Northumbria. Yet when ordered by the king to destroy Macbeth he obeyed, losing his eldest son in the ensuing battle. Whether or not Edward gave the order – more probably Harold did, as he was now the single most powerful individual in England – it does show that the southern government had real power in the north. If Harold gave the order it was probably designed to weaken Siward and Leofric still further. Harold was now moving against the other earls.

As Siward died just before Ælfgar's exile, leaving only a boy as his heir, Harold without difficulty appointed his younger brother earl of Northumbria. Indeed, Ælfgar's exile may have been a consequence of this. Ælfgar was not in exile for long. He secured Welsh and Irish support and ravaged Herefordshire. Harold led an army against him but Ælfgar took up a near impregnable position in the Black Mountains and Harold came to terms. Ælfgar got his earldom back but in 1057 Leofric died and Ælfgar succeeded him as earl of Mercia. The same year saw the death of Earl Ralf of Hereford, who though a relative of the king (that was why he was appointed) had gone completely over to the Godwins. Harold simply added his earldom on to Wessex. East Anglia, given up by Ælfgar when he succeeded his father, was divided in two and both earls were members of Godwin's family. In 1058 Earl Ælfgar was exiled yet again. The English sources say he led an expedition and secured restoration. He had Irish and Welsh allies and the help of a large Norwegian fleet. The Welsh annals stress the scale of the attack and say that England was ravaged. Ælfgar secured his position by marrying the daughter of one the most powerful Welsh princes, Gryffyd. The Welsh princes were the traditional enemies of the rulers of Mercia but in the middle of the eleventh century they were the ruler's only recourse against their new enemy, the earl of Wessex. Mercia's position was now being eroded as it became more obviously encircled by

Harold's growing authority. He had taken over the earldom of Hereford; the see, too, fell vacant and he gave it to one of his house priests. Oswaldslow was in the hands of Ealdred, who had let Harold escape to Ireland in 1051. It seems certain that Ælfgar died in 1062, though no source mentions it. He left two very young sons, Edwin and Morcar (Morkere more correctly but less familiarly) and Edwin succeeded him as earl of Mercia: but he was too young to play an independent role. The silence of the sources on the death of a man so important as Ælfgar and the obvious hatred his sons felt for Harold and his family make his death sound suspicious. Harold had found that he could not evict Ælfgar because of the harm he could do. His death was very convenient for Harold, who was now virtually the mayor of the palace.

It is obvious he had already repudiated the Norman succession. In 1054 Ealdred, the Godwins' respectable ecclesiastical tool, was sent on a mission to Germany to negotiate for a new heir. In theory Stigand was the senior English ecclesiastic as bishop of Winchester and archbishop of Canterbury but he had been excommunicated by the Pope for his intrusion into Canterbury and was not recognised outside England. It is likely that Harold felt he could not become a candidate for the crown himself. As Sir Frank Stenton pointed out,[10] as long as Ælfgar lived Harold could not hope to succeed. One of the weaknesses of the English law of succession from Harold's point of view was the power of the reigning king to nominate his successor even on his deathbed. I doubt whether Harold ever thought he could be Edward's choice. What Harold needed was a potential puppet. The obvious candidate was Edward the ætheling, the king's half-nephew. He was related to the Salians by birth and marriage and was a prominent member of a group seeking to augment German influence in Hungary. If he could speak English at all it is unlikely he could speak it very well. But it probably seemed to Harold he might do for defeating the claims of the duke of Normandy.

The negotiations were not speedy. Edward had been an important German magnate. His power now was not what it had been, but it is unlikely he was eager to exchange it for the prospect of ruling England as Harold's puppet. But Edward's position in the empire was deteriorating. After an almost certain visit to Flanders by Earl Harold he returned to England in 1057. The sources closest to Ealdred, who had been the chief negotiator, the D text and Florence all state plainly that Edward had returned because he was to be the new heir to the throne. The author of the D text says Edward was not allowed to see the king but he does not know why not. Only Harold or the king himself could have prevented their meeting but Harold had planned and effected the Ætheling's return. It must have been Edward who refused to see him, and that means he had not given up the Norman succession. The Ætheling died about the same time as Earl Leofric, and Harold and Stigand were left as the only ones who had sworn an oath to William.

It is obvious from the *Chronicle* that a sea change had occurred in Harold's position and everyone must have known it. The Abingdon chronicler falls silent. The two main, still voluble texts, D and E, are little more than accounts of the comings and goings of Harold and Tostig. After the death of Ælfgar, the Godwins dominated England from the Channel to the Border and Harold dominated the Godwins. The English must have expected that Harold would succeed Edward. This brings us to the last crisis of the reign, which has been the subject of some cavalier and capricious interpretation by modern historians. No one has attempted to explain the attitude of Queen Edith in the last months of the reign and the extraordinary venom of her encomiast towards Stigand and Harold in his account of Edward's deathbed.

It is generally accepted that at some point Harold did, as the Norman sources say he did, visit Duke William personally and swear to accept him as Edward's successor. To reject this would be to reject the virtually contemporary evidence of William of Poitiers, an allusion to Harold's oath in the *Vita Eadwardi* and the clear evidence of the Bayeux tapestry. Wherever the tapestry was hung, it was very visible and would have been seen by many who knew that it was telling downright lies if the oath and the meeting it depicts had not taken place. William of Poitiers felt about dates like T. E. Lawrence, who cited only one date in his Oxford history finals paper, 'about the middle of the eleventh century (1066)', but although he gives us little help with the date of Harold's visit, it seems impossible that it took place before 1064. This was Stenton's opinion and the date he preferred. In 1064 if Edward had died only Harold Hardrada could have challenged Harold Godwinsson's succession and the events of 1066, when he did try, suggest he would not have succeeded. All England, or that part of it that took an interest in such matters, must have known that Harold would seek the succession. Consequently we need a reason why Harold committed political suicide by going to William and performing this ruinous ritual. In 1064 there was no reason at all.

It is surely common sense that Harold went only because the king forced him to, unless one believes with Dr Barlow[11] that the idea of succeeding Edward never occurred to him until it was put there by Edward on his deathbed. I find this incredible. In many ways Dr Barlow is the true heir of Freeman, and there are worse things to be. The events of 1065 begin to offer an explanation. From spring to high summer Harold was occupied campaigning in Wales, when in late August a sudden Welsh attack had some success. The D text hints at a wider conspiracy. About a month later, whilst Tostig was with the king in Wiltshire, there was an uprising in Northumbria. A group of Northumbrian thegns mostly connected with the late Earl Siward, and thus likely to contain men of English and Viking descent, killed as many of Tostig's men as they could lay hands on. Without asking the king they invited Morcar, Earl Edwin's younger brother, to be their earl. The two brothers faced Harold at Northampton and then Oxford and made it clear that unless he accepted Morcar as earl of Northumbria there would be civil war. We are back in 1052 with the roles reversed. Harold did the statesmanlike thing – as so often a recipe for disaster – and threw Tostig over. The fact that Edwin and Morcar were prepared to risk civil war and a certain Norwegian invasion shows how desperate they felt their situation to be and how bitterly the English establishment was divided. Tostig was an abler man than his maverick brother Sweyn – who had died on a penitential pilgrimage to the Holy Land, traditionally barefoot. But in the last resort Sweyn had more sense than Tostig. Though written off by his family, and in Professor Garmonsway's splendid translation of the *Chronicle* 'having cooked his goose in Denmark', he saw that the Godwins stood or fell together. Tostig did not. He was mistaken. It cost him his life in 1066 and helped ensure that Harold fell at Hastings and most of his family with him.

It is clear from the *Vita Eadwardi* that the queen took Tostig's side. It does say that the king was very cross with Edwin and Morcar and would have led an expedition against them if the weather had not been so inclement. It also mentions, as the *Chronicle* did in 1052, the English fear of civil war, and the blunt fact that the English thegns would not fight to restore Tostig. The event seemed to create a permanent breach between Edith and Harold. Florence, who could only have got his information from Ealdred, or sources very close to the archbishop, says Tostig was unpopular because he sought to impose a more centralised authority on Northumbria and with some brutality at that. He also says that at Tostig's behest the queen had arranged the murder of a Northumbrian thegn called Gospatric, a prominent member of the house of Bamburgh. The whole Godwin family suffered from a marked lack of charm. Gospatric had been an important man, a connexion of the late Earl Siward, whose followers now controlled Northumbria. The queen, probably the only hit-woman to have sat on the English throne, was in grave danger. I have already cited

Stenton's account of the Northumbrian feud that had occurred only a generation earlier. Feuds still mattered, especially Northumbrian ones. If
Harold had done his duty to his kindred there would have been civil war.
He had preferred to abandon Tostig, who was his right-hand man. How
much less likely was he to fight for his sister? The Norman sources say that
Edith was in favour of the Norman succession. The tone of the closing
pages of the *Vita Eadwardi* is some confirmation: in any case the succession
of William the Conqueror was her safest option.

The effect on Harold's position was disastrous. Had Edward died six
months earlier than he did, I do not think either William or Harold
Hardrada could have prevented Harold's succession. Even the Northumbrians might in the end have preferred Tostig to the Norwegians. The *Vita*
says that Edward was fond of Tostig but its author speaks for the queen all
the time. He does not say that Edward was fond of Harold, and he mentions Edward's partiality for Tostig only when Tostig is in the process of
dealing Harold a mortal blow, just after Harold had dealt Tostig a mortal
blow. Edward had constantly been humiliated by the Godwins: his position was in many ways worse than his father's. Æthelred had actually made
policy, if not very successfully, but except for the one year 1051 Edward
was little, if anything, more than a figurehead. Though, and this speaks
much for him, he was never a puppet. For that one year he was his own
man and it seems to me that what he did as a free agent should serve to
control our ideas about his wishes and intentions. But now, as a result of
the Northumbrian revolt, Edward was a free agent once more and king
again, coming very near to the end of his life. Old and frail, with only
weeks to live, only one issue mattered – the succession. Willing to wound,
and not afraid to strike, he was determined that Harold was not going to
have it. Morcar and Edwin could only have lived a precarious life under
King Harold. That Edward hated the Godwins seems to me obvious but
his judgment was not entirely inflamed by hatred. He saw, I think, that
King Harold's reign would not have done the English much good. The
split between north and south, the impossibility of trust and confidence
between the house of Leofric and the house of Godwin, would have
meant another generation of the English house divided against itself.
Edward had the initiative and Harold had no choice but obedience. In the
circumstances I believe Edward forced Harold to go to Normandy and do
homage to Duke William.

Chronology is all important. The king died early in January 1066 and
the line of the Woden-descended kings passed into history.[12] He sent
Harold to Normandy soon after Tostig's flight to Flanders, which means

he must have left soon after 1 November 1065. William of Poitiers says that Harold came to Normandy when Edward was ill and not expected to live long. The *Vita Eadwardi* says Edward was taken ill at the council of Oxford when Tostig was exiled and never recovered. William of Poitiers in any case excludes most of the early part of 1065. He tells us that William took Harold with him on a campaign in Brittany to attach him to his person and remarks that the corn was still green and there was a shortage of food. A normal harvest would be gathered in late August or early September. It would be late September before the harvest was written off. I imagine William hoped Edward would die while Harold was still with him, although, had he done so, whilst Harold would have had to observe the terms of their agreement so would William. Under the circumstances a very tight time schedule was what we should expect.

William of Poitiers says Harold did homage to William and became his man. The Bayeux tapestry depicts both the homage and the oath of fealty in graphic detail. Harold as William's vassal owed him military service and he had to accompany William to Brittany and help him capture the castle of Dinan from Conan of Brittany. The term of service owed by a vassal to his lord in Normandy was forty days. William could not detain Harold any longer. It is obvious that the north French establishment was not in favour of William's promotion. The count of Flanders, though William's father-in-law, supported the Godwins to the end. The king of France made a treaty with the count of Anjou that can only have been aimed at William. I do not think William dared detain Harold longer than custom and tradition allowed.

William of Poitiers says that Harold was richer than William: since Normandy is only about the size of East Anglia and Harold held land in most parts of England, this is certainly true. English society was more hierarchical than Norman. It is sometimes said that William replaced a class of Anglo-Saxon landholders with a mere two hundred tenants-in-chief. This is based on Domesday Book but it is misleading. The majority of landholders named in Domesday book were not men of the king. It is very dangerous to equate the English landholders of Domesday with the tenants-in-chief. There were nothing like two hundred men of the topmost class in Anglo-Saxon England. The power elite was very small indeed. The reduction in the number of earls had led to the growth of the office of shire reeve or sheriff. Its holders were important and locally powerful men, and there was usually one per shire. But they were not aristocrats. English magnates did not marry sheriffs' daughters. Bishop Odo of Bayeux and Count Robert of Mortain were both closely related to a *vicomte*, the Norman equivalent of a sheriff. Harold I had been, like William the Conqueror, a bastard but his mother was as indubitably upper-class as William's mother was lower-class.

In return for Harold's homage William also made him promises. He was to be regent. He was to fortify a number of fortresses. Dover castle was the most important of them. William's own men were to garrison these castles but Harold must fortify and provision them. In return William recognised Harold's position and his fortune. None of this came to pass. Edward died very soon after Harold's return and Harold repudiated his allegiance to William, which, I imagine, surprised nobody.

Edward died in the first week of January 1066 and by All Saints' day the same year the Godwins had passed into history. We can recover something of what happened at Edward's deathbed and make an attempt at reconstructing Harold's claim to the succession and what he based it on. The first witness is William of Poitiers. We might have expected a venomous account but William seems to be fair and makes Harold offer the best case he could have made. Indeed, it is probably the case Harold did make. Harold admits that Edward had once made William his heir and that he had himself sworn oaths to William. But *in extremis* Edward had changed his mind and named Harold himself. Since the days of St Augustine English law had held that the last will should have the force of law. There is no doubt that the dying king did have an important say in who should succeed him. But it is unlikely that Æthelred II nominated Edmund (he may well have promised Emma that her son should succeed) and Cnut did name Harthacnut but without success. Harold is claiming that he, like William, is resting his claim on the king's donation but his was the latest donation and should prevail. The C and D texts are not without ambiguity if one is determined to do one's best to believe Harold. They use the same words: 'Yet the wise ruler entrusted the kingdom to a man of high rank, Harold himself.' This seems to me to mean that Edward had carried out the policy agreed between Harold and William and made Harold regent: it could just mean he gave Harold the kingdom. On an issue so important I think that if C and D had meant this they would have said it without ambiguity. The E text is ever the Godwin's propaganda sheet and says that Harold succeeded to the realm just as Edward had granted it to him. Given the nature of the E text, this must mean that that is what Harold was claiming, which is what William of Poitiers says he was.

William of Poitiers also sets out William's reply to Harold. He does not deny Edward's last-minute change of heart. I doubt if William believed Harold here, but he could offer no disproof. Harold was William's man, and that meant he must obey his lord. He must, so William claimed, carry out his agreement. The matter was bound to be settled by battle but it is not without point to look at the law. By the time of Henry II and Glanvil's law book deathbed bequests were illegal and Harold would have had no case. But long before the Conquest the dialogue attributed to Ecgberht of York shows that deathbed donations were viewed with suspicion and mistrust. A single priest could not serve to prove the genuineness of such bequests: 'so that in the mouth of two or three witnesses every word may be established, for perchance the avarice of kinsfolk would contradict what was said by the clergy were but one priest or deacon present'.

There was already suspicion, then, about deathbed bequests, and English law insisted on witnesses (in the plural). William is saying that Harold's act of homage annulled anything Edward may have said on his deathbed: the act of vassalage was crucial. Much contemporary opinion, especially French opinion, would have been sympathetic here.

However, in scrutinising Harold's claim we have a virtually contemporary account of what happened at Edward's bedside in the *Vita Eadwardi*. Dr Barlow has shown that the book was begun before the fall of Tostig and was being written when Edward was still alive. Most of the book was written before the death of Edward, and the whole book was complete before the papal legate deposed Stigand in 1070. It is not clear whether the author was actually present. He says that the queen, Harold, Stigand and Robert fitz Wimarch (who was made sheriff of Essex by William), and a few unnamed persons the king had sent for, were at the king's bedside. The author is giving the queen's version, and she was not for Harold.

Edward made a puzzling prophecy about a green tree. No one has convincingly explained what he meant. One suspects that had the deathbed scene been written up after Hastings there would have been some 'clarification'. The *Vita* says everyone was terrified by the prophecy. They all knew they were entering a very dangerous era but their fear suggests that they knew what Edward meant. Only Stigand stayed unmoved and said the old man was rambling. The author then does something completely out of character. He launches a violent, personal and emotional attack on the archbishop. The English Church is corrupt and Stigand is the root of its corruption. Although Stigand deserved every word of this abuse, its appearance in an author usually so discreet, not to say unctuous, is surprising. Only Stigand's predecessor, Robert of Jumièges, is treated to a similar diatribe, probably occasioned by his annulment of the queen's marriage and his complicity in despatching her to a more than usually unpleasing convent. It must be borne in mind that all this was written in Harold's reign, before he knew Harold was finished. Edward, we are told, first commended Edith to Harold's protection. In view of the murder of Gospatric she probably needed it. The *Vita* then comes very close to the two chronicle texts: 'I commend to you the protection of the whole kingdom.' The author knew by the time he was writing what Harold based his claim on but he does not say Edward named Harold his successor. Harold was to protect Edward's faithful French servants, either taking fealty from them if they wanted to stay or allowing them to depart if they did not, taking with them what they had. As the property was plainly portable they must have been comparatively small people. There is no mention of any long-term measures: Edward's dying speech was addressed to the interregnum. Now English law required witnesses in the case of deathbed bequests. The sole clerical witness was Stigand, but Stigand had been excommunicated by the Pope. Worse, he had twice said the old man was rambling. It cannot be said that there is much support here for Harold's case.

Edward the ætheling had left a son whom no one, save Edwin and Morcar momentarily, took seriously. Not even the Conqueror thought of him as a potential rival. He found refuge at the Scottish court, where his sister, St Margaret, married the Scottish king. She had no animus against the Normans. She corresponded with Archbishop Lanfranc and encouraged Norman influence in Scotland. Her daughter married Henry I. Her grandfather was Edmund Ironside and her great-grandson Henry II, so the house of Cerdic did not quite disappear from English history, though the house of Godwin did.

Harold had to face claims from two directions if he were to keep his crown. There was Duke William, of course, but also Harold Hardrada, king of Norway, whose claim was based on a treaty with Harthacnut. The bases of that claim may be thought tenuous but the Norwegian king probably knew that Harold II had no great hold on the affections of the English, particularly in the Midlands and the north. He gathered a considerable fleet and was joined by Tostig, who cannot have had many troops, but he was an embarrassment to his brother and he probably had good local knowledge of the north. What Tostig hoped to gain beyond revenge is not easy to see. Would he have got more out of Harold III than he did out of Harold II? It is hard not to feel that Tostig pursued a foolish and short-sighted policy.

Even with the threat of a Norwegian invasion hanging over them, a threat that must fall on them first, the Northumbrians accepted Harold only with reluctance, and only after a tour of persuasion by Bishop Wulf-

stan of Worcester. Duke William also raised an army. His now great reputation as a warrior, and the prospect of rich pickings from so great a prize
as the English crown, brought unemployed knights on the make flocking
to him. His northern French neighbours could do nothing. The king of
France was a boy and the county of Anjou was in a state of civil war. The
count of Flanders supported Tostig, who was his half brother-in-law, but
not Harold, apparently. William was his son-in-law. I imagine Baldwin
did not chose to intervene against William on his own.

William had all the luck. The wind that kept his fleet manned by many
non-Normans as well as Normans in port blew the Norwegian armada to
England and destruction. The English fleet in the Channel dispersed, the
sailors more or less mutinied and nothing barred William from a safe arrival
on the English coast. The Norwegians arrived and Edwin and Morcar had
to bear the full weight of their assault. They chose to make a stand at Fulford on the Ouse, a little to the south of York. They were heavily
defeated on 20 September 1066 and the men of York made peace with the
Norwegians on terms that showed they cared little for King Harold. Since
the Norwegians realised that they had sympathisers in Northumbria
(though they cannot have been prepared to tolerate Tostig), they delayed
marching south for some days after the battle, hoping to pick up recruits.
That was fatal. They resumed their march south and reached Stamford
Bridge probably on the evening of the 24th. Harold, after a remarkable
march, arrived with his whole army, entered York, caught them unaware
on the 25th and destroyed their whole army. It was the most shattering
defeat ever inflicted on a Scandinavian army. Both Harold Hardrada and
Tostig were killed. Stamford Bridge compares with Lechfeld as a decisive
battle.

Stamford Bridge was fought on a Monday. The following Wednesday
the wind changed and William embarked with his fleet. They were supposed to be guided by William's ship, which had a lantern affixed to a
mast. The ship was a new one, given to him by his wife. Its quality, particularly its speed, had not been appreciated and at dawn William had outsailed his fleet. Had there been an English fleet around he could well have
been killed or captured. As it was, he was able to call for breakfast and wait
for his fleet to catch up. On the morning of Thursday, 28 September 1066
his army disembarked without opposition at Pevensey. He then moved to
Hastings. All the time he bore in mind the importance of staying near his
ships.

It is probable that Harold was in York when he heard that William had
landed. Within a fortnight Harold had completed his settlement of the

north and covered the nearly two hundred miles from York to London. He managed to raise more troops and by a fifty-mile march bring them to a point near Hastings. But the speed of his march meant he could not summon his full army. Florence said he left London with only half of it. His speed of movement has been praised but his strategy faulted because he joined battle too quickly. But William was in the very heart of Godwin territory and Harold could not let his tenants be ravaged, a fact William must have been fully aware of. William marched from Hastings on 13 October to Telham Hill, the highest point of the nine miles that separates Hastings from what is now Battle. Here William learned that Harold had taken the high ground at the other end of the valley that separated them. It does not seem that when the Norman knights attacked the English army they could dislodge them from the high ground. Harold had chosen a superb defensive position but he was not William's equal as a general. William organised a feigned retreat and it drew the English off their strong position. I used to be sceptical of the feigned retreat until I visited the bat-tlefield. On that site it was a perfectly plausible manoeuvre and probably the only way the English could have been drawn to destruction. (It must also have been a fiendishly difficult manoeuvre to bring off.) It seems to have been the archers who did the damage, and it still seems probable that Harold was killed by an arrow that pierced his eye.

It was a complete and final victory. Noticeably neither Edwin nor Morcar made the faintest effort to help Harold in the south. They are sometimes excused of lack of patriotism on the grounds that Fulford and Stamford Bridge had exhausted them. They had lost many men but Edwin and Morcar still had able-bodied troops. You do not take rest days in a war. But patriotism is irrelevant here. I do not think Edwin and Morcar cared a jot for Harold and I can think of no reason why they should have. William now had no rival as king of England. Edwin and Morcar made a play at supporting Edgar the ætheling but they soon dropped him and tried cultivating William, who did not cultivate them back. Edwin was mur-dered by his own troops. Morcar fled to the fens to join Hereward the Wake and was never heard of again.

William's accession was a much less bloody affair than Cnut's. Apart from harrying the north, which was very cruel but had plenty of Anglo-Saxon precedents, William was not a cruel man. He inherited two mem-bers of the old establishment. The first was Waltheof, son of Earl Siward, whom he made earl of Northumbria in 1072 and allowed to marry his niece. The other was Ralf, the son of the Confessor's Breton minister, Ralf the Staller. William made the elder Ralf earl of East Anglia early in his reign and allowed his son to succeed him in 1069 or 1070. In 1075 Ralf, Waltheof and Earl Roger of Hereford went into rebellion. It is clear they had no very great following but not why they rebelled. It is possible that William had new notions about what an earl's function was and the three earls found themselves by traditional standards underemployed. William's earls were mostly great magnates but their power came from their wealth and the title 'earl' was more honorary than real. Their rebellion was easily suppressed. Ralf fled to his native Brittany. Roger when caught was tried according to Norman law, deprived of his lands and imprisoned. Waltheof was tried according to English law and beheaded. He was the only prominent Englishman killed by the Conqueror and he had undoubtedly committed treason.

The year 1066 was a tragic one for the Godwin family, when Harold performed a great service to his countrymen by crushing the Vikings (*pace* Freeman the only service the Godwins did anyone except themselves) in a final defeat. But it was not a tragic year for the English. William was the ablest candidate to succeed the Confessor and the only one able to cut the Gordian knot that was strangling the English body politic. What would King Harold's reign have been like? It seems unlikely that rivalry with the house of Leofric would have abated. Normandy would have been implacably hostile and the Danes would have come again. The last Danish expedition set out for England towards the end of the Conqueror's reign and dispersed without landing. I do not think they would have done that if Normandy had been friendly. We must not speculate idly but it is fair to say that the prognosis for a reign of King Harold was not favourable. If Edward was a 'holy simpleton' England could have done with a few more of them. Without resources, amid great difficulties, he formed a clear policy about the greatest problem of the day and in the very end he got his way. The Godwins were a great and powerful family and Harold was a great and powerful man, but Edward ruined them and him.

NOTES

1 The University of Manchester acquired Freeman's books. Amongst them was a decoration awarded him by King Alexander Obrenovitch of Serbia (or Servia as it was then known) for his championship of the rights of small nations. Alexander Obrenovitch was few people's idea of a democrat.

2 The D text must have some connexion with Worcester, see I. Atkins, 'The Church of Worcester from the Eighth to the Twelfth Century', 2, *Antiquaries' Journal*, 20, 1940, pp. 1–38: it also has some information about the north of England and Scotland. It is obvious that this can be explained by the intermittent connexion between the sees of Worcester and York 972–1062. It would be most likely that D was a Worcester text

with some information from York or vice versa. Dr Whitelock, *Peterborough Chronicle*, Copenhagen, 1954, p. 28, and Dr D. C. Douglas, 'Edward the Confessor', have suggested on the strength of the annal for 1051 that D is a northern source. This annal is about the greatest political crisis of the reign, when Edward temporarily exiled the Godwins from England. Edward was able to do this because he got the support of Earls Leofric and Siward: 'and the people all over these northern parts were called out thither in Siward's earldom and Leofric's'. Dr Whitelock and Dr Douglas seem to think the reference to these northern parts prove the D text is of northern provenance. But its centre of reference is Gloucester, and Mercia is included in 'these northern parts'. If this annal proves anything it points to a southern, not a northern, origin. Dr C. P. Wormald has recently reopened the debate in his Deerhurst Lecture for 1991, pp. 12 *et seq.* He rehearses most of what there is to rehearse and still plumps for a northern origin, though he agrees it cannot be York. His suggestions for other northern venues are tentative and to my mind totally unconvincing. His objection to Worcester rests mainly on the lack of reference to St Wulfstan but for most of his pontificate Wulfstan was on decidedly cool terms with his cathedral community over an important dispute resolved only on his deathbed. I have examined the lawsuit in detail in a forthcoming article 'The Church of Worcester and St Oswald'. Dr C. R. Hart, private communication, thinks there is a Ramsey connexion with the D text.

The best recent discussion of this question is R. H. C. Davis, *From Alfred the Great to Stephan*, London, 1991, pp. 105 *et seq.* I do not find the late Professor Davis's estimate of the plausibility of William of Poitiers correct or fair. He singles out William of Poitiers's considerable knowledge of classical literature as important – here he is obviously right – but makes it the ground of an attack on William's accuracy and credibility. He thinks William 'turned to the Trojan War as the most famous of seaborne invasions' as a model for his account of the Conqueror's seaborne expedition'. The Conqueror had fewer than fifty miles to sail and the campaign achieved complete success in one battle after a few days in the field. It may be, and probably was, [true] that the Conqueror's fleet was becalmed at St Valèry as Agamemnon's had been at Aulis, and that in each case a divinity had to be placated.' But the gross disproportion between the rituals the Conqueror resorted to in order to gain a favourable wind and Agamemnon's sacrifice of Iphegenia do not suggest to me any parallel here.

It is well known that Duke William in a new ship was supposed to be leading his fleet when, miscalculating the speed of the ship, he outsailed them. He, according to Professor Davis, 'subdued the crew's alarm, by settling down to a banquet'. He thinks 'we cannot help wondering whether WP was not too conscious that that was what Aeneas had done when he was shipwrecked on the coast of Africa'. But William was not shipwrecked, merely slightly inconvenienced. I do not think William of Poitiers meant to imply a banquet, the Duke was after all at sea. The late Allen Brown said he showed what in the last war were called officer-like qualities and called for his breakfast. This seems to me nearer to what William of Poitiers actually said. The urge to exaggerate this sort of episode seems to be perennial. In a recent French cookery book I found the claim that Duke William invented the gourmet dish *sole à la Normande* for this occasion. A critic suggested that if the duke did have soles for breakfast on this occasion they were probably boiled in a bucket.

'Similarly when the Conqueror is made to refuse Harold's mother's permission to bury her son, even though she offered his weight in gold, one cannot help feeling that the reality was WP's memory of Achilles and the body of Hector.' But Professor Davis forgets that Achilles did relent and gave Priam the body, deliberately conniving with the Trojan king to deceive Agamemnon and his comrades. Further, Homer makes it clear that it was important that Achilles should show mercy here, a point made neatly by, to my mind, the best of Homer's English translators, Robert Fitzgerald, when he entitled Book xxiv 'A Grace Given in Sorrow'. I can see no evidence that William was adapting history to classical models at all.

I cannot see that William was as partisan as Professor Davis says he was. 'He was … writing propaganda to show that the conquest of England was just and inevitable.' If Professor Davis means to claim the Norman conquest was neither just nor inevitable this may also be claimed to show bias. If justice is an appropriate category here, William's claim was juster than Harold's. His total victory in one battle lasting less than a day surely explains why William of Poitiers regarded it as inevitable. In general Professor Davis's interpretations of passages from William of Poitiers seem grossly exaggerated – an exaggeration concealed because he does not quote William directly.

4 Stenton, *Anglo-Saxon England*, p. 561.
5 Sir Frank Stenton observed acutely that before 1066 the Norman dukes were remarkably loyal to the French crown. Cf. David Bates, *Normandy Before 1066*, London, 1982, pp. 46–93.
6 Sir Maurice Powicke first pointed this out in his *Loss of Normandy*, Manchester.
7 R. A. Brown, *The Normans and the Norman Conquest*, Woodbridge, 1969, p. 106.
8 Douglas, 'Edward the Confessor'; Sten Körner, *The Battle of Hastings: England and Europe*, Lund, 1964; Frank Barlow, *Edward the Confessor*, London, 1970.
9 *Anglo-Saxon Chronicle*, D, *sub anno* 1066, and cf. C. P. Wormald, Deerhurst Lecture, 1991, p. 15.
10 *Anglo-Saxon England*, p. 575.
11 *Edward the Confessor*.
12 Harold II was, of course, the last Anglo-Saxon king but he was not Woden-descended. Henry II was, through his grandmother, but it hardly seems that this was remembered any more.

INDEX

This index uses alphabetical order, word-by-word, with Æ/æ following Ad/ad. People of the same name are in hierarchical order, kings first. Rulers or clerics of the same name are in chronological order.

abbatial elections, 119
Abbo, abbot of Fleury, 105, 115, 125
Aberffraw, 12, 13
Abingdon, abbey of, 115, 128
Adalbero, bp of Lâon, 120, 125
Adam of Bremen, 156
Adomnon, abbot of Iona, 18, 41, 51, 59
Ælfgar, earl of Mercia, 181, 182, 183
Ælfgifu, 'wife' to Cnut, 157
Ælfheah, archbp of Canterbury, 103, 146–7
Ælfhere, ealdorman of Mercia, 126
Ælfred, king of Wessex, 66, 68, 73, 75–80, 83–4, 101–2
Ælfred, younger brother of Edward the Confessor, 163, 165
Ælfric, abbot of Eynsham, 127, 129, 131
Ælle, king of the South Saxons, 5
Æthelbald, king of Mercia, 15, 51–3
Æthelbald, king of Wessex, 72–3
Æthelberht, king of East Angles, 54
Æthelberht, king of Kent, 17, 18, 28
Æthelberht, brother of Ælfred and king of Kent, 72
Æthelburga, wife of Edwin of Northumbria, 30
Æthelfleda, lady of the Mercians, 85, 91
Æthelfrith, king of Bernicia, 7
Æthelheard, archbp of Canterbury, 61
Æthelred I, king of Wessex, 74–5

Æthelred II, king of England, 142, 147–8
Æthelred, ealdorman of Mercia, 76
Æthelric, bp of Sherborne, 107
Æthelstan, king of England, 10, 83, 92, 93, 102–3, 110–11
Æthelstan, ealdorman of East Anglia, 95
Æthelwahl, king of South Saxons, 35
Æthelweard, ealdorman, 16, 88, 127–8
Æthelwold, son of Æthelred I, 90
Æthelwold, St, bp of Winchester, 103, 114, 115–16, 117, 124
Æthelwulf, king of Wessex, 64, 71–4
Alcuin, 15, 55, 59, 61, 62
Aldhelm, bp of Sherborne, 39–40, 51
Alexander I, pope, 22
Altitonantis (Oswaldslow) charter, 107, 108
Ambrose, St, 39
Angli, 4, 5
Anglian collection, 55
Anglo-Saxon Chronicle, 6, 79, 141, 163, 172, 193–4
Anglo-Saxon England, vii–xi, 11
Annals of St Neots, 73, 77, 89, 160
anointing, royal, 58–9
archiductor, 118
aristocracy, ix
Arnulf, emperor, 60, 76–7
Arthur, king, 6
Ashingdon, battle of, 149
Asser, bp of Sherborne, 71, 77, 85

REASSESSING ANGLO-SAXON ENGLAND

Augustine, St, bp of Hippo, 39, 41
Augustine, archbp of Canterbury, 18, 24, 28

Baldwin, count of Flanders, 176, 181
Bamburgh, 7, 12
Barlow, Frank, 171
Battle of Maldon (poem), 49, 84, 143, 145, 150
Bayeux tapestry, 173
Bede, St, ix, 4–5, 13, 15, 30, 33, 36, 41, 42, 50, 51, 52, 57
Benedict of Nursia, St, 26
    Rule of, 26–7, 37–8, 57, 68, 113, 116
Benedictine monasticism, 37, 113–14
Beowulf, 43–5, 49, 56
Berkshire, 68
Bernicia, x, 7, 13, 25, 31
Bobbio, abbey of, 24, 25
Boethius, *Consolation of Philosophy*, 78
Boffa, 45
Bolt, Robert, 42
Boniface, St (Wynfrith), 1, 51–2, 57, 58
bookland, viii, 13–14, 52–3
Breedon, abbey of, 36
Brentford, synod of, 53
bretwalda, 18, 83
Brihtwald, bp of Wiltshire, 174
Brixworth, 14
Brooks, N.P., 69
Brown, R. Allen, 177–8
Brunnanburh, battle of, 93
brytenwealda, 17, 18, 29–30, 31
Burchard, bp of Worms, 125
Burghal Hidage, 85–6, 178
burh, 84–6, 178
Byrhtferth of Ramsey, 105, 115
Byrhtnoth, ealdorman and earl of Northumbria, 10, 145
byttfyllings, 23

Cadwallon, king of the Britons, 30
caesaro-papism, 131, 134, 137
Camelot, 6–7
Campbell, J., 11, 28, 29
Canterbury, 13, 113
capitulary of Servais, 111
Carolingians, 57–8
cartularies, 108
Cassian, *Conferences*, 39
Cassiodorus, 37, 38
cattle-rustling, 110, 111
ceorls, ix, 10, 113
Cerdic, king of the West Saxons, 5, 6
Chad, St, bp of Lichfield, 34
Chambers, R.W., 'On the continuity of English prose', 55, 127
Charlemagne, sons of, 59
Charles the Bald, emperor, 68
Charles III, emperor, 60, 77
charters of the monastic reformation, 118
Chelsea, 'contentious' synod, 59
Chilcomb, hundred of, 15
christus domini, 60
Cloveshoe, 52, 61, 122
Cluny, abbey of, 27, 36, 105
Cnut, king of Denmark and England, 17, 110, 142, 151, 154–7, 159, 162
Coburg Gospels, 124
Codex Amiatinus, 14, 39
Coenwulf, king of Mercia, 61–3, 70
coins, 62, 63, 109–10
Colman, bp of York, 32
Columba, St, abbot of Iona, 51
Columbanus, St, 24–6, 28, 36, 38, 46, 63
    Regulae, 25, 26
comitatus, 56
Conrad I, emperor, 87
Conrad II, emperor, 149, 155
conversion of the English, 28–30

coronation *ordo*, 135–6
Crowland, abbey of, 14, 46
crucifix, 132–4
Cuthbert, St, 36, 41
Cuthbert, archbp of Canterbury, 51
Cwenthryth, 62
Cyprian, St, 39

Dalriada, kingdom of, 30
danegeld, 99
Danelaw, 142
Danes, 69–70
de Vogüé, Adalbert (ed.), *Rule of St Benedict*, 26
decimation of Æthelwulf, 71
Deira, kingdom of, ix–x, 7, 24–5, 29, 31
dictator, 50
Domne Earfe, 158
Dorchester, Dorset, reeve of, 66
Dorchester-on-Thames, 18, 97
Douglas, D.C., 171, 177
Dover, *burh* and castle, 178
Dublin–York axis, 66, 67, 70–1, 91, 94, 97, 109
Dumville, David, 55
Dunnere, 10, 84
Dunstan, St, archbp of Canterbury, 94–5, 99–100, 103, 114, 115

Eadfrith, monk, 39, 40
Eadgifu, wife of Edward the Elder, 110
Eadgifu, daughter of Edward the Elder, 87, 149
Eadred, king of England, 95, 99
Eadric Streona, earl of Mercia, 148
Eadsige, archbp of Canterbury, 175
Eadwig, king of England, 99
Ealdred, bp of Worcester and archbp of York, 172
Eanberht, *regulus* of the Hwicce, 53
earl, 70

Easter, calculation of, 24, 30, 31
Ecgberht, king of Kent, 54
Ecgberht, king of Wessex, 63, 68
Ecgberht, bp of York, 13, 52
Ecgferth, son of Offa, 59
Ecgfrith, king of Northumbria, 34, 35
Eddius Stephanus, biographer of Wilfrid, 32, 41
Edgar, king of England, 95, 100, 105–7, 109, 115–17, 131, 135
Edgar the ætheling, 190
edict of Pîtres, 111
Edington, battle of, 75
Edith, wife of Edward the Confessor, 171, 174, 184
Edmund I, king of England, 93–4
Edmund Ironside, king of England, 148–9
  sons of, 149
Edward the Elder, king of England, 83, 88, 90–2, 110
Edward the Martyr, king of England, 61, 120
Edward the Confessor, king of England, 60, 108, 166–7, 174, 175, 186–7
Edward the ætheling, 166, 175, 183–4
Edwin, king of Northumbria, 29, 30
Edwin, son of Earl Ælfgar, 183, 192
Einhard, *Life of Charlemagne*, 77
Elmet, kingdom of, 12
Emma, queen of England, 141, 154, 163
Encomium Emmae Reginae, 17, 151–3, 171
English law of succession, 189
Eric Bloodaxe, king of York, 95–6
Eric, earl of Northumbria, 154
Eusebius, *Ecclesiastical History*, 39
Eustace, count of Boulogne, 177
Evans-Pritchard, E.E., 2, 9
Evesham, abbey of, 14

feud, x, 9, 20, 112
five-hide unit, 10
Flanders, count of, and Godwin's
    family, 164
Fleury, abbey of, 104, 126
Flodoard of Rheims, 89, 136
Florence of Worcester, 107, 154–5,
    172–3
folc, 49
Foldbriht, abbot of Pershore, 116
folkland, viii
fortuna, 56
Fox, Robin Lane, 1
Freeman, Edward Augustus, 16, 167,
    172
Fulda, abbey of, 22, 57
Fulford, battle of, 191
fyrd as peasant army, 98

genealogies, royal, 55–6
Gerard, St, abbot of Brogne, 105
Gerbert, archbp of Ravenna, 129–30
Germanists, 7
Germanus, abbot of Winchcombe,
    120
Gildas, 6
gilds, 24
Glastonbury, abbey of, 6, 114
Goda, 110
Godescalc, 103
Godwin, earl of Wessex, 146, 157,
    163–5, 174–81
Goffart, Walter, 42
Goscelinus, 156, 171
Gospatric, 185
Grately, council of, 111
Gregory the Great, St, pope, 18, 26–9,
    38, 40, 41–2
Grimbald, 88–9
Gumley, synod of, 52
Guthlac, St, 48, 56
Guthrum, king of the Vikings, 75–6
Gwynedd, kingdom of, 13

Hallamshire, 12
Harold, king of Denmark, 154
Harold I, king of England, 110, 162
Harold II, king of England, 171, 175,
    181, 183–8, 191–3
Harold Hardrada, king of Norway,
    174, 186, 190
Harrow on the Hill, 23
Harthacnut, king of England, 110,
    154, 162–3, 164, 165–6
Hastings, battle of, 192
Healfdene, 71
Heathfield, battle of, 30
Heavenfield, battle of, 31
hegemony, 17–19
Heimatlösigkeit, 115
Hengest, viii, 4–5
Henry I, king of the East Franks, 87
Henry I, king of England, 60
    laws of, 106
heptarchy, 16
Hofkapelle, 102
Holzmann, Robert, vii
Honorius I, pope, 27
Horsa, 4–5
Humber, River, 7, 15, 54, 66
Humbert, Cardinal, 125
hundred, 15–16
Hungary, 87, 150
Hwicce, kingdom of, 14

Ibn Fadlan, 22
Ibn Rustan, 71
imperator, 18
Ingmar, 71
Ini, king of the West Saxons, 6, 79
Iona, abbey of, 29, 30, 31
Irthlingborough, xi
Isidore, bp of Seville, 40
Islandshire, 12, 13
Ivar the Boneless, 71, 74, 75

James the Deacon, 30

Jarrow, abbey of, 66
Jomsvikings, 139, 146–7
Jutes, 4

Ker, W.P., 68
Keynes, S.D., 36, 101
Kingston, council of, 63
Körner, Sten, 179

lænland, viii, 13
Lanfranc, archbp of Canterbury, 190
Latin Charters of the Anglo-Saxon Period, viii
lay investiture, beginnings of controversy, 127
Leach, Edmund, *The Hill Tribes of Burma*, 8
leading-name research, 44
Leo IV, pope, 73
Leofric, earl of Mercia, 146, 177, 180
Lévy-Strauss, Claude, 56
Liber Eliensis, 116–17, 144
Liber Pontificalis, 27
Liber Wigorniensis, 108
Lichfield, archbpric of, 61
Limerick, foundation of, 92
Lindisfarne, abbey of, 12, 31, 62, 66
Lindisfarne Gospels, 14, 39, 40
Lindsey, see of, 33
l'ivression sacré, 23
London, 29, 67, 111
Long-haired Kings, 57
Lothair, emperor, 68
Louis the Pious, emperor, 68
Luther, Martin, 7
Luxeuil, abbey of, 24, 26

Macbeth, king of Scotland, 182
McGatch, Milton, 127
Mainz, see of, 57
Maitland, F.W., 167–8
Maldon, battle of, 10, 143–5
manor, 11–12

Margaret, St, queen of Scotland, 190
marriage of a king to his kingdom, 136
Martin, St, bp of Tours, 27, 37
Mayr-Harting, Henry, *The Coming of Christianity*, 35
Medhamstede (Peterborough), 36
mensa of the monks, 108
Mercian hegemony, 64
Merovingians, 57–8
Mersey, River, 12
Michael, St, 23
Mildrith, St, 158
Minster in Thanet, 62, 158
monastic exemption, 27
Mons Badonicus, battle of, 6
Morcar, earl of Northumbria, 183, 185, 191, 192
Much Wenlock, abbey of, 158
multiple estate, 12

National Socialism, 8
nobilitas, 56
Noirmoutier, abbey of, 67
Normandy, 90, 140
Northumbria, ix–x, 7, 13, 190
Norway, 157

Occa, 45
Odin, 71
Odo, abbot of Cluny, 108
Odo, bp of Bayeux, 173
Offa, king of Angeln, 44
Offa, king of Mercia, xi, 44–5, 52–4, 59–60, 63
Offa, brother of King Oswald, 45
Offa, brother of Osred I, 45
Offa's dyke, 54
Olaf Haroldson, St, king of Norway, 157–8
Olaf Tryggvason, king of Norway, 145
Old English Bede, 79

Old Minster Psalter, 124

Oleson, T.J., 171, 180

O Neills (Uí Néill), 51, 67

Oskytel, archbp of York, 97

Oslac, *dux* of the South Saxons, xi, 53

Osmund, king of the South Saxons, 53

Oswald, king of Northumbria, 18, 30, 31, 59

Oswald, St, bp of Worcester and archbp of York, 104, 116–17

Oswaldslow, 107, 118

Oswiu, king of Northumbria and *brytenwealda*, 18, 31–2

Otto the Great, king of the East Franks, 17, 87

Otto-William, claimant to the duchy of Burgundy, 176

paganism, Anglo-Saxon, 22–3

pallium, 18

parishes and the tenth-century Reformation, 127

Parker, Matthew, archbp of Canterbury, 79

Patrick, St, 6

Paulinus, bp of York, 30

Pelagius, 41

Penda, king of the Mercians, 30

Pershore, abbey of, 120

Peterborough, abbey of (Medhamstede), 36

Picts, 4

pilgrimage, 1

Pippin, king of the Franks, 58, 60, 61

Pîtres, edict of, 111

port, 109

Portland, 67

primitive thought, 55

primogeniture, 72

Ragnar Lothbrok, 71

Ralf, earl of East Anglia, 193

Ramsey, abbey of, 108, 115

Rather, bp of Verona, 130–1

Reculver, abbey of, 62

Redwald, king of East Anglia, 23, 29–30

regula mixta, 65

Regula Pastoralis, 69, 78, 101

Regularis Concordia, 131

Ribble, River, 12

Robert the Pious, king of the West Franks, 176

Robert, earl of Gloucester, 60

Robert of Jumièges, archbp of Canterbury, 177

Robertson, H.M., 12

Rochester, see of, 29, 67

Roger, earl of Hereford, 193

Rouen, 67

royal writing office, 101–2

Rule of the Master, 37–8

Sabinus, pope, 27

sagas as history, 141

St Brice's Day massacres, 143

St Helen's church, Worcester, 108

St Mary of Egypt, 128

Sawyer, P.H., 69

Saxones, 4–5

scalping, 112

Scoti, 30, 109

secularium prioratus, 122

Selsey, church of, 35

Servais, capitulary of, 111

sexual morality and the tenth-century Reformation, 130

ships, 83

shipsokes, 106

shires, 11, 12, 106

Sigeberht, king of the East Saxons, 46

Sisam, Kenneth, 55

Siward, earl of Northumbria, 175, 177, 181–2

Siward, abbot of Abingdon, 174–5
Smyth, A.P., 70, 93
Southampton (Hamwih), 67, 86
Southern, Sir Richard, 80
Spearhafoc, abbot of Abingdon, 177
Stamford Bridge, battle of, 174, 191
Stenton, Sir Frank, vii–xi, 8, 53
Stigand, archbp of Canterbury, 174,
    189–90
stirps regia, 56
Stobart, J.C., 4
Suetonius, *Lives of the Twelve Caesars*,
    77
Sulpicius Severus, 27
Sutton Hoo, 29, 47
Sweyn, king of Denmark, 17, 140,
    146
Sweyn, eldest son of Earl Godwin,
    175, 185

Tertullian, 39
Tettenhall, battle of, 91
thegn, 10, 113
Theodore of Tarsus, archbp of
    Canterbury, 33–4, 39, 47–8
Theodred, bp of London, 103
Thietmar, bp of Merseburg, 141
Thorkell the Tall, earl of East Anglia,
    140, 146, 148, 153–4
thralls, ix, 10–11, 111–12
'The thriving of the Anglo-Saxon
    ceorl', ix
tithing group, 111
Tolkien, J.R., 'Beowulf and the
    Monsters', 44
Tostig, earl of Northumbria, 171, 176,
    182, 185–6, 190–1
totems, 56
Translatio Sancti Alexandri, 22
Tribal Hidage, 15
tribute, 145
trimoda necessitas, 52
Tuda, bp of York, 32

Turville-Petre, G.N., 23
twelfhyndeman, 10, 113
twyhyndeman, 10, 113

Udalric, prior of Cluny, 125
Uhtred, *regulus* of the Hwicce, 53
Uhtred, earl of Northumbria, 148
Uí Néill, 51, 67
unction, royal, 57, 58–9, 60
underkings, 31
urban episcopate, 30–1
Ursula, St, and her eleven thousand
    virgin companions, 88
Utrecht Psalter, 88

Valhalla, 23
value of papacy in early middle ages,
    74
Vikings, 66–7, 68–71, 89–91, 140
Visigoths, 59
Visio Caroli, 89
Vita Eadwardi, 173–4, 189
Vita Oswaldi, 143
Vitalian, pope, 33
Vivarium, 38
Völkerwanderung, 4, 7
Vortigern, 4
vouching for warranty, 111

Wagner, Richard, 23
Wallace-Hadrill, J.M., xi, 2, 56–7
Waltbrecht, count, 22
Waltheof, earl of Northumbria, 182,
    192
Walton, 12
Wantage, 68
wapentake, 16
weahlish, 12
Wenskus, Richard, 1
wergelds, 10
Wessex, kingdom of, 63
Whitby, 7, 40
    synod of, x, 31

Wicklow, 118
Widukind, duke, 22
Wight, Isle of, 35, 53
Wiglaf, king of the Mercians, 63
Wilfrid, St, bp of York, 15, 24, 28,
    32–3, 34–7, 45, 57, 63
Wilhelm, abbot of Hirsau, 125–6
William I, king of England and duke
    of Normandy, 60, 175, 179–81,
    187–8, 191–2
William of Jumièges, 173
William of Poitiers, *Gesta Willelmi*,
    173
Willibrord, 15, 57
Wilson, Sir David, 66
Winchester, 15
witan, 16, 51
Woden, 23, 28, 55–6
Wolds, x

Wollasch, Joachim, 36
Wood, Michael, 102
Worcester, 13, 85, 108
Wormald, C.P., 2
Wulfhere, king of the Mercians, 53
Wulfhere, ealdorman, 79
Wulfnoth, Anglo-Saxon viking, 146
Wulfred, archbp of Canterbury, 61,
    62
Wulfstan, St, archbp of York, 5, 108,
    112, 115, 120, 126
  demoted to bp of Dorchester, 96,
    97
Wynsige, *prepositus* of Worcester,
    108

York, 66, 70

Zusammengehörigkeitgefühl, 2, 5